All photographs courtesy of Alan M. Kirshner.

12/1/08

To Dr. Gari Browning,
With this new edition of my textbook I take great pleasure in welcoming you to Ohlone. As I tell my students, "If you don't read it at least enjoy viewing my photographs."
I look forward to working with you for many years to come.

Alan

Sixth Edition

IN THE COURSE OF HUMAN EVENTS
Essays in American Government

Alan M. Kirshner
Ohlone College

Custom Publishing

New York   Boston   San Francisco
London   Toronto   Sydney   Tokyo   Singapore   Madrid
Mexico City   Munich   Paris   Cape Town   Hong Kong   Montreal

Cover photos: courtesy of Alan M. Kirshner

Printed in the United States of America

10 9 8 7 6 5 4 3 2 1

2008480059

JK

Pearson
Custom Publishing
is a division of

www.pearsonhighered.com

ISBN 10: 0-558-05285-1
ISBN 13: 978-0-558-05285-0

TABLE OF CONTENTS

PREFACE

Why another political science textbook? This is not another political science text-book. This is my textbook! Almost every instructor using a textbook finds voids. At least I always have and so I decided to produce a book to fill in the gaps I found between my lectures and the textbooks I used.

Pride of authorship insists that a textbook written for my students will pro-vide something unique for all students. I also expect that other instructors will incorporate my material in their courses until they create their own textbooks. I will then have the opportunity to examine their works for my students.

If the last sentence suggests anything about the focus of my work, it is my firm belief in the diversity found in the discipline of political science. I may hold to a universal truth for myself, but I am aware that my faith, derived from my scholarship, belongs to me alone.

After many years of observing successful teaching, I have concluded that a common denominator exists. Accomplished professors are those individuals who express excitement about their materials and research. Instructors who pro-vide a diversity of interpretations when expressing their ideas—always being sure to differentiate between their own educated viewpoints and the thoughts of others—stimulate students to further study.

I have watched students confronted by an idea that challenges every convo-lution in their brains. They know their position is the truth, but now they need to defend their views with an intellectual argument.

Some students, frightened by diversity, cop out, drop out or pop out. My experience has proven to me that the vast majority of students rise to the occa-sion, especially when they know an educated view will be respected.

This is what education is all about—creative and critical thinking based on scholarship. Students who close their minds by continuing to accept their emotional positions without searching for an intellectual defense are simply not students.

I have written this textbook in the same manner I approach my students—by challenging their minds. Once I have caught the reader's attention, the real intent of my essays should become apparent—to provide political concepts, ideas and terminology.

In contributing to American government textbooks, I hope to provide, in an uncommon and exciting fashion, an understanding of the discipline and a basic comprehension of terminology. I have offset the major ideas and terms in italics. I have also produced a glossary of key words at the end of each chapter. I am sure that at times students will find some of their preconceived views challenged.

Since I reject the argument that college students are too young, too dumb or too fickle to decide for themselves, learning the basic concepts of political science should occur as students ponder reasonable arguments to defend their positions.

In writing my essays for *In the Course of Human Events* I have attempted to emphasize that government is people and that the events of government should be humane. I hope you enjoy my enterprise as much as I enjoyed producing it for you. I know you will find *In the Course of Human Events: Essays in American Government* far from being dull. You will probably say, "Yes, it is his textbook!" Maybe you will conclude by thinking, "I am glad he produced it for me."

Alan M. Kirshner
Mission San Jose, CA

ACKNOWLEDGMENTS

A few years ago a colleague asked me when I had had my conversion to liberalism. He told me that while serving as a priest, he rejected most of his ultra-conservative parents' values. I reported that I have always maintained the same value system—well, maybe with a few changes. He expressed his amazement.

My special thanks goes out to my parents Helen and Morris Kirshner. They provided me with the value system that enabled me to compose this series of personal essays. My grandparents gave my parents these same values and, therefore, receive my eternal gratitude. I often listened to my grandfather, Jacob Berman, argue with political commentators on the radio and television as if they would respond.

With my essays' major direction of confronting others so they might better assert their own position, I owe a debt of gratitude to my brother Edward and my sister Mikal. They constantly faced me, forcing a clarification of my views. In recent years, my wife Susan, and my sons Lev, Micah and Tov have taken over this task.

Susan E. Fisher-Kirshner deserves my eternal gratitude for translating my handwriting, clarifying my thoughts and typing a good portion of the original manuscript. However, I take complete and total responsibility for any faulty judgments or factual errors.

Dr. Howard A. DeWitt, colleague and friend, suggested this project and released my creative energies. Professor Stacy Cole, the best read individual I know, provided me with many articles that enabled me to expand my thoughts. Gigi Stengard, the editor and publisher of a local public service magazine, volunteered her time to copy edit my work. Richard Shorman, a chess teacher for my youngest sons, edited my fifth, sixth, and seventh essays. He also took the flattering photograph of me on the back cover.

Upon completion of my Ph.D. dissertation, I wrote, "Last of all, I must commend my son, Lev Yakov Kirshner, for his uncanny ability to be born and grow during the hectic year and a half this dissertation was in progress." I will now paraphrase my dissertation acknowledgment: "I must commend myself for my uncanny ability to survive to my seventies while my children's lives were in progress." Lev, now head soccer coach at San Diego State University has two younger brothers: Micah Ben Fisher-Kirshner (age 27) and Tov Joshua Fisher-Kirshner (age 26). Need I say more? Well, yes! Besides any trials and tribulations I may have suffered or caused while completing this work, my wife Susan and all three boys hold my external love as warm and sensitive humans.

Alan M. Kirshner

PART 1

A PEOPLE'S GOVERNMENT?

CHAPTER 1

Nature or Nurture: Politics and Political Alternatives

Essay I

A few years ago, a friend took me to her uncle's house that was in a relatively crime-free community in Northern California. As her uncle answered the door, I heard five clicks and noticed, upon entering the house, five locks on the door. After we exchanged pleasantries, I made a casual remark about the uncle's security system. He then insisted upon showing me the rest of the fortress. He had three locks on his bedroom door. Three loaded rifles hung on his bedroom wall and he proudly lifted his mattress to produce two handguns—"one for the little lady." Then came the coup de grace: from his closet he withdrew three hand-grenades. At this point, I inquired as to why he had this arsenal in his home. He responded: "Nobody is going to break into my house and rape my wife!" I immediately received an image of someone breaking into his house, attempting to rape his wife, and his pulling the pin and tossing the hand-grenade. I smiled to myself, and asked no more questions. I decided against any further inquiry. I felt I knew his answers to my questions based upon his obvious view of human nature. I felt I could even discern his attitude towards government.

I have read studies which show that people who view television news are more likely to lock their doors than individuals who seldom if ever watch the news broadcasts. Certainly, I could conclude that a fear of crime is generated by the daily news reports. Perhaps realism in today's society dictates that I lock my doors and I should thank the television newscasters for providing the warning.

I cannot help but remember the old adage that defines a conservative as simply a liberal who has been mugged. However, my friend's uncle had never been mugged, and yet he had a deep distrust of human beings. I doubt that it could occur to him that no one would try to break into his house. To this man, most people are naturally evil and needed to be controlled; television news broadcasts simply confirmed his attitude. To him, government continued to fail in its proper role of maintaining law and order, and therefore he had little option but to protect his property (which included his wife).

Throughout history, debates have occurred about the proper function and role of government. In most cases, when individuals disputed government's proper sphere, they argued the place of people within a political system based upon their concepts of human nature—whether people are good or evil. Except for a few notable cases, such as in the ancient Greek city of Athens, until the nineteenth century, the distrust of people and the general acceptance of the belief that people were basically evil led to *autocratic governments—systems in which a single individual asserts political power and authority. Government—the organized state's political and administrative structure*—in an autocratic system, took the form of one person exercising political power and commanding obedience while maintaining order. Bishop Jacques Benigne Bossuet (1627–1704), Louis XIV's political apologist, argued for *absolute monarchy—where a king, queen, emperor, or other regal potenate exercises the supreme powers of the state, usually acquiring his or her position through inheritance*—based on the inherent evil of humankind. He said:

> It is not enough that men live in the same country or speak the same language, because becoming unsociable by the violence of their passions, and incompatible by their different humors, they cannot act as one unless they submit themselves altogether to a single government which rules over all.

For Bossuet, the monarch was selected by God to control the passions of the masses and to provide order to the society. A monarch would act for the benefit of the state with his God-given power of reason. As Boussuet stated: "The royal authority is absolute." Absolutism, to Bossuet, never meant arbitrariness, only a higher form of reason that the people could not be expected to comprehend. As Louis XIV allegedly said: "L'état, c'est moi!"—"I am the State!"

During the seventeenth and eighteenth centuries, the concept of one individual having superior reason, being all good, and the establishment of autocratic governments, came under challenge. Enlightened philosophers argued for the perfectibility of humans, and a few like Jean Jacques Rousseau even contended that people were all good while living in a pure state of nature. Some political writers now argued for a *social contract—where people consented to enter into a government of their own creation*. From these political views came the idea of *popular consent—a concept that holds that laws are illegitimate without the consent of the people living under them*. (Further discussion of these thoughts will occur in Essay II—"Democracy Dissected.")

Arguments about human nature and the role of government raged in the late nineteenth and early twentieth centuries as individuals claiming verification from Darwin's works contended that humans and animals maintained similar base instincts. To counter these suppositions of humans reflecting fixed animal behavior, other writers emphasized the concept of *nurture—the idea that individuals become what they are because of their socio-cultural, economic, and political environments; the conditioning processes of their societies*.

From such views came the concept of government changing the environment in order to foster equal opportunity and the pursuit of happiness. Those who adhered to the notion of *nature—the idea that an individual's genetic inheritance is the basic force behind his/her behavior*—accepted a few variables in growth, but demanded a fixed political system to match the immutable nature of humans. Today, the naturist arguments for uniting physical science with political science are quite sophisticated.

Sociobiologists, as one group of naturists are called, maintain that the **DNA (deoxyribonucleic acid)**—*the molecule that contains the genetic blueprint of all living things*—molds the individual's personality. They even postulate that the human DNA has common threads that influence society's **folkways**—*the traditional patterns of life common to a group of people*—and its **mores**—*the fundamental moral values of a group*—creating common political needs.

Time magazine, in its August 1, 1977 issue, page 63, suggested that sociobiology might be the right social theory for today's culture. The article in *Time* identified people's frustration during the 1970s over the continued failure of the experiments attempting to change social behavior. *Time* believed that the view that humans are perfectible had fallen from favor. Therefore, *Time* felt, a doctrine opposing free will and supporting a human personality controlled by physical inheritance, similar to sociobiology, might be more acceptable.

A few years before the notoriety of sociobiology compelled *Time* to publish its article, George F. Gilder (whose book *Wealth and Poverty*, Basic Books, Inc., 1981, helped set the philosophical tone for the Reagan administration's supply side economics) argued in his "Sex and the Social Order" (*The New Leader*, September 3, 1973, pp. 5–10) that politicians should know they cannot confront certain inherited human characteristics. Although not a sociobiologist, Gilder maintained a similar argument when he identified an unwritten constitution of gender and the family. He saw this sexual constitution being violated by the nurturists who believed in the perfectibility of humans. He asserted that these liberals caused a severe crisis in our political order. He stressed that government must adopt a policy which acknowledged and accommodated our genetic inheritance—support of basic family values.

Nature or nurture?

Most conservatives or ultra-conservatives I know remain free-will advocates, at least verbally. They do not argue that pre-destination, either genetically or through God's will, determines why an individual is evil. They see a fair percentage of people as evil due to their own choices—people's damnation, comes from with-in, from their own choice of selecting the wrong when they knew what was right. Whenever I pursue with them their view as to a reason for what causes these individuals to make their evil choices, I almost always hear something like, "It is just in their nature."

The roots of liberal and ultra-conservative views are buried in contrary presumptions about human nature. In an August 7, 1995 article in the *New Yorker*, on the nature of twins, "Double Mystery," Lawrence Wright examines the impact of scientific studies promoting nature over nurture: "The broad movement from environmental determinism to behavioral genetics which has transformed psychology over the last thirty years has dramatically altered society's view of human development and become a part of the invisible subtratum of American politics. This can be demonstrated by comparing the climates of opinion that produced the Great Society, in 1965, and the Contract with America, in 1995."

I remember listening to a debate, many years ago, between Norman Thomas, former head of American Socialist Party, a non-Marxist, ultra-liberal group, and William Buckley, ultra-conservative publisher of *The National Review*. The topic pertained to the proper role of individuals in politics. Both individuals were extremely articulate and dynamic speakers. I soon determined that there could never be any agreement between the two because they viewed the nature/nurture of humans quite differently. Buckley thought that most individuals could never be trusted and they lacked the intellectual capacity to participate in government. He, therefore, held that government should be run by an elite in order to control the passions of the many. Thomas, a believer in the malleability and perfectibility of every person, supported a political system directed by each and every individual that provided for their general welfare.

Political Scientists—*those academic individuals who deal with the theory and practice of politics and the description and analysis of political behavior*—can also be affected by their views on nature versus nurture. For example, in his book *A Preface to Politics* (D.C. Heath and Company, 1973), David Schuman argued that ***James Madison***—*who kept a diary of the debates at the Constitutional Convention of 1787*—set the tone for our political system, one that considers people evil. Schuman wrote:

> The masses, the most of us, are potentially dangerous. We are full of violence and prejudice and had better not be trusted with deciding things for ourselves. Our virtue is in our inactiveness. We are actless, therefore we are. But the analysis is more complicated. The elites are not to be trusted, either. This vision of politics—*The Madisonian one*—reminds us over and over again that government is a necessary evil. It is necessary, in part, because of our own evilness. (Italics mine, p. 21.)

The author continued his indictment of Madison's impact on our political system by stating:

> We are structured not for cooperative acts but for private ones; we are given a form of government that calls not for the best in man but only for the minimum in him. What we must realize is that we are living a self-fulfilling prophecy: that by founding a government

geared to selfishness, we can maintain it only by being selfish. By participating within the structure, we are acting out Madison's belief that we are unworthy. (p. 26)

True, Madison claimed in *The Federalist*, No. 51 that the moving force of politics is "ambition countering ambition." This concept may have led to the study of **politics as conflict**—*where groups and individuals compete for selfish reasons in a political system and the authoritative rule of the state creates peace.* Yet, by no means would most political scientists agree with Schuman's connecting the idea of conflict and selfishness to evil, nor with his final diatribe against Madison's so-called molding of our political system: "We consider ourselves an evil people condemned to a life without trust, without power, without politics." (p. 27)

Many political scientists would hold that good people can have selfish motives as there are diverse concepts of good in any pluralistic society. Besides, **altruism**—*the unselfish concern for the welfare of others*—does not have to be the only synonym for good. The majority of political scientists see their task as being that of a disinterested scientific observer of the political process, not one of making moral judgments.

Nurture political scientists like Robert Paul Wolfe, however, visualize a just political order as good people strive to implement their partisan values through trust, power and politics. By emphasizing the perfectibility of humans, they tend to repudiate the idea of objective political science. A few nature writers, like Leo Strauss, see humans as good and politics as demeaning to the humans' true being. They contend that genetically a few individuals are superior intellectually and because of their altruism they should have the dominant role in governing. These scholars also repudiate the concept of the disinterested scientific observer, believing rather in the Platonic pursuit of truth.

From what I have written so far, I am sure many readers have become convinced that I believe all people and especially political scientists are predetermined to interpreting government and politics according to their subconscious or conscious position on the nature versus nurture or the good versus evil controversy. Nothing could be further from the truth. I feel only that the way individuals view the nature of humans has some impact on the type of government these people might desire and on the objectivity of the political scientists' studies. *My main reason for introducing the nature versus nurture debate is to introduce the reader to the disagreement that exists between political scientists about the proper scope of their discipline and the great amount of controversy over methodology. Another reason for discussing the debate is to set a convenient approach for the further study in this essay of politics, political terminology, and American government.*

If political science is a dividing discipline and political scientists disagree on the nature of politics, how do I go about defining politics. I guess as the old joke goes: "Very carefully!" Often the writer's or teacher's perspective of "What is politics?" will dictate her/his approach to classroom methodology.

In a traditional definition of politics where politics is defined as the exercise of the power of the state, the political scientist will focus on the structure and operation of the **public government**—*the institutions of the state such as constitutions, laws, legislatures, executives, and courts.* These scholars will usually avoid studying the **private government**—*the unofficial institutions like churches, trade unions, schools, etc.*

Since the late nineteenth century, many of these traditional political scientists have added some unofficial institutions to their studies. They examine such groups as political parties and pressure groups that they see as directly influencing official institutions. In so doing, they have extended their definition of politics to include those private governments that attempt to influence the exercise of the power of the American government.

Many political scientists, today, lean towards Harold Lasswell's definition of politics: "Who gets what, when and how." These scholars feel that the way to understand political power is to find out who holds it, how they have come to hold it and how they use it. These political scientists, therefore, argue for the study of the power relations in all human institutions. Since they also hold that "power" itself is an ambiguous concept, they may focus some of their studies on the impact economic, social and cultural institutions have on American government.

The late Abbie Hoffman, radical political leader of the New Left during the 1960s, who committed suicide in 1989, offered a definition of politics with which a few professors of the discipline agree: "Politics is the way you live your life." Perhaps Hoffman's suicide constituted the ultimate political act. Ignoring the nihilism Abbie Hoffman had been accused of and which might have been reflected in his decision to end politics, the way an individual leads his life includes more than the perceptions, attitudes and activities of the individual political actor. The way you lead your life includes the very individual conception that how you choose to live is a publicly important act.

When studying American government from this definition that politics is the way you live your life, the scholar would take into account for example, the impact of individual behavior in calling women "girls." If a person, male or female, sees women as immature people then he or she may try to relegate women to an infantile role in life and government. Another example could be

Politics is the way you lead your life.

individuals who care little about how much gas or electricity they use. These people could have an impact on America's energy resources, albeit minor compared to the actions of public governments.

No matter how you define it, everyone experiences politics. All people live in groups and those groups provide for some form of order and the distribution of power. Even if we ignore any private governments or individual behavior, our daily lives in America are caught in the web of government.

Our government regulates as simple a thing as the pillow on your bed. Have you ever noticed the tag that states: "Do not remove under penalty of law?" Of course, that label is for the seller, not the buyer. My grandmother was afraid she would be arrested if she tore it off. The tag lists the ingredients found in the pillow as well as the laws that control its manufacture and sale.

Realistically, political activities, either in the governmental legislatures or through executive agencies, influence almost every aspect of a person's life, ergo the pillow analogy. Why then do people make statements like: "Politics has no effect on my life," "I don't care about politics," or "I don't know anything about politics."? Obviously, some people are willing to hide from the truth about the impact of politics on their everyday life rather than admit that they are a part of a political system.

Some people feel overwhelmed by their semi-awareness of the magnitude of politics in their lives and, therefore, claim to ignore the political system. Most of the time, however, the sense of powerlessness is visible through all their protestations. A feeling of being powerless often leads to frustration about and hostility towards politics.

Many individuals who find themselves successful in their political accomplishments show a sense of internal power; they seem happier about the system as well as about themselves.

The intent of the next part of this essay is to examine some of the reasons people are negative about politics. And to try to awaken some of the readers to the realities of their own political involvement.

I have always been fascinated with politics. I suspect my interest in the discipline started around the family dinner table. My parents often discussed politics, past and present. They saw themselves as Jeffersonians and felt that President Franklin D. Roosevelt reflected the embodiment of our third President, Thomas Jefferson's, concept of democracy.

The only time I remember seeing my mother cry occurred on her learning of Roosevelt's death. My mother always seemed to be president of some organization and involved in some political campaign. I doubt if I ever heard a negative word about our government, politics, or politicians—well, maybe a few snide remarks about Republicans.

When I reached maturity and listened to the condemnation of politics by other people, I failed to understand their attitudes. No doubt, they were reared in families or political environments quite different from my household. As I listened carefully to their statements, I heard the frustrations of powerlessness I mentioned earlier in the essay. Yet, I wondered why government and politicians received the bulk of their wrath. I knew that the political system only mirrored our economic and social order.

Earlier, I identified how some people, due to their belief in the evil nature of humans, would always be negative. I recognized this naturist attitude towards politics. I failed to understand, however, why nurture oriented individuals and especially those people who believed in the natural goodness of humans perceived politics as demeaning and politicians as parasites upon society. Especially confusing to me were those individuals I encountered who insisted that anyone who entered politics became, without exception, corrupt.

When I began to professionally observe our political system, I noticed one glaring difference between government and other societal institutions—politics seemed to lack an internal positivism, causing a negative response by people towards government. After much analysis, I contributed this condition, in large part, to the politicians.

In no other occupation do people condemn each other or their products as do the politicians. Does Avis tell you that Hertz's cars fall apart or their brakes fail to work? Never! Avis informs you that they are second best, but are doing everything to be the best. To attack their competitor's product, even if such charges were true, would simply reflect on their own company. A physician seldom attacks the knowledge, learning, and training of a colleague. The professional world, similar to the business world, is well aware that to defame a colleague would only reflect on its own character.

Over the years, I have learned to avoid negative people. I found that when I am around negative people, it is much too easy for me to become negative. Since many politicians project a negative image of their profession, many people accept that view as valid and deny any connection with the world of politics. Most individuals do not want to be tied to evil and since the negative views of politics is interpreted to be evil, these people refuse to admit any connection with politics.

Despite these denials of noninvolvement in the political system, the truth is that almost everyone is in one way or another actively involved in government. Most people unknowingly involve themselves with both formal and informal governments.

During the early 1830s, Alexis de Tocqueville visited the United States on an official mission for the French government. Upon returning to France he published his two-volume *Democracy in America*. Many political scientists hold that his lucid and critical analysis of our political system is still valid.

De Tocqueville noted, among the many elements of American democracy, the amazing propensity of Americans to join private organizations. He believed that through these associations, Americans not only projected their particular interests, but also learned to work together in groups. He contended that such associations became the educational system for democracy, as people learned through practical experience the art of compromise or how to look for alternative solutions. Not only did he feel that these informal government associations prepared people for full participation in formal government, but he also perceived the interaction of these groups as a barrier to autocracy. De Tocqueville, similar to many political scientists today, believed that the United States could be classified as a pluralistic democracy.

This concept of **pluralism**—*the idea that society consists of diversified interest groups that compete for power*—is dear to the hearts of many American political scientists. When asked who rules in America, they will argue that the people rule

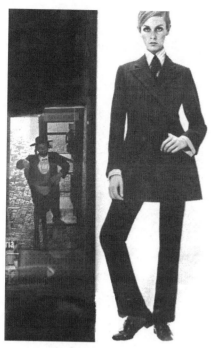

A pluralistic nation.

through their participation in interest groups, the viewpoint of De Tocqueville and also the one advocated for the preservation of liberty by Madison. This doctrine can be referred to as *democratic pluralism—the belief that group power balances group power with the result that no one group is able to dominate the American political system, enabling democracy to prevail.*

Democratic pluralists hold that democracy exists in America as various interest groups compete in an open market place, each attempting to influence government for its own selfish ends, while the government must create compromise or decide between positions. They assume that since any group has access to the halls of power, the people rule in America through their organizations. In a sense, America is therefore seen as a group democracy—democracy by the group—rather than as direct rule by the individual.

Abraham Lincoln, in his Gettysburg Address, expressed the idea of who is supposed to rule in the United States of America—"government of the people, by the people, for the people." Legitimate power in the United States ideally rests with the people.

Democratic pluralists may argue that through interest group competition we actually have a government of, by, and for the people. Political scientists who advocate *participatory democracy—the maximum direct participation in political decision making by each and every individual*—disagree. They believe that democratic pluralism is only another term for elitism. By trying to rationalize the individual's involvement in this process through interest group activities, they argue that the pluralists are upholding a government run *of, by*, and *for* the elites who control the interest groups. True, different elites may exist and vie for power, and even attain power at different times, but this is considered a perversion of the democratic principle of "one-person, one-vote."

Few if any political scientists believe that the United States is a participatory democracy where each individual's views are weighted equally in the conduct of government. However, many political scientists advocate direct action to bring rule to the people. During the 1960s and early 1970s, the *New Left— a radical-liberal movement, particularly of college students and some professors, that challenged the established political, social, cultural, and economic order*—had as a basic objective, participatory democracy. Radical groups pushed this approach, especially on the local level, as a cure for what they saw as the perversion of the democratic process by the rich and the powerful. They advocated *proportional representation—an electoral system that allocates seats in a legislative body to each group approximately equal to their numbers in society.* They believed that with this quota system the minorities and the poor would be able to share power with the white majority and the wealthy.

*Participatory democracy: Mark Rudd and SDS
take over Columbia University, May 23, 1968.*

Many of the ideas of the New Left stemmed from C. Wright Mills' book *The Power Elite*, published in 1956, although he had written articles on the subject a few years before. Mills advanced the concept that the United States was ruled by a *power elite—a relatively small group of people in the executive branch of government, the leadership of large corporations, and the top military brass, who run the country.* Mills never argued that a conspiracy between these groups existed, rather he insisted that there was an interlocking hierarchy who took command. He believed these individuals to be ruthless, selfish, and among the least enlightened citizens, blocking access to the paths of power to all but a select few, in order to advance their own positions.

Mills' view was similar to that of Henry Fairlie who coined the term "Establishment." Fairlie differed from Mills in that Mills' power elite is directly associated with power, where Fairlie's *Establishment are those people who create and maintain the power that is exercised by the elected or appointed officials.* Fairlie wrote to Mills in 1955 indicating that they might both be addressing the same phenomenon.

Both Mills and Fairlie adhered to the view that only the few rule the United States. They simply differed as to the positions of power these few commanded. Both contended that the elite achieved their power through their narrow associations. Sociologist G. William Dornhoff, fascinated by these contentions, decided to study the social backgrounds of some of our nation's power brokers. According to his 1967 book *Who Rules America?* and his 1971 book *The Higher Circles*, most of these individuals (the Power Elite—the Establishment) attended the same universities, sat on the same boards of directors of the same corporations, and attended the same fraternal clubs and social gatherings.

Political scientists often concern themselves with analyzing the role of elites in decision making. Yet these scholars seldom argue for a *conspiracy thesis—the belief that a small group of people formulate secret plans to defraud the democratic process, controlling power for their own selfish desires.* Conspiracy theories abound, especially on the political extremes. In the far left or far right literature you can read of the control of the American government by Wall Street and the "Eastern Establishment."

In many parts of the country you can still hear speakers ranting against the New York International, Communist, Faggot, Pinko, Jewish, Anti-Christ conspiracy, or attacking the Orange County, Bible Belt, Reactionary, Fascist, Mafia, Ku Klux Klan, Nazi, White-Anglo-Saxon Protestant Male plots.

In recent years, a lot of underground literature has emphasized the conspiracy of the *illuminati—alleged followers of the anti-Christ who date back to the Medieval period.* The illuminati, with their sign of the Beast (666)[1], are often linked to the so-called *Bilderbergers—an alleged conspiracy of wealthy corporate leaders and bankers—*who make decisions at secret meetings to control America's foreign policy to benefit the communists. For they, like the communists, desire the One-World Government of the anti-Christ.

This conspiracy theory seems to be more popular with the extreme right-wing. However, both right and left-wingers often contend that America's foreign policy is controlled by the *Tri-Lateral Commission—a group established by former Chase Manhattan Chairman David Rockefeller in 1973 to create a meeting place for select citizens of Japan, Western Europe and the United States to discuss solutions to their common political, economic, and security problems.*

While the evidence for the existence of the illuminati is scant to nonexistent, the Tri-Lateral Commission does exist. Whether any of these groups, real or not, rules America or is seeking to gain control of the United States government to create a new world order is unprovable. Paranoid people often feel fulfilled by believing the worst, while using whatever innuendoes or half truths they can. No one will convince them of anything but a conspiracy theory. Maybe they are right. Certainly, it never hurts to learn about their views as possibilities, even remote possibilities, just in case the paranoids really are being persecuted, and are, therefore, not paranoids.

Tied to the belief that elites rule the United States, whether through a conspiracy or by similar selfish desires is another interpretation as to who rules the United States: the *Machiavellian Interpretation—holds that certain individuals strive for power and when in control rule for their own individual, amoral benefit, characterized by their unscrupulous cunning and deception.* Niccolo di Bernardo Machiavelli in 1513 wrote *The Prince—a treatise on government in which political expediency is advocated above morality.*

Some political scientists believe former President Richard Nixon best exemplified Machiavellian rule in the United States. They hold that he ruled America in his selfish desire for power, not for the Republican Party, nor for any small group of people, and certainly not for the American public or any moral principles. If at times he provided any benefits to one group or another, they argue, he did so only to maintain his own power. He failed to be a skilled machiavellian, however, and Watergate brought him tumbling down. Nixon resigned the presidency on August 9, 1974.

---

[1]*Biblical reference.*

A few political scientists hold with the German sociologist Max Weber's *bureaucratic interpretation—the United States is ruled by the civil servants, the administrators.* Weber believed that since governments come and go, but the civil servants remain, the real source of power in any government is bureaucracy. American political scientists adhering to this view when analyzing our government often see this administrative rule as positive, in that these civil servants provide continuity and knowledge to the political system. On the other hand, some writers fear the corruption of power caused by the near impossibility of removing a civil servant from office.

A plausible case can be made for each of the five reputed sources of power in American government that I have analyzed: pluralism, participatory democracy, elitism, machiavellianism, and bureaucracy. How a political scientist, student, or the average citizen feels about who rules the United States may well relate to my earlier discussion of the positions of nature and nurture. Regardless of an individual's values or interpretations about who rules in the United States, or whether we are manipulated or are the manipulators, I am convinced that each individual in our society can express some power over her own life in relation to government.

Many opportunities exist for individuals to accomplish their goals in relation to government. Observant people have a way of taking advantage of contradictions in the political system. Every political system provides loopholes that enable individuals to achieve ends the power brokers failed to envision. The more democratic the system, the greater the alternatives for individual choice, and, therefore, the more contradictions in existence. Allow me to provide a few examples:

Madilyn Murray O'Hare, America's best known atheist, founded an atheist church. Her action to many appeared hypocritical, but it provides her church with tax exempt status. She could collect more money to better enable her to combat religions.

In the community in which I live, the City Council banned organized dances after 2 AM a number of years back. The Council allowed religious and fraternal organizations to hold dances past 2 AM. The Council had intended to prevent a local disco from remaining open after that hour because of numerous reports of illegal activities.

When the owner of the disco, however, announced his ministry in the Universal Life Church (a few dollars register an individual as a minister) and that the proceeds of the dances held after 2 AM would go to his church, the Council expressed bafflement as to what to do. After a number of months, they passed a new ordinance rather than challenge the religious freedom doctrine of the First Amendment to the United States Constitution. This new ordinance was challenged in the courts as discriminatory to minorities. The disco owner contended that our community is basically white and that his disco, in attracting minorities from other communities, was offensive to the racist members of the City Council. The Court ruled against him.

DMSO (Dimethyl Sulfoxide) is banned in most states for medical use except in a rare gall bladder infection. Yet people purchase the drug as a solvent from hardware stores, health food stores, by mail, and even at street corner stands, to speed recovery from injuries.

*Acceptable politics: Ohlone College students
work in a local campaign.*

One final example—many extremist groups run people for office in the United States even though if they ever got elected, they would try to eliminate our system of government that allowed them to achieve power.

Many years ago, when I saw the movie "The Ten Commandments," I wondered why Yul Brenner (Ramses II) never eliminated Charlton Heston (Moses) after his first plague threat. Why did he wait for nine more plagues and only decided to get rid of Charlton Heston after he let the Hebrews leave? Perhaps Yul Brenner feared the unknown might of Charlton Heston and his followers, or even the wrath of the Hebrews' god.

I believe there is another plausible explanation which I came to while viewing the film "Catch 22." The air force officers in the film decided to let Yosarian (the counter-hero of the tale) return home if only he would tell everyone how kind and generous they were. They failed to understand why Yosarian refused and would not love them for allowing him to go home. People in isolated positions of power often feel lonely and crave love, as did the air force officers in the film.

I am convinced that individuals in positions of leadership generally seek love and respect to justify their existence and will often provide boons to people who fill their emotional needs. Obviously, the method a petitioner uses in approaching a political leader must depend upon the petitioner's personality.

As I said earlier in this essay, I believe I am able to generalize about a person's political views from his/her expressed views about the nature of humans. This same analogy can help clarify some political terms and perhaps help us understand why certain individuals adhere to a specific political viewpoint.

A standard way to analyze political positions is to draw a line and place the labels left, center, and right on it. Although most people in our society would place a conservative on the right of the chart, in reality, the conservative fits in the center. The word conservative has within its generic makeup the word conserve. *Conservatives—are people who want to maintain things the way they are or they support very slow reasoned change based upon past experience.* Ideally conservatives would defend the status quo against major changes in the political, economic, or social institutions.

In American society, however, the ***ultra-conservative***—*those individuals who want to return to past institutions fairly rapidly*—have co-opted the name conservative.

Many political scientists believe that Edmund Burke, the famous late-eighteenth century English statesman, presented the most comprehensive statement on the philosophy of conservatism. He, like most conservatives, was not opposed to all change, but believed that political stability demanded that the forces of change be moderated by careful integration into tested societal institutions.

The reason Burke and other conservatives are hesitant about rapid change is their simple distrust of human nature. Their belief that human passions prevail, dictates their concern about change. Perhaps, the reason many people in our society think of conservatives as being on the right of the political spectrum is that most Americans, historically, have favored change, especially what might be termed liberal change. Let me use the concept of liberal change to further expand on the types of change the left or right want, since conservatives (in the center) want little or no change.

Earlier in this essay I wrote that liberals tended to believe in the perfectibility and malleability of humankind. A liberal or left-winger with their belief in

Moonies—An appeal to true believers?

nurture is willing to trust people and try new things. Change for the left, then, is progressive. The further left on the political scale, the more rapid the yearning to change to something new and the faster the desire to get there.

A *liberal—regards the individual as rational and believes in slow forward change without resorting to violence.* Therefore, the liberal would probably fit about half way between the center and the left-wing of the political spectrum chart.

On the extreme left would be those groups who want immediate change and are often willing to resort to violence under the pretext that the masses of good people are being restrained by the few evil individuals. Extreme leftists are often willing to exterminate the few bad under the belief that the good people would then prevail.

The right speaks: "To hell with Commies; God bless America."

Interestingly, the extreme right-wing often resorts to similar violent tactics. They do so with the belief that most people are evil. They rationalize that society is better off without many of the bad people. The right also holds that since people are evil, they need to be controlled by a strong government or individual.

People on the right of the political spectrum tend to want to return to the way things were in the "good old days." Since right-wingers generally believe that most of today's social, economic, and political problems result from democratic excesses, they would prefer to return to the days before the masses played any part in political decision making, and the deserving elite ruled society. Often right-wingers are known as *reactionaries—individuals who advocate political, economic, and social reform by returning to an earlier system as soon as possible.*

Although the terms I have used and their applications are generalizations, they should enable you to better understand the diversity of political positions and why people hold these views. However, a few individuals seem to adhere to no value positions and yet become political activists. Some of these individuals are what might simply be termed professional joiners. They seem not to care what political group they are a member of, as long as they are a member of a group. More interesting is that they often know little or nothing about their group's political theory. They have joined the group for emotional reasons, not intellectual.

Eric Hoffer studied this phenomenon in 1951 in his now classic, *The True Believer.* Hoffer concluded that certain individuals became professional joiners because of a craving to be rid of an unwanted self, unlike those persons who found an intellectual appeal in an organization because of their desire to bolster and advance their cherished self. (p. 21, Perennial Library Edition, 1966) Basically, what Hoffer argued was that in all societies there are misfits and in times of tension the number of pariahs increases as certain people lose their sense of self-worth.

These individuals, lacking a sense of their own being, cannot make value judgments on the nature of humanity. They enlist in mass-type movements to find an identity which will give them a reason for existence—what might be termed group self-worth.

Different from the individual who develops a sincere faith through intellectual self-interest and, therefore, will attempt to convert others, the True Believer must convert or eliminate everyone who refuses to follow the correct path. The True Believer's identity rests upon his/her new found faith and any questioning of this orthodoxy threatens his/her existence.

Certain groups seem to appeal to True Believer types, who recruit people through subterfuge and deception. Individuals having a true faith, be it in nature or nurture politics, have little fear in revealing their identity and they will try to convince someone through the correctness of their position. If the individual fails to understand their reasoning the true faith people will leave, believing that the unconvinced person is just a lost soul. True Believers, however, if unable to deceive an individual into joining their mass-movement, will try to eliminate the person. If they feel powerless because of their failure, they often sacrifice themselves as proof of their doctrines or as protection from their mortal enemies. The tragedy of Jonestown, Guyana in 1978 where 900 people committed suicide or were murdered exemplifies just such a fantaticism. More recently, The True Believer Branch Davidian cult of David Koresh fostered their own *auto da fé* near Waco, Texas. And, we cannot forget the strange philosophy and strange deaths of the members of Heaven's Gate a few years ago in California. True Believers all.

I have used the nature versus nurture debate in this essay to develop generalizations concerning the study of politics, political activities, and political behavior. Although I might have used other approaches to an introduction to the study of politics, I chose to develop the nature of human controversy as a means to get you, the reader, to analyze the abstract concepts of politics and realize how you are involved in a political system and also how you can become more involved through being observant. Besides the new concepts and understandings of theories pertaining to politics, I hope a side effect of my nature versus nurture approach to politics and political alternatives will have been for you to have gained a better knowledge of political terminology.

GLOSSARY

ABSOLUTE MONARCHY
Where a king, queen, emperor, or other regal potentate exercises the supreme powers of the state, usually acquiring the position through inheritance.

ALTRUISM
The unselfish concern for the welfare of others.

AUTOCRATIC GOVERNMENTS
Systems in which a single individual asserts political power and authority.

BILDERBERGERS
An alleged conspiracy of wealthy corporate leaders and bankers.

BUREAUCRATIC INTERPRETATION
The belief that the United States is ruled by the civil servants, the administrators.

CONSERVATIVES
They are people who want to maintain things the way they are or they support very slow reasoned change based upon past experience.

CONSPIRACY THESIS
The belief that a small group of people formulates secret plans to defraud the democratic process, controlling power for their own selfish desires.

DEMOCRATIC PLURALISM
The belief that group power balances group power with the result that no one group is able to dominate the American political system, enabling democracy to prevail.

DNA (Deoxyribonucleic Acid)
The molecule that contains the genetic blueprint of all living things.

ESTABLISHMENT
Those people who create and maintain the power that is exercised by the elected or appointed officials.

FOLKWAYS
The traditional patterns of life common to a group of people.

GOVERNMENT
The organized state's political and administrative structure.

ILLUMINATI
Alleged followers of the anti-Christ who date back to the Medieval period.

LIBERAL
Regards the individual as rational and believes in slow forward change without resorting to violence.

MACHIAVELLIAN INTERPRETATION
Holds that certain individuals strive for power and when in control rule for their own individual amoral benefit, characterized by their unscrupulous cunning and deception.

JAMES MADISON
The individual who kept a diary of the debates at the Constitutional Convention of 1787 and along with Alexander Hamilton and John Jay composed the *Federalist Papers* to explain and defend the Constitution.

MORES
The fundamental moral values of a group.

NATURE
The idea that an individual's genetic inheritance is the basic force behind his/her behavior.

NEW LEFT
A radical-liberal movement, particularly of college students and some professors in the 1960s and early 1970s, that challenged the established political, social, cultural, and economic order.

NURTURE
The idea that individuals become what they are because of their socio-cultural, economic, and political environments; the conditioning processes of their societies.

PARTICIPATORY DEMOCRACY
The maximum direct participation in political decision-making by each and every individual.

PLURALISM
The idea that society consists of diversified interest groups that compete for power.

POLITICAL SCIENTIST
Those academic individuals who deal with the theory and practice of politics and the description and analysis of political behavior.

POLITICS AS CONFLICT
Where groups and individuals compete for selfish reasons in a political system and the authoritative rule of the state creates peace.

POPULAR CONSENT
A concept which holds that laws are illegitimate without the consent of the people living under them.

POWER ELITE
A relatively small group of people in the executive branch of government, the leadership of large corporations, and the top military brass, which runs the country.

THE PRINCE
A treatise on government, composed by Niccolo di Bernardo Machiavelli in 1513, in which political expediency is advocated above morality.

PRIVATE GOVERNMENT
The unofficial institutions such as churches, trade unions, schools, etc.

PROPORTIONAL REPRESENTATION
An electoral system that allocates seats in a legislative body to each group approximately equal to their number in society.

PUBLIC GOVERNMENT
The institutions of the state such as constitutions, laws, legislatures, executives, and courts.

REACTIONARIES
Individuals who advocate political, economic, and social reform by returning to an earlier system as soon as possible.

SOCIAL CONTRACT
Where people consented to enter into a government of their own creation.

TRI-LATERAL COMMISSION
A group established by former Chase Manhattan Chairman David Rockefeller in 1973 to create a meeting place for select citizens of Japan, Western Europe and the United States to discuss solutions to their common political, economic, and security problems.

ULTRA-CONSERVATIVE
Those individuals who want to return to past institutions fairly rapidly.

CHAPTER 2

Democracy Dissected

Essay II

Before dissecting the topic of democracy, I feel I must state my own bias—I believe in democracy!

For most people reading this essay, this testament might not seem exceptionally radical. In fact, they would probably think it worthless for me to even have stated my prejudice, as these readers would assume that the vast majority of people in the United States adhere to democratic principles and practices. Ah, if only that were the truth. On the contrary, survey data seem to indicate that a large portion of the American public lacks a firm belief in democracy, maintaining only a weak commitment to democratic values even while expressing a faith in democracy. Of course, as in any survey, the way terms are worded or questions asked can determine the outcome of the study.

Dissecting the meaning and values of democracy becomes more complicated than a survey's distortions or bias. The word democracy is used by almost every conceivable type of government in today's world. Systems as diverse as that of the United States, The People's Republic of China, and Khaddafy's Libya all claim to be democratic. Democracy almost loses meaning when authoritarian and totalitarian governments can justify their repression of human rights in the name of democratic principles and values.

I guess the obvious question is: "What do I mean when I use the word democracy?" Before answering that question let me warn you that my use of the word scares groups such as the communists or the John Birch society; the meaning I give to democracy makes even many middle of the road Americans twist their heads, doubting whether such a system can ever work.

When people are confronted with inflation, recession, unemployment and high crime rates, they have difficulty understanding my democratic faith.

I could generate fear with a simple traditional textbook definition of *democracy—a government of the people, by the people, and for the people*. In other words, I believe in *popular sovereignty—a vesting of the ultimate political authority in the people*. The word democracy derives from the Greek word for people—*demos*, and their word for rule—*kratos*—the people rule.

America wants you'se.

I hear the skeptics whispering: "Still not very radical." True, so permit me to continue.

My belief in democracy stems from my faith in the individual's basic goodness—whether inherited or learned. For, to have faith in democracy, I must trust the people and respect each and every person's worth and dignity. I do! And, now I can read the lips of those worrywarts saying: "Don't you recognize that there are in our society a large number of **sociopaths**—*those psychopathic personalities with aggressively antisocial behavior?*" Of course I do—well, maybe not a large number—but every democracy must decide who can participate, who are the people who should rule. I will discuss these points later.

My belief in democracy also rests upon a firm tolerance for diversity in our society. Certainly, I have strong opinions and prejudices that bias my attitude toward specific groups or people.

My tolerance rests on a willingness to argue with their positions. I do not intend to eliminate them through censorship even if I should some day be a part of the majority. A democracy depends on the principle of majority rule with respect for minority rights and the institutional guarantees that a minority may some day become a majority. Underlying this concept is that each and every individual is more important than the state and his/her rights must be protected from governmental arbitrariness.

And what are those rights? The "unalienable rights" mentioned in the Declaration of Independence are "life, liberty, and the pursuit of happiness." Please note that **Thomas Jefferson**—*chief architect of the Declaration of*

Independence and third president of the United States—failed to include property as had *John Locke—the English philosopher whose most important works are* The Essay Concerning Human Understanding *(1690) and* Two Treatises on Civil Government *(1690).*

Locke wrote that men are born with the natural rights of life, liberty and property. He emphasized the preservation of property as pursuant to a just government.

The democratic creed set forth in our Declaration of Independence insists that the pursuit of happiness is a major principle government must uphold in order for justice to prevail. Tied to the unalienable rights of life, liberty, and the pursuit of happiness advanced in the democratic creed that I support in my conviction, is the idea that "all men are created equal." Now, with a few of your heads perplexed, attempting to mull through these abstract terms called natural rights, let me summarize a little of democracy's history before I go into the conditions necessary for a democratic government to exist.

Our first recorded knowledge of a democratic government stems from Ancient Greece. A number of Greek city-states developed democratic governments, Athens being the most predominant. Almost every form of government we know today existed in miniature among the Greek city-states. The Athenian *polis—the Greek term for a city-state*—prided herself on having evolved through almost all of these systems of government, achieving the highest form, democracy, by the fifth century before the Christian era.

Like many of her counterparts, Athens started out as an *absolute monarchy—a form of government where a king, queen, emperor, or other regal potentate exercises full ruling powers (monarchs usually inherit their position through birth).* Athens then developed a *constitutional monarchy—a form of government where the monarchs share the ruling power with elected representatives or are merely figureheads.*

Athens' monarchy soon evolved into an *oligarchy—a form of government where only a few rule, usually an elite, based upon military power or wealth.* (Our newspapers usually refer to a military oligarchy as a Junta.) In the seventh century before the Christian era, Athens found herself ruled by *despots—rulers with unlimited power*—and *tyrants—rulers with absolute power who tend to govern harshly or cruelly.* Some of these despots provided the Athenian people with certain rights and privileges, enabling them to participate in the city's government. Finally, a despot named Solon (c. 640–c. 558 BC) bestowed on Athens a democratic constitution.

Today the word *solon is often used synonymously with legislators.* The laws Solon codified created a *direct democracy—where the people make the decisions directly.*

Although in some parts of the United States town meetings are held and state constitutions provide for other forms of direct democracy, our system is known as an *indirect* or *representative democracy—where the people elect representatives to act as their agents in the law-making process.*

Athens only contained 43,000 citizens, a small enough figure, some people argue, to make direct democracy feasible. Actually, the Athenian population was quite a bit larger, but women, aliens, and slaves were not accorded citizenship rights.

A few writers have suggested that the United States could become a direct democracy with our computer technology. Using special ID cards and computers in each home, every citizen could propose and vote on laws directly. Like Athens' Council of 500, drawn by lot, we could still have a legislature to supervise the business of state, arrange for elections, receive foreign embassies and steer resolutions to the general populace.

In Athens, no business could come before the Assembly of all the people unless it had first been debated in the Council. Our executive could be similar to Athens' ten generals, with different responsibilities assigned to each individual. Of course, I am not sure if any of these suggestions are feasible considering the status of politicians and their control of legislation in the United States, but I felt it was at least worth giving some space in this essay.

William Buckley, a conservative writer, once said that it was not an issue of providing more democratic participation, but of taking the vote away from most American citizens. He felt that they lacked the knowledge to participate in the political process. Perhaps Buckley and other ultra-conservatives would support direct democracy if, like Athens, the United States abandoned its recent principle of "one person-one vote."

In the mid-1990's a new ultra-conservative movement emphasizing the theme of a tyrannical federal government arose. Leaders of this movement, often members of private militias, have demanded County Supremacy or State Sovereignty. The most fanatic of these groups seemed to be in the Western United States. The fanaticism has been manifested as threats, intimidation and violence toward federal employees. Helen Chenoweth, a former Republican Congresswoman from Idaho, personified the rise of this radical fringe in legitimate politics. She said: "We have democracy when the government is afraid of the people." While Representative Chenoweth's rhetoric emphasizes empowering people, I must question her support of diversity and individual rights. Her District office in Boise, Idaho displays on the wall a quotation from Patrick Henry proclaiming the Christian essence of this nation.

Democratic principles demand equal access of people to the political process no matter what their faith, creed or race. But, who are people? Athens excluded women, slaves and aliens from citizenship and equal access to government. In our early history, many states excluded anyone but male property holders from participation, believing they were the only ones who had a justifiable stake in society. *Thomas Paine (1737–1809)—the author of* Common Sense *and* The Crisis Papers, *which inspired the American independence movement*—once asked something like: "If property worth fifty pounds is necessary for a man to vote, and a man owns a jackass worth fifty pounds, enabling him to vote, but the jackass dies and the man can no longer vote; who voted, the man or the jackass?"

Even in the not so distant past, our nation placed limitations upon access to the political process to women, blacks, Indians, and eighteen year olds. I doubt if anyone would question certain residency requirements or argue that small children, illegal aliens, or the insane should vote. Arguments have been made, however, to provide equal access to the political process for imprisoned criminals, convicted felons, and illiterates.

Some view the U.S. as a totalitarian nation.

All democracies set some criterion of competence. I feel the fewest possible limitations on access to the political process provide for the expansion of liberty and enhances the pursuit of happiness. I do adhere to the protection of civil liberties (see Essay III) and access to the political process for those noncitizens, those under eighteen (our legal voting age—in Athens it was twenty), and for illiterates, but I cannot support their right to vote. I have mixed emotions about convicted felons who have served their time being denied access to the political process.

History books, when discussing Athens, make comparisons with her chief adversary, the polis of Sparta. The Spartans were an *aristocracy—a ruling elite, classified as the "best" citizens, usually based upon birth status.* They numbered about 25,000 and ruled over one million peasants. Sparta created a military society and could be compared with modern day *totalitarian governments— where the state has total control of the institutions of society and generally maintains command with a political ideology.* Sparta, like totalitarian states today, indoctrinated all her citizens through the use of propaganda and promoted the concept that the state was more important than the individual. The highest duty of a citizen was to give his life for the state.

Athenian *imperialism—the control (sometimes by finance capital) of one political community over another—*clashed with Spartan expansionism in 431 BC. The war lasted until 404 BC when Sparta finally proved victorious. Magnanimously, they installed an ultra-conservative oligarchy in power. The flame of the world's first democracy flickered and in fifty years would be extinguished by Philip of Macedonia, father to Alexander the Great, when he conquered all of Greece.

Athens and other Greek cities had founded colonies in many regions along the Mediterranean Sea, including southern Italy. Perhaps some of the Greek principles of freedom and equality influenced the development of Rome. The next contact we have with a form of democracy occurs there.

In 509 BC, the people of a small city (ten miles by twenty-five) called Rome established a *republic—in simple terms this means the absence of monarchy, however, the word is also associated with representative government; a debate exists as to whether a representative knowing what is best decided for the common good, or literally represented the will of the people (indirect democracy)*. Descendants of the founders of Rome known as *patricians—today this word refers to people of high social rank or noble families*—controlled the political process throughout the early centuries of Roman expansion in Italy.

Patricians ran their city through the Senate, open only to them, where they served life terms. The Senate handled the finances and created the law, supposedly representing the interests of all classes.

Other citizens, not descendants of the founding families, known as *plebeians—today this word refers to the common people*—had an Assembly (actually two, but only one had any real possibility of power). Seating in the Assembly depended upon wealth and it was quite easy for the patrician class to maintain control of any Assembly actions.

Rome had two consuls who acted as the executive branch of government. Elected by the Assembly, the consuls had to be patricians.

The plebeians provided the chief source of capital for the constant Roman wars and many lost their land or became debt slaves. The plebeians, according to legend, went on strike, leaving the city to protest the unjust laws. As a concession to their power, the patricians granted the plebeians the right to elect their own officers, called Tribunes, who eventually gained the right to sit outside the door of the Senate and shout "I forbid" when they opposed something. The Roman word the Tribunes shouted, *veto—refers, in the United States today, to the power vested in the President to cancel or postpone the enactments of the Congress.*

Gradually, the plebeians increased their rights; however, Rome never became a direct democracy. With Julius Caesar's murder in 44 BC, assassinated by those believing he intended to terminate the Republic, and with the ascension of Caesar's nephew Octavian (Augustus) to power in 27 BC, the Roman Republic gave way to the Roman Empire.

We would be hard put to find any vestiges of democracy in the next thousand years. During the Medieval Period a number of citizens rebelled against their Lords or bought charters from their monarchs and created communes, as these city-state republics were called. Most of these communes were *plutocracies—where the ruling class exercised power by virtue of its wealth.*

One medieval Italian city-state, Rome, for a while had a democratic *theocracy—where the religious leader and the political leader are the same.* The commune of Rome elected the Pope by virtue of the cheers of the masses of people in the city's streets. By the later part of the Middle Ages, the college of Cardinals took responsibility for the election of the Pope. This system of electing the Pope still exists today, and although Rome is a part of Italy, a part of Rome called the Vatican is an independent polity ruled by the Pope as head of the Catholic Church. Some other Medieval cities developed *theocratic systems—where the religious leader and the political leader are separate, but the enactment of laws is based almost totally on religious doctrine.*

As the Medieval Period waned, the communes were absorbed into the new Absolute Monarchies. In 1689, England created a constitutional monarchy under principles enunciated by John Locke (see my earlier discussion of Locke's ideas on a social contract). Locke's views, along with those of other writers and philosophers of the eighteenth century, had a direct influence on the intellectuals of the American Revolution.

Jefferson's Declaration of Independence reflected the eighteenth-century philosopher's faith in human reason. The ideas expressed in this document, issued on July 4, 1776, challenged the absolute monarchies' contention that governments were established by divine will and that in serving these governments men were somehow serving God. Jefferson wrote:

> We hold these truths to be self-evident; that all men are created equal, that they are endowed by their Creator with certain unalienable rights, that among these are life, liberty, and the pursuit of happiness.

> That, to secure these rights, governments are instituted among men, deriving their just powers from the consent of the governed;

> That whenever any form of government becomes destructive of these ends, it is the right of the people to alter or to abolish it, and to institute new government, laying its foundation on such principles, and organizing its powers in such form, as to them shall seem most likely to effect their safety and happiness.

Jefferson expressed the creed and the founders of the United States reestablished the ancient Athenian principles of democracy. On July 4, 1776, John Hancock, as President of the Second Continental Congress, placed his name first on the document and later other representatives of the thirteen colonies signed these revolutionary tenets. America declared her independence and in a sense John Hancock served as the first President, as he was head of the Congress.

A more formal government became necessary and in July, 1777, the Congress sent to the states the Articles of Confederation. To prevent the formation of an autocracy like the one the revolutionaries believed they lived under as British colonies, they created a *confederation—a government structure with a limited central government and with most of the power residing in the sub-divisions of the polity.*

Most of the state governments under the Articles provided their citizens with liberal constitutions, incorporating bills of rights, liberalizing property requirements for voting, abolishing most religious qualifications for serving in government, and establishing indirect democracy. In fact, some states like Massachusetts incorporated into their constitution the principle of equality as set forth in the Declaration of Independence. In 1783, the Massachusetts Supreme Court declared slavery to be illegal under the provision in their constitution that proclaimed that all men were created equal.

All of the state legislatures passed the Articles of Confederation by 1781. With the end of the Revolutionary War in 1783, as is often the case with revolution, conservative forces reasserted their power. The league of friendship of the weak central government of the Articles of Confederation along with the advancement of democratic principles in many of the states distressed the *plutocrats—the merchants, money-lenders, the large landowners.* These "rich and well-born" became convinced, especially with *Shays's Rebellion—a revolt of farmers in Massachusetts in 1786–1787, led by Daniel Shays, seeking relief from debts and mortgage foreclosures—*that the state governments by themselves could not protect life and property. Historians debate whether Shays's Rebellion actually caused the call for revisions to the Articles of Confederation, but the event certainly underlined the economic fears among the creditor and commercial interests. Other leaders feared that the new nation, with a weak central government, was a tempting prize for a foreign nation.

During the summer of 1786, delegates from five states met at Annapolis, Maryland, to discuss possible amendments to the Articles relating to trade and navigation. Individuals like Alexander Hamilton supported changing the Articles to create a strong national government. Lacking numbers, the few delegates present moved to request the various state legislatures to authorize representatives to go to Philadelphia in May, 1787 to consider basic amendments to the Articles of Confederation.

The Confederation Congress reluctantly concurred and moved to have the states appoint delegates for the "sole and express purpose of revising the Articles of Confederation." Please note the wording, for what transpired at Philadelphia during the late spring and summer of 1787 proved a violation of the commission assigned by Congress.

The fifty-five delegates (nineteen failed to appear and Rhode Island refused to send delegates, fearing a conspiracy by "the rich and well-born") created a totally new constitution. The convention acted illegally by sending the final draft to state ratifying conventions, specifying that only nine states needed to approve the Constitution before the new document went into effect. The Congress had specified that any revisions necessitated their approval and must be confirmed by all of the state legislatures.

It could be argued that the Constitution of the United States, created in 1787, ratified in 1789 by nine states, was an illegal document. When all thirteen states approved the Constitution by 1791, it became legal *de facto*—*it exists in fact and the legal establishment is no longer necessary or relevant.*

In recent years, some Americans have called for constitutional conventions to propose amendments to the Constitution providing for a balanced budget or to overturn the Supreme Court's decision of one person-one vote. The Supreme Court decision demanded equal distribution of population in all state Senates as well as in their Assemblies. Some thirty-five legislatures have approved this latter call, as they believe that they have been unfairly restricted in not permitting their upper houses to represent districts. However, 38 state legislatures must ratify an amendment for it to go into effect.

Many people fear this call for constitutional conventions because the only experience our nation has had with such a convention failed to live up to its mandates. Despite reassurances that a new convention would only deal with the issue at hand, the previous convention created a totally new constitution. The critics of the convention movement argue that there is nothing to stop a new convention from doing the same thing.

Liberals, especially, oppose such a convention. They believe that because of the tensions in American society today, the convention delegates would be ultra-conservatives willing to eliminate many of the civil-liberties protections guaranteed Americans under the Bill of Rights and The Fourteenth Amendment.

Perhaps the legality of the original Constitution lacks relevance, but its counter-revolutionary importance needs to be discussed. I am too deficient in historical expertise, however, to become directly involved in the controversy surrounding Charles A. Beard's *An Economic Interpretation of the Constitution of the*

United States in which he leaves the impression that many, if not most, of the framers created the Constitution from motives of monetary self-interest. His views have been contested by many notable historians.

From my perspective, there is no question that the distinguished gathering at Philadelphia contained only the "rich and the well-born"—lawyers, bankers, planters, and successful merchants. And although it is true that most of the signatories to the Declaration of Independence attended the convention, there were the notable exceptions of some of the more liberal and sometimes radical endorsers—Thomas Paine, Patrick Henry, Sam Adams, and Thomas Jefferson. Even those who had expressed their support for the principles of liberty and equality as enunciated in the Declaration of Independence were eleven

Federalism: Separation and unity.

years older and the heat of the Revolution had dissipated. There is an old Spanish proverb which goes something like this: "If you are young and not a liberal, you have no heart. If you are old and not a conservative, you have no head." I am convinced the heads prevailed, as the Constitution of the United States set forth a system that emphasized liberty but not equality.

The framers of the Constitution continually expressed their disdain for the common people. Alexander Hamilton spoke of the "folly and wickedness of mankind." James Madison emphasized the "infirmities and depravities of human character." Elbridge Gerry, a delegate from Massachusetts, believed that the problems faced by the Confederation were due to too much involvement of the people in government. He said: "The evils we experience flow from the excess of democracy." Most of the framers agreed with Gerry and saw democracy, with its emphasis on equality as well as liberty, as *mobocracy—the belief that when people rule they rule through passion and not reason.*

In closed sessions, at Philadelphia, the framers moved to control the passions of the mob—that democracy which they saw as threatening to their liberty and property—as well as to maintain the Articles' limitation on autocracy. We call this system federalism. A *federal system—means a sharing of power between the central government and its sub-divisions.*

The intent of the framers went beyond this sharing of power. They were determined to provide a system of government where no one group would become too powerful. Through this system they hoped to preserve liberty. To accomplish this goal they created an intricate system of checks and balances and a separation of power between the executive, legislative, and judicial branches of government.

In a sense I agree with the ultra-conservative John Birch Society's contention that the framers established a Republic, not in the indirect democracy sense, but with the concept that the people should elect representatives who determine what is best for the common good. This is far from the democratic thesis I advocated and described earlier in this essay. I cannot but abhor the John Birch Society's desire to return this elitist government. An examination of just a few of the sections of the original constitution will explain the elitism of the Federal Republic advanced by the framers.

Article I of the Constitution established a legislature that was *bicameral—a two-house legislature*. Most states, since colonial days, had bicameral legislatures. A compromise at the convention produced an upper house, the Senate, that gave each state two delegates who would serve six years. This agreement satisfied the fears of the small states about large state domination of the new nation. State legislators were to elect the Senators as they needed to represent state issues and the framers believed that the state legislators would know better than the voting public which individuals would best serve state interests. Because of pressure from the democratic movement of the early twentieth century, an amendment to the constitution in 1913 provided for the direct election of Senators by the people.

A lower chamber, the House of Representatives, would be based on population. This satisfied the large states. A compromise became necessary to determine just who the people were. Southern states insisted that slaves were people, at least for population purposes. The framers finally agreed that a slave was at least three-fifths of a person when it came time to allocate seats in the House of Representatives. Indians failed to be granted even partial status as individuals, for the framers decided that Indians, not taxed, could not be counted in the census determination, nor could they vote.

Article III of the Constitution outlined the judicial branch of the proposed government. The framers decided to place federal judges above politics and the influence of the people by allowing the President, with the approval of the Senate, to appoint them for life (actually the Constitution says good behavior). They also stipulated that their salaries could not be reduced during their time in office.

In developing the executive branch, the framers had difficulty deciding upon a method of electing the President. They did not trust the people's knowledge and finally agreed to a unique compromise—the creation of the electoral college. According to the Constitution:

> Each State shall appoint, in such Manner as the Legislature thereof may direct, a number of Electors, Equal to the whole Number of Senators and Representatives to which the State may be entitled in the Congress: but no Senator or Representative, or Person holding an Office of Trust or Profit under the United States, shall be appointed an Elector.

What the electoral system amounted to, for most states, was a system telling people in their localities to vote for those people who knew better than they did who should be President of the United States. Let me attempt to explain the electoral system with a few examples. Imagine that the author of this textbook is well versed in politics, and that the year is 1788. I will take us back in time.

On your local ballot you would see, among the names of those individuals running to elect a President, an Alan Kirshner. I had met the state's requirements to be an elector. No, Kirshner is not running for the office of President. I would only be asking you to vote for me as I knew better than you did who should be President of the United States. If I should win, I would then cast my ballot for my favorite candidate.

Who did I vote for? Well, you trusted me to make the right decision, so I am not telling! Not satisfied? Exactly what happened in most states. People began to insist upon knowing beforehand for whom the electors would vote.

When my name appeared on the ballot again, next to my name would be written my choice for President. For example, you would read: "Kirshner— Thomas Jefferson."

Over the years the number of electors became too numerous to place their names on the ballot. California, the largest state in population, has 55 electoral votes. If ten candidates ran for the office of President, the ballot would need space for 550 names, as each candidate would have 55 loyal supporters sworn to vote for his/her candidacy.

Electors are not required by law in most states to cast their votes as pledged. In very few instances has an elector voted different from his/her promise. It takes a majority of the electors to elect a President. Their votes are counted in front of Congress usually on the third of January every fourth year. There are 538 electors who vote for President (the District of Columbia has been granted three electors as if they were a state with two senators and one representative). A minimum of 270 electoral votes are necessary to elect a President.

If you are thinking that the electoral college system is not a direct democracy because you are not voting directly for the President, you are quite right. Remember, I informed you earlier that the framers never intended to provide for a direct democracy. Four times in our history—1824, 1876, 1888 and 2000—the individuals who received the greatest number of popular votes failed to be elected President. Andrew Jackson, in 1824, fell short of a clear majority of the popular and electoral vote. Through the provision of the Constitution pertaining to a case where neither candidate obtains a majority of the electoral vote, the election fell to the House of Representatives. They elected John Quincy Adams President (John Quincy Adams had 12-1/2 percent less popular votes than Jackson). In 1876, an electoral commission threw some disputed electoral votes to Rutherford B. Hayes, making him President despite Samuel J. Tilden's 51% in the popular vote. Grover Cleveland in 1888 clearly beat Benjamin Harrison in the popular vote, but Harrison won a strong victory in the electoral college due to his winning the populous states. In 2000, Al Gore won a small victory among the nation's voters, but lost to George W. Bush in the electoral college.

Polls today consistently indicate that 80% of the voters and nearly the same percentage of politicians believe the electoral system should be eliminated or drastically modified. Even though the people and the politicians express a desire for more direct democracy, all attempts to change the electoral college have failed miserably. I am still amazed that after the 2000 election there was little push to eliminate the electoral college.

Federalism still prevails in the smoke filled rooms of the salons. The electoral college system continues to provide benefits to the state governments. Candidates for the presidency must guarantee state politicos various benefits to get them to work for their election. State politicians look for promises to their state of items such as defense contracts, dams, post offices, or road construction funds.

A presidential candidate, in appealing directly to the people, would seldom emphasize such programs. He would most likely pledge to reduce unemployment, end inflation, and provide a strong national defense. These latter issues could be broadcast through the airways and a candidate's appearance in the states could be minimized. State politicians like the coat-tails of presidential candidates to help them get elected, especially when they can point to the projects they obtained for the people of the state.

To paraphrase myself—many political leaders feel that by maintaining the electoral college system, we continue the principle of a Federal Republic with its balance of power between the states and the national government, as well as its limitations on the power of any one group, be it the people or the chief executive's appointees. If the people elected the President directly, his commitment might be totally to them and not to the states.

Political leaders fear that the power of the two-party system would diminish with the elimination of the electoral college system. An independent candidate, like Ross Perot in 1992 and 1996, might defeat the Republican and Democratic candidates through appealing only to voter-oriented issues.

Some supporters of the electoral college system warn about the dangers inherent in an election by a *plurality—where a candidate receives less than 50% of the vote, but obtains more votes than any other candidate.* During the 1980 Democratic Congressional primary in San Diego County, California, the head of the local Ku Klux Klan won the nomination because two popular candidates split the vote. Democratic party leaders then got behind the Republican candidate to assure the defeat of Grand Dragon Metzger. What the supporters of the electoral college are arguing is that the system allows mainstream candidates to be elected.

I want to be clear that my presenting the arguments for upholding the electoral college does not signify my support. I have declared my faith in democracy and this necessitates my own adherence to the elimination of the electoral college with its replacement by a direct election for the President. Sure, I appreciate the alarm of those who fear that by changing a system that works we fail to know what will happen.

I guess I am just not an upholder of undemocratic traditions even if they do work. I believe a runoff between the top two candidates, as occurs in France, would be a more honest expression of popular will than the electoral college.

I trust the people and I do agree with the critics of the Washington bureaucracy that we have turned over too much power to the national government in recent years, almost creating a **unitary system**—*where most of the power rests in the central government with little or no power in the sub-divisions.* Since the Great Depression of 1929 and Franklin Delano Roosevelt's New Deal legislation, the central government created an extensive **bureaucracy**—*a body of officials and administrators whose responsibility it is to interpret and carry out legislative law.*

The increase in bureaucratic agencies is due to the growth of demands for social services, human rights, and military defense. With the centralization of government comes federal control over many local issues. Framers of the constitution, such as Alexander Hamilton, distrusted the people and wanted a more unitary system. Liberals, like Thomas Jefferson, trusted in local control to provide for the liberty and equality of the people.

The liberals called for an addition to the Constitution of a **Bill of Rights**—*the first ten amendments to the Constitution of the United States with its emphasis on human rights and liberties.* Without the framers' agreement to add a Bill of Rights, the state conventions would probably never have ratified the Constitution. In New York, the vote was so close that Alexander Hamilton, James Madison, and John Jay produced **The Federalist Papers**—*a series of essays explaining the purpose and issues of various sections of the Constitution of the United States.*

Some leaders continued to oppose the new constitution as being an attempt to return to autocracy. Patrick ("give me liberty or give me death") Henry of Virginia wrote:

> Consider our situation sir: go to the poor man, and ask him what he does. He will inform you that he enjoys the fruits of his labor, under his own fig-tree, with his wife and children around him, in peace and security. Go to every other member of society,—you will find the same tranquil case and content; you will find no alarms or disturbances. Why, then, tell us of danger, to terrify us into an adoption of this new form of government? And yet who knows the dangers that this new system may produce? They are out of sight of the common people: they cannot foresee latent consequences. I dread the operation of it on the middling and lower classes of people: it is for them I fear the adoption of this system.

Since the end of the nineteenth century, liberals (as Patrick Henry could have been called in his day) have looked to Washington to expand the rights of the "middling and lower classes of people." Liberals felt, and many still feel, that the "rich and well-born" took control of the state legislatures. These selfish vested interests, the liberal democratic movement believed, refused to deal with social and economic problems affecting the common person. One political scientist, William H. Riker, in his *Federalism: Origin, Operation, Significance* (Boston: Little Brown, 1964), argued that federalism perpetuated racism and protected big business. Opponents of federalism contended that the states could not effectively deal with the complex economic and social problems of modern America because of the disparity of wealth among states.

Federal grants-in-aid programs have been an approach by moderates to balance the differences in state wealth while maintaining the principles of federalism. **Grants-in-aid**—*allocate federal funds to states for support services.* They often carry with them the provision that the state provide matching funds. Individuals supporting grants-in-aid have dominated Washington until the presidency of Ronald Reagan, from 1981 through 1989. President Reagan held that the national government attached too many specifications to these grants and they simply served as a way for Washington to annex the reserved powers of the states.

President Reagan called his philosophy *The New Federalism—President Ronald Reagan's view that federal programs should be dismantled and the states be allowed to take care of their own needs*. President George Bush, the First, who took office on January 20, 1989, continued the New Federalist argument that the power to deal with social and economic problems must remain with the states. Newt Gingrich, the Republican Speaker of the House of Representatives during the Clinton Administration, followed the traditional Republican demand for State's Rights. The mainstream Republicans have never advocated the total dismantling of the federal government as a few of their more reactionary colleagues have. One example, the *County Supremacy Movement—goes beyond States' Rights and advocates the elimination of the federal government leaving almost all decisions to the will of the people in their counties; they also want to eliminate all federal ownership of land*. With the death of communism new devils have to be found and the fanatics are looking inside America for the new Antichrists. For those who need a scapegoat for whatever they see wrong in their lives, the federal government fulfills their needs. Political correctness is giving way to a new p.c., patriotic correctness.

Where do I stand? With the radical-liberal belief that the federal government must distribute a major portion of its budget for social services and continue to protect access to the economic market for all humans. I do favor local control over these programs. Bureaucracy needs to be dismantled and humanized. This can best be accomplished by limiting the power of vested economic interest groups at the local level. I am still a Jeffersonian with a belief that smaller government units allow more citizens to participate and advance the democratic ethic, but I would never favor an elimination of federal power. I could support the relocation of many if not most of the federal agencies from Washington to diverse sites in the United States. I believe such a relocation of the federal bureaucracy would derail the power of interest groups. The interest groups could no longer afford to sustain their access to power as they would out of necessity have to maintain numerous offices. Some refer to this philosophy as devolution—returning power back to the people of the states.

A new populism seems to have arisen. *Populism—was a political, economic and social reform movement at the end of the nineteenth century, mostly of Western and Southern farmers against what they perceived as the control of government by Eastern business interests; the protests of the common person against the privileged few*. The populist and *progressive movement—a series of political, social and economic reform movements active during the early twentieth century*—were responsible for the introduction of direct democracy into many city and state constitutions, especially in the west. Perhaps the addition of a few of these reforms into the Constitution of the United States—recall, initiative, and referendum—would enhance the new populist movement and the cause of democracy.

California is one of those western states that includes such direct democratic processes in their constitutions. *Recall—is defined as the power of the voters to remove an elected officer*. On the national level, the voters cannot remove an elected office holder. California's two senators and 53 congressmen are national office holders and can only be removed by their colleagues.

Impeachment proceedings apply only to the President, Vice-President, Cabinet Officials, Federal Judges, and other civil officers. The impeachment and trial on the charges brought by the impeachment are carried out by Congress. The House of Representatives impeaches and the Senate tries the case. It takes a two-thirds vote in the Senate to convict and the penalty is removal from office, inability to hold another federal office, and denial of appeal. The people of the nation have no say in this process.

Recall requirements vary from state to state; in California:

Jane Fonda speaks to Ohlone College students

> A petition to recall a statewide officer must be signed by electors equal in number to 12 percent of the last vote for the office, with signatures from each of 5 counties equal in number to 1 percent of the last vote for the office in the county. Signatures to recall Senators, members of the Assembly, members of the Board of Equalization, and judges of courts of appeal and trial courts must equal in number 20 percent of the last vote for the office.

Once the signatures are certified, an election must be called within 80 days and a majority vote is sufficient to remove the person from office. The recall of local officers is also permitted, usually with the stipulation that fifteen or twenty percent of the registered voters of the district sign the petition.

An *initiative—is the power of the electors (voters) to propose laws and amendments to the Constitution and to adopt them.* The federal Constitution does not include any provision for the people to introduce legislation or constitutional amendments. Two-thirds of the state legislatures can call for a special convention to propose amendment to the Constitution, but the people can only "petition the Government for a redress of grievances" according to the First Amendment. The government is not required to respond.

In California:

> An initiative measure may be proposed by presenting to the Secretary of State a petition that sets forth the text of the proposed statute or amendment to the Constitution and is certified to have been signed by electors equal in number to 5 percent in the case of a statute, and 8 percent in the case of an amendment to the Constitution, of the votes for all candidates for Governor at the last gubernatorial election.

After the Secretary of State verifies the signatures, the initiative must be submitted to the people at the next general election or the Governor may call for a special election. In the local communities, an initiative may be placed on the ballot with 10 percent of the signatures of the registered voters.

It is to the advantage of the petitioners to obtain enough signatures to place a proposed amendment on the ballot rather than a statute (law), as the legislature can always change a law. A Constitutional amendment can only be changed by another amendment which must be passed by a majority of the people voting.

In many states the word referendum is synonymous with initiative. California defines *referendum—as the power of the voters to approve or reject laws or parts of laws.* In California, the Constitution prohibits the rejection by referendum of tax levies or appropriations for state expenses.

Once again, the Federal Constitution fails to provide any method by which the voters can have a direct say in accepting or rejecting legislation. Such decisions are left solely to the members of Congress and to the President.

The Constitution of California reads:

> A referendum measure may be proposed by presenting to the Secretary of State within 90 days after the enactment date of the statute, a petition certified to have been signed by electors equal in number to 5 percent of the votes for all candidates for Governor at the last gubernatorial election, asking that the statute or part of it be submitted to the electors.

The Secretary of State has 31 days to submit the referendum to the voters after it qualifies or the Governor may call a special statewide election. Referendums are also permitted on the local level. To appear on the ballot, a petition to remove a law must receive ten percent of the signatures of the registered voters in the district.

The California Constitution provides more democracy than the Federal Constitution. I suspect the real issue for many is whether with all the Constitutional provisions, separation of powers, checks and balances, federalism in the United States is actually democratic, direct or indirect.

In my first essay, I developed some concepts as to who rules in America. *In this second essay, I have espoused my faith in democracy and advanced some ideas as to how I think a democratic system could be improved. I have indicated that I believe the Declaration of Independence advanced a democratic creed. And, though the framers of the Constitution established a federal republic, I held it was a reaction to democracy, returning to a modified elitist system. I showed how democratic principles and practices have been enhanced with the progressive and populist movements. However, I do not intend to try and analyze how much of a democracy our nation has become. I will leave that up to you. But I will provide you with some criteria for an analysis.*

I can only try and make my criteria as clear as I can. A democratic government must satisfy the principles of liberty and equality in order for citizens to give their active, and even passive, consent to its existence.

Liberty—in the context of democracy, means the quality or state of being free or freedom from arbitrary or despotic control. In simple terms, I would associate liberty with freedom and define *freedom—as the ability to choose between alternatives.*

In a democracy, liberty (freedom) cannot mean license. In this context, license refers to an individual's belief that s/he can do anything that s/he wants. How many times have I heard: "This is a democracy, I can do anything I want!"? No! Freedom demands responsibility. The responsibility of taking into account the impact of your actions on yourself and on others. Without self-restraint, chaos results and democracy ceases to exist.

Equality—in a democratic context refers to equal opportunity to achieve one's potential in order to participate fully in the political process. Alexis de Tocqueville in his *Democracy in America* (see Essay 1) warned that the principle of equality as misinterpreted in many segments of American society could bring everyone down to the level of mediocrity. He feared people demanding an egalitarian society rather than one that provided equal opportunity for each individual to reach their full potential and participate on an equal basis in the political process. The tyranny he feared was one that demanded conformity of the minority to the standards of the majority. The English philosopher John Stuart Mill, in his *On Liberty*, also expressed fear for minority rights in a democracy.

Kurt Vonnegut, in a series of short stories called *Welcome to the Monkey House,* has one piece on an egalitarian society, where the masses demanded the elimination of quality and people never merited their success. Showtime made this short story, "Harrison Berginan," into a full length movie a few years ago. In this future egalitarian society a prima ballerina could be no better than the corps de ballet. To assure this equality, she had to wear heavy weights. An articulate speaker in this equal society must discourse with marbles in his/her mouth so s/he would not impress anyone with his/her rhetoric. An imaginative thinker received electrical shock every time her/his mind began to create. In this manner the society remained stable. In such a society, with all people literally equal, lacking individuality and superiority, the liberty to achieve ceases to exist. No democracy can survive unless individuals are permitted to develop their full potential. No democracy can survive unless minority rights are respected. No democracy can survive unless pluralism continues to exist. And, no democracy can survive unless the unique creative ability of people allows them to merit their positions.

Neither liberty nor equality can exist unless children are reared in a democratic environment. I vividly recall attending a gathering a number of years ago while I was teaching at a university in the south. A young child, maybe a year old, had crawled to an end table, lifted himself up, and knocked over an ashtray. The grandmother picked up the boy and proceeded to smack the child around viciously. I shouted at her to stop and asked her what she thought she was doing. She replied angrily: "No grandchild of mine is going to grow up to be a hippie, nor talk back to his parents!"

I stared at her for a short while, incredulous at her words. I could think of nothing else to say but: "You mean your children never talked back to you after you hit them?" "Oh yes, they did," she informed me, "but I am hitting my grandchild harder so it won't happen to his parents." A child raised in a dictatorial family will grow up expecting and even wanting control, or s/he will rebel violently against authority.

On the other extreme, and perhaps more prevalent in some parts of our nation today, is the child who grows up lacking any controls. A few years ago, while shopping in a local general store, I observed an eleven year old and his mother. Every time he wanted candy or cookies or sugar cereals she said, "No!"

Symbol of freedom for millions.

And, every time his mother said no, he proceeded to throw the items in the shopping cart. They remained there until she paid for them with her charge card. Is it any wonder that some children today believe the world belongs to them and they can say, write, and do whatever they choose and whenever they desire?

A democratic environment fosters responsibility through guidance and direction. People must be given the opportunity to grow and develop through consistent discipline, the kind that creates responsible citizens able to choose between alternatives, trying to reach their potential while participating in government decision making.

For this growth to occur, a democratic government, with its principles of liberty and equality, must permit all citizens the right to formulate their preferences. Tied to the citizens formulating their preferences is their inalienable right to express their views. A true democratic government has institutions which provide that the citizens' positions are weighted equally in the conduct of government. Among these institutions are a free media which can provide alternative sources of information, free speech and the right to free assembly. Elections need to be conducted that allow for majority or plurality determination, while protecting the rights of the minority. These institutions must allow the people to hold government leaders accountable for their actions and give the people the right to become leaders or form and join organizations to promote their cause. Democratic institutions must guarantee that the sum of the parts is always greater than the whole—the sum of individuals in the state more important than the whole of a nation's political leadership. When these conditions exist, the country might rightfully be called a democracy.

GLOSSARY

ABSOLUTE MONARCHY
A form of government where a king, queen, or emperor, or other regal potentate exercises full ruling powers (monarchs usually inherit their position through birth).

ARISTOCRACY
A ruling elite, classified as the "best" citizens, usually based upon birth status.

BICAMERAL
A two house legislature.

BILL OF RIGHTS
The first ten amendments to the Constitution of the United States with emphasis on human rights and liberties.

BUREAUCRACY
A body of officials and administrators whose responsibility it is to interpret and carry out legislative law.

CONFEDERATION
A government structure with a limited central government and with most of the power residing in the sub-divisions of the polity.

CONSTITUTIONAL MONARCHY
A form of government where the monarch shares the ruling power with elected representatives or is merely a figurehead.

COUNTY SUPREMACY MOVEMENT
Goes beyond States' Rights and advocates the elimination of the federal government leaving almost all decisions to the will of the people in their counties; they also want to eliminate all federal ownership of land.

DE FACTO
Meaning that the legal establishment is no longer relevant as it exists in fact.

DEMOCRACY
A government of the people, by the people, and for the people.

DESPOTS
Rulers with unlimited power.

DIRECT DEMOCRACY
Where the people make the decisions directly without representatives.

EQUALITY
In a democratic context, refers to equal opportunity to achieve one's potential in order to participate fully in the political process.

FEDERAL SYSTEM
Means a sharing of power between the central government and its sub-divisions.

THE FEDERALIST PAPERS
A series of essays explaining the purpose and issues of various sections of the Constitution of the United States.

FREEDOM
The ability to choose between alternatives.

GRANTS-IN-AID
Allocate federal funds to states for support services.

IMPERIALISM
The control (sometimes by finance capital) of one political community over another.

INDIRECT (REPRESENTATIVE) DEMOCRACY
Where the people elect representatives to act as their agents in the law-making process.

INITIATIVE
The power of the voters to propose laws and amendments to the Constitution and to adopt them.

THOMAS JEFFERSON
Chief architect of the Declaration of Independence and third President of the United States.

JOHN LOCKE
The English philosopher whose most important works are *The Essay Concerning Human Understanding* (1690) and *Two Treatises on Civil Government* (1690).

LIBERTY
In the context of democracy, means the quality or state of being free or freedom from arbitrary or despotic control.

MOBOCRACY
The belief that when people rule they rule through passion and not reason.

NEW FEDERALISM
The view of Ronald Reagan and his supporters that federal programs should be dismantled and the states take care of their own needs.

OLIGARCHY
A form of government where only a few rule, usually an elite based upon military power or wealth.

THOMAS PAINE—(1737–1809)
The author of *Common Sense* and the *Crisis Papers,* which inspired the American independence movement.

PATRICIANS
Today this word refers to people of high social rank or noble families.

PLEBEIANS
Refers to the common people.

PLURALITY
When a candidate receives less than 50 percent of the vote, but obtains more votes than any other candidate.

PLUTOCRACIES
Where the ruling class exercises power by virtue of its wealth.

POLIS
The Greek term for a city-state.

POPULAR SOVEREIGNTY
A vesting of the ultimate political authority in the people.

POPULISM
A political, economic, and social reform movement at the end of the nineteenth century, mostly of Western and Southern farmers, against what they perceived as the control of government by Eastern business interests; the protests of the common people against the privileged few.

RECALL
The power of the voters to remove an elected officer.

REFERENDUM
The power of the voters to approve or reject laws or parts of laws.

REPRESENTATIVE (INDIRECT) DEMOCRACY
Where the people elect representatives to act as their agents in the law-making process.

REPUBLIC
In simple terms this means the absence of monarchy, however, the word is associated with representative government.

SHAYS'S REBELLION
A revolt of farmers in Massachusetts in 1786–1787, led by Daniel Shays, seeking relief from debts and mortgage foreclosures.

SOCIOPATHS
Psychopathic personalities with aggressively antisocial behavior.

SOLON
Is often used synonymously with legislator.

THEOCRACY
Where the religious leader and the political leader are the same.

THEOCRATIC SYSTEM
Where the religious leader and the political leader are separate, but the enactment of laws is based almost totally on religious doctrine.

TOTALITARIAN GOVERNMENTS
Where the state has control of the institutions of society and generally maintains command with a political ideology.

TYRANTS
Rulers with absolute power who tend to govern harshly or cruelly.

UNITARY SYSTEM
Where most of the power rests in the central government with little or no power in the sub-divisions.

VETO
Refers, in the United States today, to the constitutional power vested in the President to cancel or postpone the enactments of the Congress.

CHAPTER 3

First They Came For . . .

Essay III

Many moons ago, while I was teaching at a university in Florida, the police arrested a professor in the university system for using a four-letter word—not l-o-v-e—in a speech protesting the Vietnam War. Convicted of the charge, a judge sentenced him to a number of years in prison. After five years of lost appeals, I understand that he finally went to jail. The mistake this instructor made, apparently, was to curse in a non-political context even though he used the four-letter word in a political speech.

Individual freedoms—civil liberties—the topic of this chapter, are guaranteed by the Constitution, depending upon how the courts interpret those rights. Regarding "offensive speech," the Supreme Court ruled in *Cohen v. California* in 1971 that to use a curse word in a political context failed the test of obscenity. Paul Robert Cohen had appeared in the Los Angeles County Courthouse wearing a jacket bearing a four-letter word followed by "The Draft."

Justice Harlan, writing for the Court, argued that not all speech is protected. Obscenity may be punishable, but Justice Harlan said: "Obscene expression must be, in some significant way, erotic. It cannot be plausibly maintained that this vulgar allusion to the Selective Service System would conjure up such psychic stimulation in anyone likely to be confronted with Cohen's crudely-defaced jacket."

Concerning California's contention that Cohen's jacket contained "fighting words" tending to provoke violence, Harlan wrote: "While the four-letter word displayed by Cohen in relation to the draft is not uncommonly employed in a personally provocative fashion, in this instance it was clearly not 'directed to the person of the hearer.' No individual actually or likely to be present could reasonably have regarded the words on the appellant's jacket as a direct personal insult."

Implied in this decision is the concept that the government's role is to protect dissidents, not arrest them. Harlan quoted Justice Frankfurter in an earlier court decision: "One of the prerogatives of American citizenship is the right to criticize public men and measures—that means not only informed and responsible criticism but the freedom to speak foolishly and without moderation."

43

Vulgar, political or lyric?

I can agree with Justice Harlan when he said: "While the particular four-letter word being litigated here is perhaps more distasteful than most others of its genre, it is nevertheless often true that one man's vulgarity is another's lyric." I fail to find the word in question lyrical and recall Elihu Root's observation while walking through a squalid Siberian village during the Russian revolution, which I will try to paraphrase. He said something to the effect that he was a firm believer in democracy, but never liked filth.

I gave my testament to my belief in democracy in Essay II and I also do not like filth. But, I also hold that democracy cannot exist without civil liberties and that may include the protection of filth, again remembering Justice Frankfurter's words about "the freedom to speak foolishly and without moderation."

Sometimes "the freedom to speak foolishly and without moderation" extends to symbolic speech. On July 21, 1989, the United States Supreme Court announced a decision that caused more dissent than any I can remember in recent history. The Court ruled in *Texas v. Johnson* that the public burning of an American flag is protected by the First Amendment to the U.S. Constitution and constitutes free political expression. A national poll immediately found 65 percent opposing the decision with 71 percent of the people favoring a constitutional amendment banning flag burning *(Newsweek,* July 3, 1989, p. 18).

In mid-October, 1989, President Bush allowed the Federal Flag Protection Act, which authorized the prosecution of individuals who desecrated the American flag, to become law without his signature. He wanted a constitutional amendment. Scholars and politicians seem to agree that the statute was meaningless without an amendment to the constitution. Congress appeared to need its own symbolic speech to appease the protest and to allow reason to prevail in time.

If a jerk wants to burn the flag, that remains a constitutional right. For, if the First Amendment fails to protect offensive expression, it fails to protect anything. And, this is the way the Supreme Court ruled in *Texas v. Johnson*. Justice William J. Brennan wrote: "If there is a bedrock principle underlying the First Amendment, it is that the Government may not prohibit the expression of an idea simply because society finds the idea itself offensive or disagreeable."

The Supreme Court rapidly overturned the Federal Flag Protection Act of 1989 in the *United States v. Eichman* (1990). Attempts in Congress to amend the Constitution, and thereby "override" the Supreme Court, prohibiting flag burning failed. Most Democrats and many members of President Bush's own Republican party were fearful of tampering with the Bill of Rights.

I am led to the purpose of this essay—the role of civil liberties in our government. After explaining the necessity of civil liberties in a democracy, I will attempt to define the term in relation to government. Yet, a simple understanding of the term becomes meaningless without examining the different approaches to interpreting civil liberties. In this context I will look at the absolute, clear and present danger, dangerous tendency, and balancing of interest positions. Finally, I intend to study the meaning of civil-liberty protections as embodied in the Constitution and the Bill of Rights.

Civil liberties are rights that go to the heart of the democratic process. Certainly, democracy requires the articulation of community needs, a community consensus, but as I indicated in my second essay, democracy also demands the protection of minority rights in order to prevent a tyranny of the majority.

In 1721, Benjamin Franklin's brother James, a Boston printer-editor, found himself in prison for insulting the colonial government. Ben, sixteen at the time, decided to continue the publication of the *New England Courant*. Ben, using the pseudonym Cato, published excerpts from two London writers who had beautifully expressed the relationship between democracy and liberty:

> Without freedom of thought, there can be no such thing as public liberty without freedom of speech. . . . This sacred privilege is so essential to free government that the security of property and the freedom of speech always go together; and in those wretched countries where a man cannot call his tongue his own, he can scarce call anything else his own. Whoever would overthrow the liberty of a nation must begin by subduing the freeness of speech.

James and Benjamin Franklin lived in a land which bred freedom. They were familiar with the English historical tradition of censorship, a tradition remaining alive in our armed forces today, where dissent is associated with rebellion—the heritage of an authoritarian existence. One that demands an esprit de corps—uniformity—at the expense of liberty or individuality.

A military society fails the test of democracy. The English absolute monarchy had provided some lip service to liberty since the ***Magna Carta***—*A charter granted by King John in 1215 confirming the privileges of the feudal barons; limiting the king's power over the nobles.* It became the symbol of democratic liberty over autocracy.

In reality, few civil liberties existed for the average person under the English monarchy. Only a century before the Franklin brothers insulted royal authority, a John Stubbs had his hand chopped off for attacking a proposed royal marriage.

English law, at times arbitrary, had provided for jail and the confiscation of a person's property for anyone who wrote or talked "seditiously" against the government. A second offense led to life imprisonment and an unrepentant offender received a sentence of death.

Such has been the story of censors throughout history—an anathema to democracy. Democracy demands an enlightened citizenry who can choose between alternatives and express their preferences. With the acquittal of John Peter Zenger in 1735 on charges of seditious libel against the royal governor, "the germ of American Freedom, the morning star of that liberty" rose, to quote the words of a leading American Revolutionary, Governor Morris.

Zenger's attorney, Andrew Hamilton, shocked the court by admitting his client had actually printed the statements. Ignoring the judge's admonitions that the law provided guilt simply through the act of publishing, he convinced the jury to find Zenger not guilty because "the words themselves must be libelous—that is false, scandalous and seditious." Governor Morris found the acquittal of Zenger to uphold the inborn human trait of liberty so essential to a free government. Yes, there is a certain optimism demanded by a belief in democracy—the people will eventually choose well for themselves. I definitely prefer that right to choose for myself and that reinforces my strong advocacy of civil liberties.

Many Americans verbalize their support for civil liberties, but as Charles W. Dunn identifies in his *American Democracy Debated* (Scott, Foresman and Company, second edition, 1982, p. 12), "they frequently do not when they are faced with the realities of specific provisions." He uses a 1970 CBS television network survey to show how people can accept individual rights in the abstract but oppose them when they disagree with the individual's views. The television survey showed that 55 percent of those queried held that "newspapers, magazines, and television should not have the right to report any story if the government feels it's harmful to our national interest"; 75 percent held that "if someone is suspected of treason or other serious crimes, he shouldn't be entitled to be let out on bail"; 50 percent held that "a book that contains wrong political views cannot be a good book and does not deserve to be published." As C. Wright Mills wrote in *The Power Elite* (New York: Oxford University Press, 1956, p. 334): "It is much safer to celebrate civil liberties than to defend them."

I must celebrate and defend civil liberties, perhaps because of my Jewish ancestry. The words of the German Theologian Martin Niemueller stick in my memory. Reverend Niemueller welcomed the Nazis to power in 1933, but in 1937 they confined him to a prison in Berlin. After the war, Reverend Niemueller wrote something to this effect: "First they came for the mentally retarded and I didn't say anything because I wasn't mentally retarded; then they came for the homosexuals and I didn't say anything because I wasn't a homosexual; they came for the Jews and I didn't say anything because I wasn't a Jew; then they came for the communists and I didn't say anything because I wasn't a communist; then they came for the trade union leaders and I didn't say anything because I wasn't a trade union leader; then they came for the priests and I didn't say anything because I wasn't a priest; and then they came for me and there was nobody left to say anything."

As the old adage goes, "I may not agree with what they say, but I will defend to the death their right to say it." I might note that while I defend an individual's right to free speech, I do not have to hold any respect for his idiotic views.

A free-speech rally.

I have no other choice but to defend all speech. I live with a heritage of fear that says if "they" go, I may be next.

Judge Bernard M. Decker of the Illinois Supreme Court expressed my sentiments about civil liberties quite succinctly in the *Village of Skokie v. the National Socialist Party of America* (1978) decision:

> It is better to allow those who preach racial hate to expend their venom in rhetoric rather than be panicked into embarking on the dangerous course of permitting the government to decide what its citizens may say and hear. . . . The ability of American society to tolerate the advocacy even of the hateful doctrines espoused by the plaintiffs without abandoning its commitment to freedom of speech and assembly is perhaps the best protection we have against the establishment of any Nazi-type regime in this country.

This statement embodies a major principle of those who defend civil liberties—the view that truth will prevail when freedom of expression is upheld. Certainly, any of the civil liberties can be considered inadequate because they are abstractions and depend upon governmental institutions to define and enforce them, but as an individual citizen I can only survive by saying something when individual rights have been violated. I must maintain a sense of indignation or I may be the next person who they come for.

I loved the Acknowledgments in Nat Hentoff's *The First Freedom: The Tumultuous History of Free Speech in America* (New York: Del Publishing Co., 1981, p.v.). His words touched my soul even though his experience may have differed a touch—only a touch—from mine:

> For my abiding concern with the First Amendment, I am particularly indebted to those officials at Northeastern University in Boston who tried to censor the writings of the staff when I was editor of the *Northeastern News* in the early 1940s. Most of us finally resigned in protest, and *I never lost my sense of rage at those who would suppress speech, especially mine.* (my emphasis)

Civil liberties are abstractions made real through institutional interpretations brought on by individual pressure. They are amorphous, elusive issues, hard to harness and even more difficult to understand. And, that is why I have failed, so far, to provide you with a direct definition. I felt that it would be better to discuss the term civil liberties in the abstract and hope that in a gestalt fashion (learning through the whole rather than the specific properties) you would reach an understanding of the term. Now, I believe, the time is right to provide you with a simplistic definition of *civil liberties—those individual rights protected from the arbitrary power of government.*

The definition is simple but the concept is not. Civil liberties pertain to the citizen's right to be protected from government, and that is quite different from an individual's right to be protected from another individual or non-governmental criminal activity.

Criminal laws protect us from one another. Protection from criminal activity is an essential social necessity as some might see fire prevention or medical care, but not that same type of right—the right to live as a free person in a free society. And, these rights are also laws and their enforcement the proper role of law enforcement agencies, as would be the statutes against any crime. Except in the case of the lawlessness associated with violations of civil liberties, the agents of the government are the offenders.

How, then, does one ensure that governmental institutions that interpret abstract, amorphous and elusive rights designed to protect citizens against that same government are law abiding? As I implied earlier—by individual and group scrutiny; by standing up for the rights of others as you stand up for your own rights; and, by developing a sense of rage when an individual's rights are violated and by saying something.

Going in his own direction.

James Madison warned, in a letter to Thomas Jefferson, that rights could too easily be snuffed out. A government, especially a democratic one, can too easily fall sway to the will of the majority, as easily as an autocratic system can eliminate liberty through the will of one person. As Madison wrote in his letter: "Wherever the real power in a Government lies, there is the danger of oppression. In our Government, the real power lies in the majority of the Community, and the invasion of private rights is chiefly to be apprehended not from acts of Government contrary to the sense of its constituents but from acts in which the Government is the mere instrument of the major number of Constituents."

James Madison supported adding a Bill of Rights to the

Constitution to protect the majority as well as the minority, even a minority of one. Madison knew that through specific constitutional provisions, individuals' rights might be placed beyond the reach of any branch of government and hoped that through a checks and balance system these liberties could be preserved. He knew that even then the possibilities for violations existed. Madison felt by delineating the rights, the United States could avoid some of the centuries of abuses generated by the unguarded privileges in the British constitution.

As the democratic ethic grew with the maturity of our Republic, a movement developed to advance *civil rights—those individual rights of equal treatment under the law with respect to life, liberty, and the pursuit of happiness.* In the second half of the twentieth century, the civil rights movement demanded that government institute regulations and statutes to guard rights which were previously unguarded and to ensure equal treatment of minorities in society.

Where civil liberties protect individuals from government, civil rights demanded that the government protect the previously unprotected. Where civil liberties demand that government stay out of our lives, civil rights require that government become active in preserving such rights as voting, abortion, employment, health care to the mentally and physically handicapped, and the protection of innocent people from the threat to their health and lives caused by drunken drivers, air pollution, hucksterism, and manipulative advertising on children's television programs.

The early civil rights movement directed its energy to removing the legal supports of racial discrimination. The passage after the Civil War of the Thirteenth, Fourteenth and Fifteenth Amendments to the Constitution was only a beginning. *The Thirteenth Amendment—outlawed slavery. The Fourteenth Amendment—stipulated among its provisions that "all persons born or naturalized in the United States" are full citizens of the nation as well as of the respective states and that due process of law could not be denied.* The equal protection of the law section of the amendment, later used by the courts to declare applicable certain parts of the Bill of Rights to the states, is:

> No State shall make or enforce any law which shall abridge the privileges or immunities of citizens of the United States; nor shall any state deprive any person of life, liberty, or property, without due process of law; nor deny to any person within its jurisdiction the equal protection of the laws.

The Fourteenth Amendment became the cornerstone of the civil rights movement during the second half of the twentieth century. Blacks employed it as their major constitutional weapon in their struggle for equality. The Amendment has also been construed to proscribe gender and ethnic discrimination.

After the Civil War, Congress passed the first Civil Rights Act, forbidding states to discriminate against their citizens because of color or race. Not sure of the constitutionality of their legislation, they incorporated the main principles in the Fourteenth Amendment.

Almost 100 years passed before new civil rights legislation enhanced the provisions of the Fourteenth Amendment. In 1957, the law established a federal Civil Rights Commission to investigate alleged violations of civil rights. This legislation gave the federal government the power to seek court injunctions on behalf of individuals claiming that their right to vote, freedom of speech, or assembly had been denied.

The Civil Rights Act of 1960 created "voting referees" to investigate the denial of voting rights to qualified Blacks in the South and desegregation was ordered in the armed forces. Congress passed the most far-reaching Civil Rights Act in 1964. This statute outlawed racial discrimination in public accommodations and facilities; prohibited employers and unions to practice racial discrimination; the Attorney General could initiate suit on behalf of complainants in school desegregation and other cases involving racial discrimination; the federal government under the law could halt funding to programs in which racial discrimination persisted.

The third Civil War amendment, **the Fifteenth Amendment**—*states that "the right of citizens of the United States to vote shall not be denied or abridged by the United States or by any State on account of race, color or previous condition of servitude.* However, because of legal schemes to circumvent and thwart the objective of the Fifteenth Amendment, civil rights advocates took to the streets and to Congress to force a reaffirmation of the constitutional commitment.

The 1957, 1960 and 1964 Civil Rights Acts were steps in the right direction but still fell short of providing full franchise to America's blacks. In 1964, the Twenty-fourth Amendment to the Constitution outlawed the *poll tax*—*an individual had to pay a tax to vote; this scheme devised by a number of southern states had, by the 1890s, effectively prevented poor blacks and whites from voting.* In 1966, the U.S. Supreme Court made the Twenty-fourth Amendment applicable to the states by declaring Virginia's $1.50 poll tax for state elections, which did not apply to federal elections, in violation of the equal protection of the law guaranteed under the Fourteenth Amendment. Now a poll tax could not be charged for any election, federal or state.

The federal battle to assure the enforcement of the Fifteenth Amendment had only begun. Many blacks continued to be disenfranchised by state voting laws requiring literacy and other tests. The Voting Rights Act of 1965 finally made a significant impact on providing the full franchise to blacks.

The United States Commission on Civil Rights found in 1975 that 1.1 million new black voters were added to the rolls in seven southern states between 1964 and 1972, an increase from 29 percent to 56 percent of eligible blacks. Significant gains have been achieved, but I hold with those who argue that full participation of blacks, minorities, and women in the political process is a goal still to be realized as we enter the 21st century.

The tragic setback for the Equal Rights Amendment (it failed to meet the June 30, 1982 deadline for ratification), repeating the events of 1923 when a similar attempt to provide full citizen status for women went down to defeat, only underlines the lack of commitment of many segments of the American public to civil rights. It is beyond my comprehension how such an innocuous amendment could be defeated. The exact wording follows:

> Section 1. Equality of rights under the law shall not be denied or abridged by the United States or by any State on account of sex.
>
> Section 2. The Congress shall have the power to enforce, by appropriate legislation, the provisions of this article.
>
> Section 3. This amendment shall take effect two years after the date of ratification.

The Nineteenth Amendment—passed in 1920 gave women the right to vote. Yet, the Alabama State Constitution prohibited women from voting in state elections until 1996. Even though such provisions were generally unenforceable since most state elections coincided with federal elections, feminists pointed to this and many other legal barriers to full citizenry for women as reasons for the need for an Equal Rights Amendment.

A handful of women oppose not only an Equal Rights Amendment but believe that the Nineteenth Amendment has harmed America and needs to be repealed. The leader of the pack is Ann Coulter, a right-wing Republican pundit. In an interview with the *New York Observer*, October 2, 2007, she stated:

> If we took away women's right to vote, we'd never have to worry about another Democrat president. It's kind of a pipe dream, it's a personal fantasy of mine, but I don't think it's going to happen. And it is a good way of making the point that women are voting so stupidly, at least single women.

In a June 16, 2008 interview on a Colorado radio show, she held that giving women the right to vote "explains the destruction of America."

A few men still argue that women are naturally inferior especially since once a month they get so emotional they cannot make logical decisions and, therefore, function as rational citizens. The majority of people, however, who argue against an Equal Rights Amendment rationalize their position on the grounds that women are already protected under other provisions of the Constitution and the courts have upheld women's rights in the majority of cases.

When the framers of the Constitution finished their product, Noah Webster argued that it was unnecessary to add a Bill of Rights as these privileges were inherent and since the Constitution failed to outlaw them, people had such rights. Most Americans failed to be convinced by such rhetoric, especially with our natural distrust of government. I suspect that if Noah Webster had had statistics to prove that ninety percent of the court cases upheld individual liberties, the people of our early Republic would still have demanded a Bill of Rights. They wanted to see it in writing and legal, not just de facto. Obviously, feminists, of both sexes, feel no different than the civil libertarians of 1789—women's rights, like all other liberties, must be spelled out in no uncertain terms.

Any argument made as to the simplicity and abstractness of the Equal Rights Amendment could be made towards any of the provisions of the Bill of Rights. Individuals, and from my perspective women are individuals, must be protected from the arbitrary actions of governments. As the old saying goes, "The battle may be lost, but the war is not over."

Racial and ethnic groups, women, gays and their supporters will continue the fight to provide protection through law for their liberties. Certainly, with the realization that even when written into law, court decisions will determine the extent of the enforcement of civil liberties and civil rights. As I earlier indicated, civil liberties are abstract and amorphous due to the simplicity of the wording of the Constitution and provide for numerous interpretations.

The late Abbie Hoffman, that Yippie leader of the New Left, once wrote, "Freedom of Speech is the right to yell theater in a crowded fire." His humorous statement questioned the validity of accepting simplistic adages often quoted from court decisions to justify limitations on individual rights. Abbie intended,

The right to yell Theatre in a crowded fire?

with his quip, to ridicule the famous statement by Justice Oliver Wendell Holmes, delivered as the unanimous opinion of the U.S. Supreme Court in *Schenck v. United States* (1919): "The most stringent protection of free speech would not protect a man in falsely shouting fire in a theater and causing panic."

Abbie Hoffman, like Charles Schenck before him, opposed war and conspired to print, mail, and circulate material aimed at having young men resist the draft. Hoffman's statement, that I paraphrased, simply pointed out the ludicrousness of the government's ability to use words to justify the violation of an individual's rights—in this case Charles Schenck's resistance to World War I.

I do not believe anyone would question the danger and illegality of actually yelling fire in a crowded theater when there was no fire, but what has that to do with an individual's right to call for others to oppose what s/he felt to be an unjust war. Even the Court in 1919 agreed that Schenck would not have been convicted "in many places in ordinary times."

It rests with government to determine the places and ordinary times, as well as whether an individual might have really thought there was a fire or might even be insane and therefore, not responsible for his/her actions. It rests with the people to keep government aware that they are concerned about the upholding of civil liberties and not with double talk that permits violations of individual rights. However, people and government often differ on which liberties or rights should be given first priorities.

Let me cite a few cases in which civil liberties have conflicted and the courts had to determine the greater importance. In 1969, the Supreme Court confronted racial discrimination at a private recreational facility (The Lake Nixon Club). Interpreting the public accommodation section of the 1964 Civil Rights Act, the Court ordered integration, thereby supporting the black person's right to use the facilities over the white owner's control of his own club.

The U.S. Supreme Court has usually held that a person's right to a fair trial supersedes the freedom of the press. Yet, as in the case of trying to decide the whys and wherefores of a person yelling fire in a crowded theater, the Court has decided each case on its own merits. For example, in *Gannett v. De Pasquale* (1979) the Court excluded the press from the courtroom to ensure the defendant's right to a fair trial. But in *Richmond Newspapers, Inc. v. Virginia* (1980) they reversed a lower court order barring the press and followed suit permitting television coverage of court trials in *Chandler v. Florida* in 1981. Apparently, such access is permitted as long as it cannot be proven that public exposure would impair the fairness and effectiveness of the trial.

Judgment on individual rights are always subject to diverse interests and someone gains or loses depending upon the specific outcome. The Courts, the Congress, the President, administrative officials and other decision-making institutions interpret, mold, and manipulate the Constitutional guarantees.

Decisions regarding civil liberties or civil rights are never final. At any point in time a new precedent may develop from the specific application of a case and the philosophy of the examining body.

The natural inferiority of women???

Generally, these doctrines can be placed in four categories: Absolute, Clear and Present Danger, Dangerous Tendency, and the Balancing of Interests interpretations. I will discuss each one and express my views regarding their application.

Absolute Interpretation—refers to the concept that civil liberties must be upheld without qualification. Supreme Court Justices Hugo Black and William O. Douglas followed this position. Some students of individual rights like Lucius J. Barker and Twiley W. Barker, Jr. (*Civil Liberties and the Constitution: Cases and Commentaries*, Englewood Cliffs, N.J.: Prentice-Hall, 1982) discuss a *Preferred Position—the idea that civil liberties are so vital to the democratic process that any legislation should be scrutinized with extreme care to make sure that individual rights cannot be violated.* I, personally, see little distinction between the two doctrines. Both adhere to Justice Rutledge's statement in *Thomas v. Collins* (1945), "That priority gives these liberties a sanctity and a sanction not permitting dubious intrusions."

The *American Civil Liberties Union (A.C.L.U.)—is the organization best known for fighting to maintain an absolute interpretation of the constitutional guarantees of individual rights.* Conservative and ultra-conservative individuals and groups maintain a constant attack on the A.C.L.U. as the destroyer of American values.

Former Attorney General Edwin Meese called the A.C.L.U. a "criminals' lobby." Similar charges have been leveled against the A.C.L.U. for over fifty years. To these individuals and to many others, the A.C.L.U., in protecting constitutional rights of criminals, hinders law enforcement.

Lost in the smears against the American Civil Liberties Union is the concept of civil liberties I developed earlier—to protect the individual against a lawless government. The A.C.L.U., in defending an absolutist approach to the Constitution, holds that rights are laws and must be upheld for democracy to prevail. Government, they believe, must be held accountable for its actions or law enforcement becomes meaningless.

People in totalitarian societies can walk the streets securely, but lack human freedoms. Benjamin Franklin once said: "People willing to give up a little freedom to gain security will have neither freedom nor security." A.C.L.U. lawyers are fond of quoting Justice Oliver Wendell Holmes in his dissent from the

Court's decision in *Gitlow v. New York* (1925): "If there is any principle of the Constitution that more imperatively calls for attachment than any other it is the principle of free thought—not free thought for those who agree with us but freedom for the thought that we hate."

In more cases than I would like to admit, I have fervently disagreed with A.C.L.U. stands. Two that come to mind are a brief filed to stop the execution of a mass murderer who wanted to die and the support of Nazis in full regalia demonstrating in Skokie, a suburb of Chicago that is forty percent Jewish with a large number of concentration camp survivors. From my perspective, if a mass murderer wants to die, I wholeheartedly defend his right to suicide.

I have an emotional response to the Skokie case. If the Ku Klux Klan demanded police protection to demonstrate in Harlem, I doubt there is a court in the land that would grant them protection. I believe the A.C.L.U. would defend their right. What I am convinced of is that in the Skokie case, and my example, the right of freedom of speech or assembly invites a Clear and Present Danger. The Nazis and the KKK have acted on their beliefs in the past and their uniforms are designed to spit in the faces of the Jews and the blacks and fall within the definition of "fighting words" used in numerous cases to provide *prior restraint—to forbid in advance speech, publication or assembly.*

The Illinois Appellate Court ruled in July, 1977, that the fighting words doctrine applied to the Nazis' demand to demonstrate in Skokie. The Court said that the swastika was "a personal affront to every member of the Jewish faith, in remembering the nearly consummated genocide of their people committed within memory of those who used the swastika as their symbol. This is especially true for the thousands of Skokie residents who personally survived the Holocaust of the Third Reich." Their avowed purpose is only to incite emotional violence and obtain as much publicity for their cause as possible.

What bothers me is my feeling that the Illinois Supreme Court, overturning the Appellate Court upholding the Nazis' right to demonstrate wearing the swastika, saw Jews as passive people who went into the gas chambers without violence. Since blacks are often viewed as emotional, uncontrollable people, I am sure that the KKK would never be permitted to demonstrate in Harlem. Of course, the descriptions I have used of blacks and Jews have little reality to their actual being, but only to certain prejudices. I have no doubt that such preconceived views can determine the outcome of a civil liberty decision. Still, I fully understand and support the A.C.L.U.'s reasons for defending such unpopular causes, even if I feel they are misguided.

From my perspective, if the extremist, if the kooks, did not have their defenders, then they could easily be eliminated. If that happened, a new extreme and new kooks would appear and they would be eliminated. Sooner or later, my views and maybe even yours become the extremes. We return once again to Reverend Niemoeller's statement that first they came for . . . and I was not a . . . , so I didn't say anything. Finally, there will be no one left to say anything.

Once a government succeeds in creating absolute uniformity, eliminating the individual, democracy ceases to exist. No, the A.C.L.U. is not a criminals' lobby, but one of the strongest advocates for democracy our nation contains, even if I cannot abide many of the positions they take.

In my discussion of the A.C.L.U. and the Absolute Interpretation of constitutional rights, I alluded to my support of the *Clear and Present Danger*

Interpretation—*the view that civil liberties can be restrained when there is a clear and present danger that a substantive evil will result.* The Supreme Court in *Schenck v. United States* (1919) adopted the clear and present danger test and it has been the most widely applied.

In *Schenck*, Justice Oliver Wendell Holmes wrote the famous words, "free speech would not protect a man in falsely shouting fire in a theater, and causing a panic." Holmes, speaking for a unanimous Court, rejected the Absolute Interpretation of freedom of speech, assembly, or the press. Obviously, words like "clear and present danger" and "substantive evils" are open to interpretation, but at least they provide some guidelines.

The words of Justice Holmes, this time in the minority, in another 1919 case, *Abrams v. United States*, speak vigorously for cautiousness in using the Clear and Present Danger Doctrine and the need to defend free speech and indirectly, I would say, other civil liberties in a democratic nation:

> When men have realized that time has upset many fighting faiths, they may come to believe even more than they believe the very foundations of their own conduct that the ultimate good desired is better reached by free trade in ideas,—that the best test of truth is the power of the thought to get itself accepted in the competition of the market; and that truth is the only ground upon which their wishes safely can be carried out. That, at any rate, is the theory of our Constitution. It is an experiment, as all life is an experiment. Every year, if not every day, we have to wager our salvation upon some prophecy based upon imperfect knowledge. While that experiment is part of our system I *think that we should be eternally vigilant against attempts to check the expressions of opinions that we loathe and believe to be fraught with death, unless they so imminently threaten immediate interference with the lawful and pressing purposes of the law that an immediate check is required to save the country.* (my emphasis)

The eloquent words of Justice Holmes ring in my ears every time I hear the advancement of the **Dangerous Tendency Interpretation**—*the view that civil liberties lose their constitutional protection when they tend to lead to a serious evil.* Some political scientists refer to this doctrine as Bad Tendency rather than Dangerous Tendency. From my viewpoint, the Dangerous Tendency Interpretation leads to a dangerous tendency.

Since freedoms do not have to present an actual threat before being limited, but only tend to be dangerous, this doctrine could too easily open gates to concentration camps. The Dangerous Tendency test simply provides too much latitude in determining the circumstances permissible to ban a civil liberty.

In recent years, we have been confronted by self-appointed censors who are demanding that governments forbid what they authoritatively determine to be evil and, therefore, dangerous. The New Christian Right would appoint itself the sole arbiter of proper conduct and morals. They would have the government protect us against our dark side by instituting prayer in the public schools, censoring library and school books, and watching over our sexual behavior.

In the July 19, 1981 *San Jose Mercury News*, page 2c, Gilbert Feldman argued that the Christian Right's support for a Family Protection Act, which while professing to get government out of our lives, in reality is simply a ploy to return to old fashioned wife beatings and the abuse of children. As an example, the Christian Right would have the government act as a censor, barring public

A dangerous tendency?

schools from using such books as those depicting women in the factory instead of the kitchen.

Similar attempts to have government act as a censor because of the dangerous tendency to lead to an evil have also come from the left and ethnic and minority groups. Some blacks have organized to have public schools remove books which degraded their people. Under pressure, a school named after Mark Twain removed Huckleberry Finn because of the word "nigger." The Superintendent of Schools later ordered the book restored. Some Jews have protested the use of Shakespeare's *The Merchant of Venice* in high school English classes because of the derogatory approach towards Jews.

In such cases, the historical merit of the readings and the manifest right of our citizens to learn and make their own moral judgment is ignored. When some feminists move to ban magazines like *Playboy* from newsstands because in degrading women, which they do, they tend to lead to violence against women, they reject the individual's choice and free inquiry.

A pluralist society like our own, if any of these groups prevailed, would soon evaporate into a dictatorial state. When one person or group determines what are proper values, we are on the road once again towards—"First they came for . . . and I was not a . . . so I didn't say anything . . . and then they came for me." Since I do not intend to end up in a concentration camp, I will continue to fight for civil liberties and civil rights, even though others are convinced they tend to lead to substantive evils, unless I can be shown beyond a reasonable doubt that a clear and present danger will "imminently threaten immediate interference with the lawful and pressing purposes of the law."

Censorship is a perplexing question—where do I draw the line? I am aware that at some point a decision needs to be made regarding the limitation of the rights of one group over another or chaos might result. Censorship has been relatively rare in recent years despite attempts by self-righteous groups to push their authoritarian values on the whole society, ignoring our pluralistic tradition.

A humorous look at both diversity and factional censors in America today appeared in *Time Magazine* ("Crybabies and Busybodies") on August 12, 1991: "In San Francisco last month, a motley flock turned out to picket the classic Disney movie 'Fantasia.' One man complained that the spooky 'Night on Bald Mountain' scene had terrified his child. Members of an organization called Dieters United objected to the tutu-clad hippos frolicking to the music of 'Dance of the Hour'; the protesters felt the sequence ridiculed fat people. Conservationists were appalled at the waste of water in 'Sorcerer's Apprentice.' Fundamentalist Christians bewailed the depicting of evolution in 'Rite of

Spring.' Antidrug forces suspected something subliminally pro-drug in the 'Nutcracker Suite' episode featuring dancing mushrooms."

Yet, a legitimate question is raised by these groups and even by many civil libertarians: How pluralistic can we be without creating chaos? I provided one answer in my advocacy of the Clear and Present Danger Doctrine while expressing understanding and guarded support for the Absolute Interpretation. To be sure, some advertisements, displays of violence, and even books have corrupted individuals. And, I have never encountered anyone who held without reservation that public authorities never ought to interfere in some fashion to protect individuals from other individuals and themselves.

I wish I could believe that free competition in the cultural marketplace would always produce, as Justice Holmes implied in the above quote from *Abrams v. United States*, the power of truth and goodness, to win out. With these contradictions within myself—my support for civil liberties and my fear of corruption to democracy—years ago, I viewed myself a bit hypocritically. A student came to the rescue by providing me with a *Reader's Digest* (January, 1975, pp. 93–96) condensation of Irving Kristol's book, *Where Do You Draw The Line? An Exploration into Media Violence, Pornography and Censorship*.

Kristol distinguished between repressive censorship and what he called liberal censorship. I believe the thrust of his ideas— and if I am incorrect it is at least the thrust of my ideas—is that liberal censorship would ban not the product but its advertising. He notes that in Britain, for example, plays judged obscene could be performed but only in private theatrical clubs.

I remember visiting—only for observation purposes mind you— The Block in Baltimore, Maryland. Pornography had been basically relegated to one small section of the city into which you did not wander by sheer accident.

A person's right to choose is sacred, especially if you have faith in humanity and in the strength of responsible parents to develop responsible children. I have such faith.

Freedom of religion?

I was offended a few years ago, however, when I took my son to get a soda at a local 7-Eleven store. In front of the machine, in full view, were pornographic magazines (at least, by my standards). I objected to my child having to be confronted with such obscenity at his age, against my will. I could make the choice not to enter that store again or speak to the owner to prevent the open display. The owner understood and covered the pornographic magazines even though they remained near the soda machine. Now anyone could buy them, yet innocent victims would be protected.

As a civil libertarian, I oppose suppression and support regulation. I am also aware that one person's regulation may be another's suppression, so I am back in that unending circle of abstract, ambiguous terminology civil liberties are dependent upon.

The fourth doctrine used to test civil liberties is the **Balancing of Interests Interpretation**—*The view that a society's interest outweighs an individual's rights.* When the decision-making institutions of government use this doctrine, they hold that the interests of the nation in stifling freedom is greater than the interest of people exercising them. For example, if a speech might disturb order then that speech could be banned. Not because the speech posed a Clear and Present Danger or might tend towards an evil, but simply because the speech might disturb order. This doctrine must be very cautiously used in a democratic society.

Twenty years ago most people would have objected to airport searches. Today we go through machines and allow devices to be run near our bodies, generally without question, because of the recent history of terrorist hijackings. Due to robberies and muggings in many city parks, they are closed after dark as we lack the resources to protect innocent people.

The laws in California that make it a crime for anyone under eighteen to be on the streets unaccompanied by an adult after 10 P.M. reflect the Balancing of Interests Doctrine. The law assumes that these youths will be up to no good and replaces the authority of the parents with the authority of the government. These laws exist even though in most of these California communities there had been no rash of crimes by minors.

On June 23, 1982, President Reagan, following the Balancing of Interests Doctrine, signed into law the Intelligence Identities Protection Act. The law makes it a crime to identify spies, even if the information is gleaned from public records. The administration lobbied for the bill to prevent disclosure of such information, as they believed it would interfere with covert operations so necessary to our national security.

Forty five days after the terrorist attack September 11, 2001 on the World Trade Center, Congress passed the USA Patriot Act. While the Act is a perfect example of the Balancing of Interest Doctrine, many parts of this sweeping legislation take away checks on law enforcement. Civil liberties groups like the ACLU hold that the USA Patriot Act threatens the rights and freedoms that we as Americans have struggled so long to protect. They continue to oppose vehemently the revived Patriot Act of 2006.

Perhaps the ultimate application of the Balancing of Interests Doctrine is **Martial Law**—*which refers to the replacement of all civilian laws, authorities and courts by military government.* Martial Law may be accompanied by the suspension of all civil liberties. It is an exercise of government authority that is totally arbitrary and unfettered.

The Constitution fails to provide direct authority for the President to declare Martial Law. The Courts have, however, upheld his right to do so under Article 1, Section 9.2, which permits the suspension of the writ of habeas corpus "in cases of rebellion or invasion (when) the public safety may require it."

Presidents have invoked Martial Law on rare occasions. Abraham Lincoln placed southern and border states under Martial Law and Franklin Roosevelt did the same in Hawaii following Japan's attack upon Pearl Harbor. Franklin Roosevelt's Executive Order 9066, which relocated all the mainland Japanese to concentration camps, under the guise of it being for their own safety, remains one of the most infamous abuses of the power of Martial Law and the Balancing of Interests Doctrine in our history.

In 1950, Congress passed the Internal Security Act, popularly known as the McCarran Act. After declaring that a world communist conspiracy existed with the objective of establishing a communist dictatorship in the United States, the law provided for the establishment of eight concentration camps throughout the nation to be activated under Martial Law when the communists attempted their revolution. To preserve order in society, the act provided for the registration of "communist-action," "communist-front," and "communist-infiltrated" organizations with a Subversive Activities Control Board. Other provisions virtually prohibited immigration to the United States of individuals with communist connections and made it illegal to discuss with others the establishment of a "totalitarian dictatorship" in America. The Communist Party finally had their day in court and registration procedures were declared unconstitutional based on the Fifth Amendment's protection against self-incrimination.

After *Look* magazine in 1968 published an extensive photo-story about the existence of American concentration camps, which blacks and antiwar demonstrators believed would be used for their detention, Congress eliminated these stockades.

While the possibility of abuse of the Balancing of Interests Doctrine and Martial Law remain, the United States has had a history of rapidly eliminating such rare decrees, laws, or interpretations. The black marks that spot our history, these violations of civil liberties in the name of government order, are few.

When Adolf Hitler declared Martial Law in 1933, under the provisions of the Enabling Act of the Weimar Constitution, it remained in effect until the Allies, during World War II, overthrew his regime. Order was balanced as the prisons and concentration camps of the Nazis overflowed with people. The interest of society was interpreted according to the theological doctrines of Adolf Hitler— and nobody said anything because they were not a. . . !

The Weimar Republic's Constitution that Hitler overthrew by declaring Martial Law contained civil liberties protections similar to those of our own Constitution. Despite the Martial Law decrees in our history, our Constitution remains because of our long history of defending civil liberties and our belief in human rights. The Germans lacked that kind of heritage. Their democratic experiment was less than fifteen years old when Hitler abolished it.

Our defense of individual rights goes back to our colonial history and became codified in the Constitution in 1787 and the Bill of Rights added in 1791. I believe it is time to take a cursory look at the specific civil liberty provisions of these documents.

As I indicated earlier in this essay, most of the framers of the Constitution felt it unnecessary to include a Bill of Rights in the original document. They held that the people had all the freedoms not prohibited by the Constitution. However, they did deem it necessary to deny government a few powers and so inversely protected certain rights.

The government could not suspend the *writ of habeas corpus*—*an order by a judge that an individual being held in prison be brought before him/her to show cause for the detention*. The writ could be suspended, as I discussed under the Balancing of Interests Interpretation, "when in cases of rebellion or invasion the public safety may require it."

Congress could not pass a *Bill of Attainder*—*an act of a legislature having the effect of punishing a person without a trial*. Congress in 1959 passed the Labor-Management Reporting and Disclosure Act. The law made it a crime for a member of the Communist Party within the past five years to serve in any major capacity in a labor union. In *United States v. Brown* (1965) the U.S. Supreme Court, in a five to four decision, found the act unconstitutional as a bill of attainder for it imposed punishment through legislative action for past membership in the Communist Party.

In a sense, the act also violated the Constitutional restriction against *ex post facto laws*—*retroactive punishment in the sense that legislation has made unlawful, prescribing punishment, for an act which was lawful when it was committed*. The Constitution also prohibited states from passing bills of attainder or ex post facto laws. Congress also was denied the power in cases of treason to legislate *corruption of blood*—*when an individual's blood relatives (past, present or future) are punished for his/her acts*. Article III of the Constitution did decree that criminal trials should be by jury.

To assure the passage of the Constitution, the framers agreed to add a *Bill of Rights*—*The first ten amendments to the Constitution of the United States with its emphasis on human rights and liberties*. An "eleventh amendment," which James Madison believed to be more important than all the others, failed to be ratified: "No state shall violate the equal rights of conscience, or of the freedom of the press . . . because it is proper that every Government should be disarmed of powers which trench upon those particular rights." In other words, the states, regardless of their constitutions, would have to protect freedom of thought and press.

I suspect many of my readers will reason that the "eleventh amendment" was unnecessary since freedom of speech and press were already embodied in the First Amendment which required the states to protect these liberties. I also would have thought this until I became a student of civil liberties. I learned, much to my dismay, that the Bill of Rights originally applied only to the federal government.

In *Barron v. Baltimore* (1833), Chief Justice John Marshall wrote: "The Constitution was ordained and established by the people of the United States for themselves, for their own government, and not for the government of the individual states." Although Justice Marshall specifically singled out the Fifth Amendment, the implication was obvious that the whole Bill of Rights restrained only the national government and lacked application to the states. Later court decisions reaffirmed this principle.

Even after the passage of the Fourteenth Amendment in 1868, which held that "no State shall make or enforce any law which shall abridge the privileges or immunities of citizens of the United States," the Supreme Court refused for more than half a century to apply the Bill of Rights to the states. In 1925, the historic decision came in *Gitlow v. New York* when the Court finally held that the states must uphold the principle of freedom of speech as embodied in the First Amendment to the Constitution. The respective states now had to protect an individual's free speech not because of the First Amendment, but because of the Fourteenth Amendment.

Again, I must warn the reader that court decisions are quite limited and the incorporation here only applied to freedom of speech. However, this did begin the application of specific provisions of the Bill of Rights to the states—what scholars call the process of **selective incorporation**—*making most of the principles outlined in the Bill of Rights applicable on a case by case basis to the states.*

Even today, the Court continues to determine that many provisions of the Bill of Rights are not applicable to the states, only to the federal government. *The Second Amendment*—"A well regulated Militia being necessary to the security of a free State, the right of the people to keep and bear Arms, shall not be infringed"—has never been incorporated.

Early in 1982, a federal judge in Illinois denied the contention of the National Rifle Association that the village of Morton Grove by prohibiting the purchased and ownership of guns had violated the Second Amendment of the U.S. Constitution. The judge ruled that the federal courts had no jurisdiction as the Second Amendment and the plaintiffs would have to take the case before the Illinois courts. The United States Supreme Court had implied in a 1939 case that there might not be an individual right to bear arms, only a collective right. The words "a well regulated Militia" might mean that "the right of the people to keep and bear Arms" only applied to an official government Militia. On June 26, 2008, the *U.S. Supreme Court in the District of Columbia v. Heller* for the first time in its history ruled on the question of an individual's right to keep and bear arms.

The Court indicated that the individuals in Washington D.C. had the right to keep handguns and it also struck down the provisions in the law that required all firearms be kept "unloaded and disassembled or bound by a trigger lock." The decision was far from decisive in that only five of the nine Supreme Court justices voted in the affirmative. The majority felt that the Washington D.C. ban contradicted the intent of the framers of the Second Amendment to allow arms within the home for self-defense purposes. In other words, that there is an individual right to "keep and bear Arms." The dissenting justices, as articulated by John Paul Stevens, held that it was obvious that the framers of Second Amendment created only a collective right by using the term militia and that they, based upon some state laws at the time, would not have limited the tools available to elected officials for limiting the civilian use of weapons. The Court majority did not attempt to overturn all gun control laws nor establish a precedent states must follow. The question of whether the individual right to keep and bear arms must be incorporated with the states will have to be decided in a future Court case that introduces this issue.

The Supreme Court has never incorporated the Third Amendment: "No soldier shall, in time of peace, be quartered in any house without the consent of the owner, nor in time of war, but in a manner to be prescribed by law." In the Fifth Amendment only the clause requiring indictment by grand jury has never been made applicable to the states. The double jeopardy clause—"nor shall any person

Choice

be subject for the same offense to be twice put in jeopardy of life or limb"—the self-incrimination clause and the clause requiring that private property cannot "be taken for public use without just compensation" have all been applied to the states. Although the federal courts have ruled since 1962 that the states cannot inflict cruel and unusual punishment, they have still not incorporated the Eighth Amendments prohibition against excessive bail or fines.

Most of the incorporated cases pertained to the principles expressed in the **First Amendment**—*protects freedom of religion, speech, press and assembly as well as the right to petition government on the federal level.*

To develop all the nuances of the court decisions and legislation applicable to these amendments would take another essay, if not a book. For those who would like to study these amendments in greater depth, I can recommend the books I have mentioned in my essay and to these I would add Alfred H. Kelly and Winfred A. Harbism, *The American Constitution: Its Origins and Development* (New York: W.W. Norton and Company, 1970) and Robert F. Cushman, *Leading Constitutional Decisions* (Englewood Cliffs, N.J.: Prentice-Hall, 1976).

Of the ten amendments to the United States Constitution known as the Bill of Rights, I have so far neglected the last two. The Tenth Amendment does not really pertain to civil liberties as it delegates those powers not given to the federal government in the Constitution, "nor prohibited by it to the States," to the states, *"or the people"* (my emphasis). Such subjects as education, control of crime, and health standards were traditionally controlled by the states, but in more recent times "the people," represented by the federal government, have assumed this power.

The Ninth Amendment reads: "The enumeration in the Constitution, of certain rights, shall not be construed to deny or disparage others retained by the people." Recent court decisions citing the Fourth and Ninth Amendments have determined that individuals in both federal and state jurisdiction have a right to privacy. The Supreme Court has held that the right to privacy includes the right to obtain birth control information and contraceptives.

To date, the Court has seldom cited the Ninth Amendment in its decisions, nor to my knowledge been confronted with many cases of liberties not spelled out in the Constitution and its first eight amendments. Some homosexuals have argued that the Ninth Amendment protects their right of sexual preference. And as in many marriages, extremely controversial issues, I suspect it will be a long time before the Supreme Court touches the civil liberty of sexual preference or same sex marriage.

A WARNING!

As always, I have taken advantage of my civil liberties to express my views on individual rights. My civil libertarian views, I hope, have aided your understanding of the necessity of preserving these rights in a democratic society. If you disagreed with any of my points, and it would be unusual if you did not, you have lived vicariously the thrill of the right of free thought. How you would approach permitting the publication of my words, you now should understand, would depend upon your adherence to one of the four doctrines I discussed: Absolute, Clear and Present Danger, Dangerous Tendency, Balancing of Interests. Once confronted with my bias, the actual intent of this essay should have become clear to you: to leave you with a better comprehension of the meaning of civil liberties and civil rights; to provide you with a cursory knowledge of the specific provisions of the Constitution and the Bill of Rights that protect you from living under a lawless government; to inform you of how Constitutional guarantees only pertained to the federal government until the passage of the Fourteenth Amendment and how slowly the United States Supreme Court moved to apply these rights to the people of the respective states and the extent of this incorporation.

Masking free speech!

In conclusion, let me remind you that the whole concept of civil liberties is based on the realization that the possessors of power, left unguarded, may wield their power in the name of goodness to deprive individuals of the basic rights to life, liberty, and the pursuit of happiness. To preserve these "unalienable" rights, Thomas Jefferson wrote in our Declaration of Independence, we must always remember that governments derive "their just powers from the consent of the governed." Governments may also derive unjust powers from the passive consent of the people. Many years ago, the Catholic philosopher, Teilhard de Chardin wrote: "It is too easy to find an excuse for inaction by pleading the decadence of civilization, or even the imminent end of the world." Reverend Martin Niemueller learned the hard way, that by turning his back on his fellow human beings he was deprived of his life, liberty, and pursuit of happiness, for they soon came for him.

GLOSSARY

ABSOLUTE INTERPRETATION
Refers to the concept that civil liberties must be upheld without qualification.

AMERICAN CIVIL LIBERTIES UNION (A.C.L.U.)
Is the organization best known for fighting to maintain an absolute interpretation of the constitutional guarantees of individual rights.

BALANCING OF INTERESTS INTERPRETATION
The view that a society's interest outweighs an individual's rights.

BILL OF ATTAINDER
An act of a legislature having the effect of punishing a person without a trial.

BILL OF RIGHTS
The first ten amendments to the Constitution of the United States with its emphasis on human rights and liberties.

CIVIL LIBERTIES
Those individual rights protected from the arbitrary power of government.

CIVIL RIGHTS
Those individual rights of equal treatment under the law with respect to life, liberty, and the pursuit of happiness.

CLEAR AND PRESENT DANGER INTERPRETATION
The view that civil liberties can be restrained when there is a clear and present danger that a substantive evil will result.

CORRUPTION OF BLOOD
When an individual's blood relatives (past, present or future) are punished for his/her acts.

DANGEROUS TENDENCY INTERPRETATION
The view that civil liberties lose their constitutional protection when they tend to lead to a serious evil.

EX POST FACTO LAWS
Retroactive punishment in the sense that legislation has made unlawful, prescribing punishment for an act which was lawful when it was committed.

FIFTEENTH AMENDMENT
States that "the right of citizens of the United States to vote shall not be denied or abridged by the United States or by any State on account of race, color or previous condition of servitude."

FIRST AMENDMENT
Protects freedom of religion, speech, assembly, press, and the right to petition government on the federal level.

FOURTEENTH AMENDMENT
Stipulates among its provisions that "all persons born or naturalized in the United States" are full citizens of the nation as well as of the respective states and that due process of law could not be denied; also holds that a state may not deprive its citizens of their privileges and immunities.

HABEAS CORPUS, WRIT OF
An order by a judge that an individual being held in prison be brought before him/her to show cause for the detention.

MAGNA CARTA
A charter granted by King John of England in 1215 confirming the privileges of the feudal barons; limiting the king's power over the nobles.

MARTIAL LAW
Refers to the replacement of all civilian laws, authorities, and courts by military government.

NINETEENTH AMENDMENT
Passed in 1920; gave women the right to vote.

POLL TAX
An individual had to pay a tax to vote; this scheme devised by a number of southern states by the 1890s, effectively prevented poor blacks and whites from voting.

PREFERRED POSITION
The idea that civil liberties are so vital to the democratic process that any legislation should be scrutinized with extreme care to make sure that individual rights cannot be violated.

PRIOR RESTRAINT
To forbid in advance speech, publication, or assembly.

SECOND AMENDMENT
"A well regulated Militia being necessary to the security of a free State, the right of the people to keep and bear Arms, shall not be infringed."

SELECTIVE INCORPORATION
Makes most of the principles outlined in the Bill of Rights applicable on a case by case basis to the states.

THIRTEENTH AMENDMENT
Outlawed slavery.

CHAPTER 4

Don't Bother Me With the Facts . . .

Essay IV

In 1983, the United States invaded the small Caribbean island of Grenada. The Reagan administration feared that the island would become a communist outpost with a major military airbase. The reason they gave for the attack was the protection of American medical students studying on the island.

Rather than face the negative media impact of words like invasion, attack, war or aggression, the Pentagon tried to neutralize *public opinion—those views expressed by large groups of people who try to influence the political process*. The Pentagon called the invading army the "Caribbean Peace Keeping Forces." They also proudly announced that they had carried out a "pre-dawn vertical insertion." Now, how could anyone object to a "pre-dawn vertical insertion?"

William Lutz described this colorful, meaningless and morally neutral language in his 1990 book, *Doublespeak*. Politicians have used *doublespeak—language that pretends to communicate but really doesn't*—forever. Doublespeak, however, has exploded on the political horizon in the last thirty years because of the advent of the *Media Age—the recent era in which politics are increasingly intertwined with the media*. I hold that all political institutions today are inseparable from the *media—books, magazines, newspapers, movies, recordings and, above all, television, which convey facts and ideas through images*.

The term doublespeak is derived from what George Orwell called Newspeak. In his classic novel *1984*, Newspeak was the official state language. Newspeak provided the means of expression for *doublethink—the mental process that allows an individual to hold two contrasting ideas and believe in both*. An example of doublethink in Orwell's novel was the slogan "War is Peace." Doublespeak often creates the doublethink that forms the images that limit thought. Others have called the process of doublespeak Watergatespeak or Washingtonspeak.

Doublespeak is the language of the Media Age. In an advertising controlled, information processing, high-tech communications society where news is instantaneous, doublespeak provides the politician with a language that conceals and prevents thought. Doublespeak is language designed to deceive.

Print will always be!

Doublespeak is in reality a non-language. Doublespeak avoids meaning by the avoidance of words that have negative, moral or unpleasant connotations. Doublespeak—Washingtonspeak, Watergatespeak—provides the non-language that, according to William Lutz, "makes the bad seem good, the negative appear positive, the unpleasant appear attractive or at least tolerable." Politicians consciously or subconsciously use these weasel words to duck or shift responsibility in our factional and fragmented political society. In an image-producing world that demands a language that would hopefully extend critical thinking, doublespeak gives importance to the insignificant, aids the development of desensitization towards evil and prevents the necessary moral indignation towards wrongs.

William Lutz delineates four doublespeak approaches. First, is the ***euphemism***—*an inoffensive or positive word or phrase used to avoid a harsh, unpleasant, or distasteful reality.* Second, is the use of ***jargon***—*specialized language of a trade or profession.* Third, comes the ***gobbledygook***—*piling on words to overwhelm an audience.* Finally, Lutz identifies the ***inflated language***—*designed to make the ordinary appear extraordinary; the simple appear complex.* This language as non-language reminds me of my college sociology course, where the professor seemed to hide his ignorance behind big words.

George Orwell foresaw the doublespeak age in his 1946 essay, "Politics and the English Language." He wrote: "Prose consists less and less of words chosen for the sake of their meaning and more and more of phrases tacked together like sections of a fabricated henhouse." I suspect the analogy of the fabricated henhouse fails to project a meaningful image to the 1990s student, so let me provide some examples of the non-language that tries to keep us in a synthetic coop.

In the Media Age, politicians do not lie. They provide strategic misrepresentations, disinformation, misinformation, inoperative statements and plausible deniability.

For the C.I.A., for the military, killing no longer occurs. Individuals are not unlawfully or arbitrarily deprived of life. They are eliminated with extreme prejudice, or just neutralized. The Pentagon describes the expected loss of millions of lives in a nuclear war as collateral damage, a term also applied to any civilians killed in a conventional war.

When members of the Nixon administration authorized break-ins and burglaries, the President called them surreptitious entries in the name of political expediency. He and his co-Watergate conspirators often used the euphemism national security to justify their illegal activities. According to Watergate testimony, members of Richard Nixon's reelection campaign never destroyed documents, they deep sixed them, a naval term referring to sinking objects.

Reality #1?

Doublespeak pretends to communicate, but really misleads. It is a non-language of non-responsibility. The political establishment has taken its cue from the world of advertising, which sells products with deceptive appeal: "Real Counterfeit Diamonds," "Genuine Imitation Leather." When a product hype can describe a couch as "Virgin Vinyl," then why not refer to an invasion as an "Early Morning Vertical Insertion."

When the Peace Corps kicked me out, they never fired me. Like many government and business employees today, I was selected out. We hear firings described with the weasel words: non-retained, released, dehired, non-renewed, or downsizing.

Such is the non-language of the Media Age that circumvents the unpleasant and prevents moral value judgments. This non-language allows government and politicians to avoid responsibility for their actions and hinders the public's indignation. When political leaders double talk, can we expect less from the average citizen? In 1987, Steve Strunk, after winning the amateur Mr. Universe title, called anabolic steroids a pharmaceutical training aid.

Lest it appear that the purpose of this essay is a condemnation of politicians and government officials for using doublespeak, let me be clear that my concern is that we will lose our ability to critically think, to make moral judgments and

An instinctive or linear sport?

to become indignant. Critical thinking *is thinking about what you are thinking while you are thinking, to know what you are thinking; reading between the lines.* In the visual media world I would define critical thinking as viewing images in a minimum of three dimensions. When Tucson, Arizona officials claim to have pavement deficiencies and not potholes I can only laugh. No, I do not condemn the politicians or the government officials. I am scared of our future as creative thinking beings because we are blinded by this non-language.

Other monographs and textbooks deal quite well with the abuse of language. Many books question whether the government manipulates or coerces through control of the media. Some authors even argue that we, the people, manipulate or coerce government by our use of the media.

Political scientists often discuss how the media causes *political socialization—the impact of society on the development of an individual's political views and values.* Many studies report that individuals selectively perceive the news. A few scholars even argue that the corporate establishment manipulates the system. I am more interested in how we, the people, respond.

I am not writing to condemn the media or the political process, nor to demand a return to a pre-media age. I love technology and believe the communication era, the information processing age is here for quite a while. I do not believe we can regress, but only progress. My interest is to advance the human spirit that I hold is rooted in the human intellect. My emphasis in this essay is to examine the changes that have occurred in the media, especially the visual media, in the last thirty years.

I intend to explain why we accept the imagery of non-language and go on to advocate a human growth, a political process, fertilized through critical thinking. I am most interested in promoting an education, that allows us to defend ourselves against the "seduction of eloquence," as the philosopher Bertrand Russell used to advocate. Today we must also build defenses against the seduction of imagery.

We now live in a ***Visual Media Age***—*a world of media images that bombards our senses with emotions.* The Visual Media Age is a fragmented world, colorized, synthesized, pastel-shaded, heard in quadraphonic dolby digital 64 bit surround-sound and watched in quick-time images. A revolution is taking place in how we process information. The last such dramatic change occurred with the development of the printing press in the fifteenth century. At that time, society transformed from an oral tradition to a print dominated culture.

Now, we are eliminating the printed page for image processing. The Media Age brought with it a visual-image oriented culture—a culture where a hypercard program probes subject matter with visual depth. The modern person is beginning to live in a multi-dimensional computerized world of virtual reality. Today we find chaos structured through the striking beauty of the fractional dimension of the Mandelbrot set.

Using computers, Benoit Mandelbrot developed ***fractal geometry***—*a study of the repetition of the geometric patterns of nature that were once considered chaotic.* The old geometry studied smooth spheres, even curves, straight lines. A more careful examination of the irregularities of nature has produced a geometry of imagery. The earth, dimpled with craters, canyons, oceans, rolling hills and jutting mountains, can never again be viewed as a simple sphere. Neither can we view lives in linear terms—science in the Media Age has progressed too far. We must make sense of the multi-dimensional structured chaos as we process it through the imagery of the visual media, especially as it impacts our political culture.

In an interview in the *San Jose Mercury News* (May 5, 1991, 5C), Camille Paglia, a professor of humanities at the Philadelphia College of the Arts and a cultural historian, compared the print world to the ***Fractal Era***—*a term coined by Professor Kirshner to refer to the modern multi-dimensional world of image processing.* She said that the pre–World War II era American sport was baseball. A sport, she said, that academics, who love print, love. Baseball, she felt, was "the ultimate academic sport—linear, logical, slow." She holds that in the Fractal Era "football, especially as remade for T.V." attracts her 1980 generation. She argued: "There's a lot of writing about baseball but hardly any good stuff about football. When a quarterback pulls back from the line and quickly checks out the field, he's not thinking, he's scanning, the very thing we do when we watch T.V."

She used other examples to make her point that in the Media Age, in the Fractal Era, people function more by intuition than by logic. They read the field and react by instinct. Instantaneous decisions become the basis of the factionalized, fragmented world of structured chaos. Maybe that is why the political establishment sought the vote of the "Soccer Moms" in 1996 and not the "Little League Moms" previous politicos fought over. Soccer, an image processing and visual sport, is the emerging game of the Fractal Era.

Ellen Goodman, in "The Fuss Over 'JFK'" (*San Francisco Chronicle*, January 2, 1992, A17) commented on the revolution from print to visual processing: "Those

Attention grabbing.

of us who are print people—writers and readers—are losing ground to the visual people—producers and viewers. The younger generation gets its information and infotainment from television and movies. The franchise over reality is passing hands."*Infotainment—refers to how the entertainment industry provides information that mixes fact with fiction.*

Studies continuously report that American children spend more time in front of the television set than in school. Information provided by the media provides the base for their learning of current events, of the political process.

Television is the primary source of news for the average American. People express considerable disillusionment with television and the quality of the programs, but they still trust this medium of communication more than any other. Television is the means of mass communication that provides visual images to all—the rich, the poor, the young, the old, the politician, the voter, the academic, the illiterate, the children. The Internet (the Web, the Information Superhighway, Cyberspace) is beginning to challenge the dominance of television in bringing visual images to the masses. Hundreds of millions of people now access this anarchistic communications medium.

An imaging culture, exploited by product and political advertisers, is winning over the historical culture. A 1988 study reported that children and adults knew the names of more beers than they did the names of Presidents. Those who would write down and conserve the past are losing to those living in the present. Most newspapers, not just *USA Today*, are written to be more like television infotainment. Even the staid *New York Times* has added color to its photographs and pages.

Newspapers, in their desire to attract the television generation, are appealing to the fragmented short attention span of the visual person. Today's television fare pays little attention to concepts, situations and characters; it deals with problems for little more than a few seconds at a time.

Robert MacNeil, writing in *The National Forum* ("Is T.V. Shortening Our Attention Span?," Fall, 1987, 21) heightened my concern for a society that accepts doublespeak or political imagery without an ability for critical analysis. He said: "I think it has become fashionable to think that, like fast food, fast ideas are the way to get to a fast, impatient public reared on television."

Robert Hughes, writing in *Time* ("Fraying of America," February 2, 1992) felt the end of the print era people would develop a nostalgic attitude towards books: "Before long, Americans will think of the time when people sat at home and read books for their own sake, discursively and sometimes even aloud to one another, as a lost era—the way we now see rural quilting bees in the 1870s."

Yes, change is a constant. Changes in the last few decades, however, have been revolutionary—quantum changes.

I grew up in the world of the print media, baseball and the radio. I was ten years old when my parents got a television—the first in the neighborhood. When most of my present students were ten years old, their parents bought them Nintendo's Sony Playstations, Xboxes, Wiis. I asked a student recently what books he had read to obtain his excellent knowledge of history. He shocked me by reporting that his knowledge came from video games.

The late 1990's ten-year-olds, besides having Nintendo 64's, Sony Playstations and Sega Saturns, had more sophisticated desktop computers in their houses— PC's or Mac's. Even if they lacked a computer in their home to play or work with, the younger siblings of my college students had computer labs during the week in their elementary schools. Computers dramatically changed the education curriculum of the new century. The way young people today interact with the visual media differs drastically from the ancient times of my youth.

In the early years of television, similar to a scene in the movie "Avalon," we often sat around simply watching a test pattern on a nine-inch black and white T.V. screen. The visual images mesmerized us. We had the patience to wait for one of the few T.V. shows that would be on the air that day.

We waited, watching a geometric design, because we looked forward to an exciting future. As the number of T.V. shows increased, many political discussion programs appeared. We listened to people discuss issues for hours on end. The speakers often rambled on about mundane and even stupid issues. Yet we would sit glued to the set, fascinated.

Today, listening to commentators, not to mention politicians, talking calmly and rationally for any length of time, is near impossible. Most of us have trouble viewing a mini-series; forget watching a calm and collected discussion.

The T.V. fare of the contemporary era can only hold our attention through fragmentation, through segmentation. No plot can continue with one theme for half an hour; forget an hour. There must be many subplots and diversions. A recent popular T.V. show bragged about being nothing: Seinfeld. Each weekly episode went from one non-related non-plot to another.

Today's talk shows follow the same pattern—subplots and diversions. These programs are really entertainment designed to stimulate an audience with impressions. The fragmented talk show or news program mimics the modern culture, a society divided into small segments, each reflecting only pieces of reality. Our contemporary world lacks a consistency—a constancy.

CNN's former "Crossfire" show was a telling example of this fragmented sensationalized issue imagery entertainment. No simple exchange of views there. Individuals attacked and cut each other off. They must interrupt. I remember watching "Crossfire's" commentator from the Right, Pat Buchanan, and the visiting critic from the Left, Mark Green, do a typical interview one night. Their guest, angry over their constant interjections, said, "I will be the first person on this show to finish a..." He never got the word "sentence" out. Individuals in the Fractal Era are prevented from completing their thoughts.

Interview shows thrive on emotion. How does it go? "Today on Geraldo, 'Nudists who live in glass houses!'" "Live on Oprah, 'Men who have sex with vegetables!'"

During T.V. news interviews in the 1950's, the host would rationally discuss an issue with a guest for thirty minutes or more. Today, most interviews do not last more than a minute. News commentators feel the need to go on to a new subplot for fear of losing their audience. Interviewees must present their viewpoint, their position, their answer to a question, their thoughts in under a minute. And, so we enter the world of *sound bites—short catchy phrases that sound good and that may or may not convey insights into a political issue.*

Sound bites are the perfect sort of small packaged oversimplifications that reporters in the Media Age love. An analysis of the evening television newscasts in the later stages of the election campaigns of 1968 and 1988 revealed that the average sound bite fell from 42.3 seconds in 1968 to 9.8 seconds in 1988. Can you imagine trying to get your position across to voters in 9.8 seconds? No wonder the modern candidate has to be quick on his toes, sharp with his tongue and, as is more the case, have speech writers who have a comedian's sense of timing. The same study, incidentally, also identified that T.V. networks dramatically increased their visuals of the candidates between 1968 and 1988, while ignoring their words.

The ever present media.

Michael Dukakis, Democratic candidate for President in 1988, two years after his loss, said that his major mistake in his campaign was underestimating the importance of the television sound bite. Fox Butterfield reported in the *New York Times* on a talk by Governor Dukakis at the University of Hawaii in April, 1990. The former candidate admitted: "I made a lot of mistakes in the '88 campaign. But none as damaging as my failure to understand this [sound bite] phenomenon and the need to respond immediately and effectively to distortions of one's record and one's position."

Barack Obama took these words to heart in his 2008 campaign for President. He established a process of near instantaneous retorts to distortions of his positions and record.

Perhaps the most remembered sound bite of the 1988 campaign did not come from Governor Dukakis' opponent. His running mate, Senator Lloyd Bentsen's, remark during the vice-presidential candidates debate with Senator Dan Quayle remains etched in the annals of classic sound bites. Senator Quayle compared his own experience with that of John F. Kennedy before his election as President. Senator Bentsen, prepared for just such an equation, dealt a killing blow that fed the media's sound bite appetite for that night: "Senator, I served with Jack Kennedy. I knew Jack Kennedy. Jack Kennedy was a friend of mine. Senator, you're no Jack Kennedy." Some political analysts hold that Senator Bentsen's pithy sound bite caused the Bush campaign to place Senator Dan Quayle in deep freeze until after the election.

Memorable sound bites from recent campaigns abound. Who can forget George H.W. Bush's "Read my lips, no new taxes?" during the 1988 presidential campaign? Ann Richard, then Texas State Treasurer, in her keynote address at the Democratic Convention in 1988, tore into Bush's upper-class background and tendency toward verbal gaffes: "Poor George. He can't help it. He was born with a silver foot in his mouth." Her sound bite seemed destined to harm Mr. Bush's campaign, but Michael Dukakis failed to maintain the momentum set at the convention. His own words, that I quoted earlier, attest to his lack of understanding of the importance of the sound bite in modern politics.

In the Democratic primary of 1984, a catchy phrase allowed Walter Mondale to destroy his closest opponent for the party's nomination. During a televised debate between the candidates, Mondale shot, "Where's the beef?", a slogan from a Wendy's Restaurant T.V. advertisement, at Gary Hart. This sound bite reinforced the Mondale strategy of imaging Hart as lacking substance in his positions. Gary Hart, however, had produced a book of extensive and well-developed policy statements and programs. How could he provide any realistic insights to his positions on issues in the minute allotted him to respond to Mondale's "Where's the beef?"

During the presidential campaign of 1984, Walter Mondale had struck some damaging blows on the incumbent Ronald Reagan in their first debate. President Reagan arrived at the second debate ready to brush aside one of the major attacks, his age. When Walter Mondale tried to stick the age issue to the President, Reagan struck back with that evening's most memorable sound bite: "I'm not going to exploit for political purposes my opponent's youth and inexperience." Reagan was the master of the political equivalent of the Johnny Carson monologue—strings of randomly assembled one-liners and anecdotes. He went on to win the election by a landslide.

The media referred to the 2008 presidential campaign as a "sound bite war." Both Barack Obama and John McCain used sound bites to question the other's fitness to be President. My favorite Barack Obama sound bite: "McCain is running for Bush's third term!" I loved this sound bite from John McCain: "I admire and respect Senator Obama. For a young man with **little experience** he's done very well."

While the sound bite can create some superficial sense of political issues, it cannot provide the listener with a solid command of information or in-depth knowledge of the politician. In the Fractal Era, abbreviated forms of communication abound, thwarting substance. With the response speed to questions down to a few seconds, the listener—the viewer—has little substance to analyze. Politicians often ignore rational deliberation and avoid expressing themselves, the past essence of the political process.

The first broadcast presidential primary debate occurred in May, 1948 between the Republicans, Governor Thomas E. Dewey and Governor Harold E. Stassen. This dialogue took place before the Oregon Republican primary and was the last debate limited to a single issue: "Should the Communist Party be outlawed?"

John F. Kennedy and Richard M. Nixon locked horns in the first televised general election debate in 1960. Neither candidate pursued any single subject in much depth. Surveys after the debate found that for those who heard it on the radio, Nixon won. In contrast, for those who saw the debate on television, the polls reported that Kennedy won. The Visual Media Age had arrived full blown.

Richard Nixon learned his lesson well from his narrow loss to John F. Kennedy in 1960, which most analysts believed stemmed from his negative television image. In his successful campaign for the presidency in 1968, Richard Nixon managed and orchestrated the images to play well on the evening television news. He started the era of staged media events that flowered with Ronald Reagan's presidency in the 1980's. The actor turned President used the able advice of professional advertising experts. Michael Deaver, the most talented of his PR strategists, helped perfect the techniques of the video presidency.

Early every morning, Deaver would sit down with other presidential aides to shape what was to be broadcast on that night's television news. They recognized that they would receive no more than a thirty or forty second spot and set their agenda accordingly. Although the reporters had selected the sound bites and the visuals for their news broadcasts, now the White House staged the media events.

When Ronald Reagan lacked a daily script, he avoided being caught in gaffes by feigning an inability to hear questions. Any annoyance the public might feel about Reagan's avoidance of answers was mitigated by the elaborate *photo ops*—*carefully staged photographic opportunities designed to promote beautiful optimistic images to boost a politician's visual stature*. Often the media referred to Reagan as the Teflon President because no damaging substance would stick to him.

Political campaigns in the 1980's now depended upon sophisticated staging and backdrops. Media gurus provided the scripts and recommended the camera angles for the photo opportunities. George H.W. Bush kicked off his 1988 presidential campaign with a Labor Day appearance at Disneyland, a perfect network event—not a presentation of substantive issues, but a visual performance designed for television. CBS's Bob Schieffer reported on the "Disneyland backdrop and the pictures with the Disney gang." Bob Schieffer might have viewed this campaign as "frivolous, even silly at times," but his network loved the pictures.

Bush had provided the photo ops while avoiding any thoughtful message. All the networks jumped at the opportunity to telecast this political entertainment—the number one priority of the modern campaign. Disneyland, the entertainment capital of the world, where all are happy and young at heart. Politics as Universal Studios, as impression management, is seldom enlightening, but can win votes.

Of course, not all staged photo ops benefit the politician. Michael Dukakis, trying to ward off the Bush campaign's attack videos, picturing him soft on defense, climbed aboard a tank. He looked very uncomfortable and out of place in an ill-fitting military outfit as the tank made circles like a dog

Reality #2?

around a fire hydrant. Dukakis became the butt of jokes and a whole new round of attack videos imaging Dukakis's artificial behavior.

Kiku Adatto, writing in *The New Republic* ("The Incredible Shrinking Sound Bite," May 28, 1990, 20–23), revealed the new dynamics between the politician's media gurus and the network news. He observed: "So attentive was television news to the way the campaign constructed images for television that political reporters began to sound like theatre critics, reporting more on stagecraft than the substance of politics."

Media handlers have been around since the 1952 presidential campaign. Both Adlai Stevenson and Dwight D. Eisenhower hired advisors. Joe McGinniss exposed the expanded role of media advisors in his 1968 book, *The Selling of the President*. McGinniss' publication of his sense of disillusionment and outrage, however, did not stem the use of these media gurus.

By 1988, in place of independent fact collaboration, reporters sought out media advisors to comment on a politician's effectiveness and truthfulness. The politicians soon took advantage of the realization that they could put their spin on the news. They hired squads of **spin doctors**—*individuals retained by politicians as public relations people to speak with reporters and appear on the networks to favorably influence what the media presented.* Realizing that the media representatives might just miss or overlook the prepared zingers and the staged photo ops, these PR people, "spin doctors," sought to spin or doctor the evening news for their politician or their political party.

Reality #3?

Skilled political handlers now identify the "hot-button" issues by electronically recording the reactions of sample groups of voters to various themes. They then prepare the ads, the photo ops, the attack videos and the sound bites for the spin doctors to manipulate the media presentations. Is it any wonder that in 1988, *Newsweek* called for a return to "the days when reporters and editors picked the sound bite?"

Since I am one who believes that change moves forward—you cannot return—I have a different call. From my perspective, sound bites, controlled by the politician or the media, deny intellectual analysis. In the Fractal Era, in the Visual Media Age, critical thinking becomes even more urgent. My main concern is to avoid the negative, but to express my belief that critical thinking is a major element of being human. I hold that being human means using our ability to reason and to not be like the pea-brained dinosaurs.

We must design an educational system, a media, and a political process, that train us to use our intellectual capacity with both the print world and the visual world. Many educators, writers and thinkers today are discussing this issue. Primary and secondary school educators are adding critical thinking to their curriculums. Before graduation at my college, students must complete a course that includes critical thinking. Obviously, one course cannot teach critical thinking. **Critical thinking**—*thinking about what you are thinking while you are thinking*—must infect every part of our lives. We cannot survive in a world of instantaneous happenings without a capacity to process everything through our data base with the speed of the most rapid computer. We must meet this challenge within a global village.

A generation ago, Marshall McLuhan in *Understanding the Media: The Extensions of Man*, (1964) coined the term **global village**—*a borderless world in which the communications media transcend the boundaries of nations.* He wrote: "Ours is a brand new world. . . . 'Time' has ceased, 'space' has vanished. We now live in . . . a simultaneous happening."

Time magazine (January 6, 1992), in its cover story on its Man of the Year, Ted Turner, observed: "The very definition of news was rewritten—from something that *has happened* to something that *is happening* at the very moment you are hearing it." Events become momentous because people see them happening.

We have traveled light years in technology since the 1988 Bush-Dukakis presidential race. Politicians must respond instantly to events seen live. They no longer have time to ponder a response. The event occurs instantaneously and the medium is the message, to use Marshal McLuhan's words. Events have a thousand times the impact of previous decades.

I sat fascinated after President H.W. Bush's State of the Union Message (January 28, 1992) when seven million people tried to participate in a simultaneous happening on CBS. They wanted to express their views on his remarks. Only 300,000 callers got through on the new fiber optic television lines that night. Dan Rather said that they expected that the lines would soon handle all callers.

See the reporters question President Clinton about an alleged affair while he is ready to bomb the hell out of Iraq (1998). Watch the live telecast of the sizzling O. J. Simpson trial (1995). See Gorbachev and Yeltsin ward off the Evil Empires Return (August, 1991). Come behind enemy lines and hear Peter Arnett report while the smart bombs hit their targets with video camera rolling in the warheads (January, 1991). Let's all join the simultaneous happening as the Berlin Wall comes tumbling down (November, 1989). Let's all watch in abject horror as planes slam into the twin towers (September, 2001). Call or fax a talk show host. E-mail your legislator. Discuss any issue you want at any time of the day on the Internet.

President John F. Kennedy pondered for six days in 1962 what to do about the missiles in Cuba. The White House during the Iraqi War of 1991 responded in a few hours to events and reportedly felt the need to reply in minutes. The military often got its information about where missiles landed and what was occurring from CNN television network downfeeds.

Since the politician and the viewing public no longer have time to analyze the instantaneous facts, they must rely on belief systems. The Visual Media Age inundates us with facts that have extended the number of belief systems. Our conflicts are no longer between beliefs, but conflicts about beliefs. Walter Truett Anderson in his *Reality Isn't What It Used To Be* (1990) holds that "beliefs about beliefs . . . will become a central part of the worldview of most people. It will be the core of the first global civilization." He adds: "But it is not yet a core. It is more a seed of discontent. It fills our daily lives with uncertainty and anxiety, renders us vulnerable to tyrants and cults, shakes religious faith, and divides societies into groups contending with one another in a strange unfamiliar kind of ideological conflict." Todays ideology groups have different beliefs about belief itself.

Walter Truett Anderson continues his assessment of the Fractal Era by arguing that the "metaconflict about beliefs" is now a central theme in politics. Because individuals now assert their own reality, Anderson says: "We can also see an increasing theatricality of politics, in which events are scripted and stage-managed for mass consumption, and in which individuals and groups struggle for starring roles (or at least bit parts) in the dramas of life."

Virtual reality—an emerging three dimensional technology that provides the illusion of being physically surrounded by video images and interacting with them—has appeared on the commercial market. William Bricken ("Virtual Reality: Directions of Growth," *Technical Report No. HITL-90-1*, Human Interface Technology Laboratory, 1990, p. 16) says that virtual reality marks the true beginning of the essence of the computer revolution. He states: "The most important thing to realize about VR is that it is more than reality, more than a simulation of reality. You add physical realism to a virtual world." I will be fascinated to see how, in the next decade, the political PR gurus use this revolution development in media technology.

Politicians with their PR people love to give us the happy ending scripts, avoiding the bad news. Except in a campaign, when they feel the compulsion to air attack videos.

The art and science of image management saturates politics. A while back, I saw the British musical "Chess" at the San Jose City Light Opera. I realized that the story had changed from my original-cast recording. Soviet deception and deceit had given way to a semi-happy ending. In 1913, the French poet, Paul Valery wrote: "The future isn't what it used to be." In the Visual Media Age, "the past isn't what it used to be," or as expressed in the title of Walter Truett Anderson's book, "reality isn't what it used to be."

As old belief systems collapsed, or became the subject of extensive debate, the political story-makers moved in. The Political PR people continued to fill the gaps of realities by creating new multi-dimensional realities. These feed the needs of voters for value construction in a world of contradictory facts. Simplistic answers to complex issues, sound bites, photo ops and political theatrics seldom educate the voter—unless the individual can critically analyze what is presented. Critical thinking can expand our moral or intellectual understanding, constructing new public realities in the mass democracies of the Fractal Era.

David Glidden, in the *Los Angeles Times* (December 11, 1988), wrote: "Understanding is the only way of seeing through the facts that inundate us, the circumstances that fail us, the grief that pains us." He continued: "And a just society requires understanding why immorality is wrong. If memory banks replace understanding, then our future is in peril. We will have forgotten how to think."

From my perspective, a prime danger to our human essence and to our democracy in the visual image world of colorized, glitz, quadraphonic, pastel shades, would be the loss of our moral indignation. If doublespeak, sound bites and photo ops lead to desensitization, our ability to cry out against wrongs and injustices will cease.

A Nazi leader once said: "You don't find Hitler with your mind, you find him with your heart. The intellect deceives. Emotion leads you to truth." Once you accept emotion as a path to truth, ignoring your intellect, I think you destroy the reason for being human.

The Visual Media Age not only emphasizes pictures over words, but it also stresses sensationalism. Sensationalism opens the door to desensitization as each exaggerated event appears commonplace. A desire may then appear for more exciting stimuli. As the stimuli becomes the message, the belief system, you can easily lose a sense of right or wrong. The couch potato can readily accept phrases such as "plausible deniability" and "surreptitious entries for political expediency" without batting an eyelash.

Reality #4?

"Please just entertain me and do not enlighten me" becomes the slogan of the desensitized person. Moral issues and ethics are ignored in the search for fulfilling images.

Sensationalized entertainment sells programs and newspapers in the same manner a politician hawks his wares. He uses doublespeak, sound bites and photo ops. Even the *New York Times,* with its slogan "all the news that's fit to print," joined the competitive sensationalist media market a few years ago. While other newspapers refused to print the name of the alleged rape victim in the William Kennedy Smith case, the *New York Times* named her.

The media moguls argue that they are only giving the public what they want. They rationalize that if the public wants entertainment and sensationalized images, they must follow. I suspect my calling for media responsibility and leadership would simply be haggling over to which belief system individuals should subscribe. Yet, I do believe that if the media acted more responsibly, instead of searching for the almighty dollar, then the politician would need to deal with issues.

Behold the field day the media had with the charges of marital infidelity directed against Arkansas Governor Bill Clinton during his 1992 presidential primary campaign. The media spent even more time arguing over whether they should be emphasizing Governor Clinton's personal life and neglecting his position on issues. Their debate provided even greater entertainment.

By avoiding content and focusing on emotional trivia, the media makes it difficult for the voter to respond intelligently. Certainly, the politicians and their media gurus are going to avoid mobilizing the public around issues and play on attractive images.

I wrote earlier that I did not feel we could return to the print era. Instantaneous reports, spontaneous happenings, sensationalized events are probably here to stay. In the next media stage we may be able to program events to our liking. A few buttons on the T.V. would allow us to focus close or far, focus on specific people or scenes or even enter the happening through Virtual Reality.

I continue my argument that change must come from the education system. Students, the future voters, will have to learn to analyze and interpret the world of images at megaspeeds—not fall into the trap of blind acceptance.

Education must provide the means for the next generation to become responsible and knowledgeable citizens. Walter Lippmann, a political commentator a few generations ago, said that people "who have lost their grip upon the relevant facts of their environment are the inevitable victims of agitation and propaganda."

In the world of media make believe, we can lose our sense of reality, as well as our ability to make value judgments. As we become bombarded with image stimuli, inundated with sense stimulation, we can lose our ability to become shocked, to become incensed—we can lose our moral indignation. With the loss of moral indignation comes the destruction of imagination and creativity.

In the Visual Media Age, reality becomes entertainment and entertainment becomes reality. When we no longer fear reality, we will no longer recognize reality.

On November 22, 1963, Americans entered the world of reality as entertainment television—John F. Kennedy's assassination. We also saw Jack Ruby shoot

Education in Crisis.

Kennedy's assassin, Lee Harvey Oswald (excuse me Oliver Stone). Television began a new era.

The Vietnam War provided us with immediately processed films and instant replay tapes of violence and death. Would these soldiers killed on the small screen return on a different soap opera to be killed again? Or, would they next appear in a sitcom loving a beautiful woman instead of covered with stage blood?

Imagination becomes unnecessary—in a docudrama or in a live report from the Gulf War. We can view all the parts of the body hanging out. In entertainment as reality, people don't die. They aren't really injured. Go watch "Goodfellas" and see violence that leaves nothing to the imagination. Imagination is unnecessary—everything is in living color.

A lot could be said for those films and programs which let your imagination take over. Your mind and senses receive a creative workout. The original movie "Psycho" was scary as hell even though it lacked vivid violence. A desensitized viewing public now demand blood and gore. What is left to the imagination in the "Friday the 13th" and "Scream" series?

Sex receives similar treatment and lacks redeeming social value. Late night T.V. starts in the afternoon. You can view "R" rated films that are really triple "X" on Showtime or HBO, forget the Playboy channel. Hardly simulated sex! Nothing is left for your creative imagination.

Why not appeal to fantasies, to fears, to base instincts, when advertising? Newspapers, T.V. stations, the movie industry feel the pressure of competitive market. They worry that if they can't compete they will fold. So they try to out-sensationalize each other. The market for advertising is quite profitable. A prime time T.V. thirty-second advertisement can bring in upwards of $350,000. A thirty-second time slot during the 2005 Superbowl cost $2.5 million. No wonder T.V. news becomes entertainment and the station owners pay newscasters entertainers' salaries.

Actually, some of the visual media is designed to neutralize rather than excite. Michael Parenti, in his *Inventing Reality* (1986), states: "While we think of the press as geared to crisis and sensationalism, often its task is just the opposite, dedicated to the graying of reality, blurring popular grievances and social inequities." He also argues: "Instead of neutralizing themselves as observers, reporters and editors are more likely to neutralize their subject matter, giving it an innocence it may not deserve."

Media moguls, when not sensationalizing or neutralizing, often spread myths popular to the current political climate. Susan Faludi's *Backlash: The Undeclared War Against American Women* (1991) exposes how the media, during the conservative 1980's, presented distorted, faulty and plainly inaccurate information. She calls on women to act in their own behalf.

We must all act on issues that concern us. But, first we must learn to siphon the myths and visual images into rational belief systems.

Once again, schools must set the stage for critical thinking. They must provide for visual literacy as well as print literacy. A curriculum that allows students to structure knowledge and create frames of reference is the basis of critical thinking. Critical thinkers have the insights to reveal and reject irrational beliefs.

In their attempts to figure things out for themselves, critical thinkers can reject unjustified authorities, distorted information and sensationalized appeals. They will maintain a sense of moral indignation that will help prevent the politicians abusing their power. They will have the potential for enhancing and advancing democratic institutions. Developing critical thinkers who can sort and process visual media information at quantum speed will advance democracy in a global village.

Many schools are already offering courses for the Fractal Era with names such as "Media Literacy," "Visual Literacy," or "Critical Viewing." My local newspaper (*The Argus,* December 9, 1990) reported: "Students from kindergarten through high school . . . are learning to analyze television and the other media that pervade their lives." In Ontario, Canada, since 1986, educators have required all students, from the 7th through the 12th grade, to study the messages of television.

In 1990, media studies became a required part of the school curriculum in Great Britain. American educators still shy away from recommending a media literacy requirement. Yet pressure is mounting to teach thinking skills through visual literacy courses.

Educators cannot add true critical thinking to a curriculum like they can add driver's education. Teaching the art of reasoning, of problem solving, of critical viewing, must become integrated within a total school program.

Jane M. Healy, in her *Endangered Minds: Why Children Don't Think and What We Can Do About It* (1990), says that a generation with short attention spans must have a curriculum that unites talk with visual presentations. However, "hands-on" activities and projects are not the lone answer. She notes: "Potentially great

Welcome to fantasy!

minds are also encouraged to 'mess around' with real-life challenges—and with great ideas. Neither have neat, tidy edges."

Jane Healy then goes on to provide specific suggestions on how to structure a critical thinking curriculum. I also recommend *What Curriculum for the Information Age?* (1987), a series of articles published by Lawrence Erlbaum Associates, for anyone who desires more suggestions for education in the Visual Media Age, the Fractal Era.

Every day, in the expanding world of telecommunications, we make greater demands on the intelligence of citizens. Media moguls and political PR gurus, meanwhile, expend their energy sending out meaningless images and idiotic stories. Politicians continue to rest their stature and their campaigns on double-speak, attack videos, sound bites and photo ops. Yet, despite my presentation of these negatives and of the ramifications of the kaleidoscope of information, I remain optimistic.

Curriculums preparing people for critical thinking in the visual media world are increasing. We now can transmit, at the speed of light, information in any form—print, voice or image. A few of you may even be reading my book of essays for an on-line computer class. Individuals can gain political information with minimum control. Fewer dictators exist on today's planet, as they can no longer control information. Activities of governments and political leaders occur within a global village as the whole world watches.

Cellular telephones and wireless fax machines dump information unceasingly to all parts of the world. The Internet provides instantaneous information about any subject. So far, political leaders have failed to limit this distribution of knowledge and pseudo-knowledge—rumors and conspiracy theories abound, especially in the chat rooms and in the news groups. Political leaders have, themselves, found the Internet a useful tool for spreading their propaganda. Among the first American politicians in the early 1990s to create web pages were Representative Newt Gingrich and Senator Ted Kennedy. By 1996, candidates for almost every office in our country from the Ohlone College School Board to President of the United States sold their wares through their web sites. Many politicos answer questions through chat rooms established by different servers like America On Line (AOL). Some have even used Instant Messaging to communicate with their constituents.

E-mail travels within nano-seconds to all corners of the globe. Computer geeks now refer to normal mail delivery—that which arrives the next day—as snail mail. Dictatorial governments can control snail mail. They can open it and examine it for subversive content. While private servers like AOL can filter out certain words, most mail over the Internet travels in an anarchistic manner. Governments, so far, are unable to limit the ability of their nationals to use E-mail to communicate with friends in other countries. Yes, the politicos could simply ban computers, but international business in the global marketplace demands the use of modern technology.

John Naisbitt in his book *Megatrends* stated that in a high tech world people need high touch. E-mail provides this high touch need using high tech. Every day I receive jokes and pithy messages from friends throughout the world. It appears that my friends in the high tech industries are mainly responsible for this humorous E-mail that clutters my box. Since I have never been one who appreciates canned jokes—I like spontaneous humor—most of this mail goes unread. In most cases it is the communication—the touch—that counts. And, this touch has enabled former students and old friends to finger me—search out my E-mail address. I love the restored contact as it provides me, a high tech person, with high touch.

The need for high touch appears to have spawned a movement to tribal emotionalism among some of my college students. Benjamin R. Barber in his article "Jihad vs. McWorld" (*The Atlantic*, March 1992) sees the political conflict in the contemporary era between the centrifugal power of tribalism and the centripetal force of internationalism. I will discuss this further in my chapter "The Unicorn vs. The Lion: Foreign Affairs." However, suffice it to say that in a technological globe knotting people together behind the Apollonian machine, a Dionysian rebellion is bound to occur. Apollo was the Greek god of the intellect, rationality, controlled thought and structured action. Dionysius was the Greek god of wine, song, dance, feeling, spontaneity and emotion.

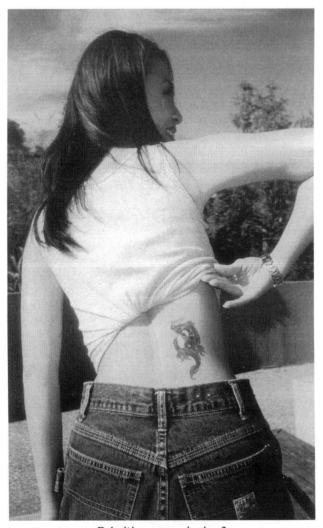

Primitive expressionism?

When I was a college student the only tattoos and body piercing I saw were in *National Geographic* magazine photographs. In recent years, about 20% of my students are sporting tattoos and piercing every part of their anatomy. One of my students told me about her friend who had her clitoris pierced with a ring so she could walk around feeling pleasure most of the time—certainly a different form of the high touch in a high tech world. Are the tattoos, piercings and all the survivor TV shows just an attempt to bring out our primitive emotional touch in the cold world of high tech?

Other generations in developed nations have attempted to escape the rigors of the modern world through alcohol or drugs. The pop out drop out youth of the 1960's and early 70's reflected this rebellious spirit. But, something else appears to be taking hold in the Fractal Era of the 21st century. The contemporary youth are not dropping out or cropping out, they are reverting. These are the modern *Luddites—a group of British workers who between 1811 and 1816 rioted and destroyed laborsaving textile machinery in the belief that such machinery would diminish employment.* The Fractal Era tattooed pierced youths are not concerned with unemployment. They are simply raging against the machine. They are taking a stand against a centralized technocratic world directed by suited political managers. Interestingly this tribal youth is using the decentralized chaos of the World Wide Web to hack away at the faceless bureaucrats. While they rage against the machine they communicate through the anarchy of the web to keep the city and

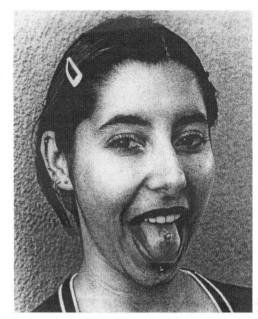

A statement to modernity?

forest people informed of what is happening in the bounded world. In some ways, I would argue that the news media is no longer "the watchdog of democracy." E-mail, chat groups, instant messaging, blogs for the fractal youth generation have taken over that role. Sadly, while the fractal computer literate youth have helped prevent the dictators from flourishing, they have also disseminated disinformation and paranoid rumors through the net. So once again, I must return to my theme of promoting critical thinking.

I do believe it is necessary to reduce things to their essence. I am glad the media provides pastel colored photographs and stereophonic stories. I am grateful to the tattooed indignant hackers and bloggers who want to keep touch in our technological lives. But, to maintain the human spirit, to preserve democracy, we need more—we need Apollo and Dionysius. The picture on the T.V. or on the computer screen must be worth 1,000 analyzed words or in the long run the *solons—legislators—*as well will forget they must be responsive to the people.

Never has the chance for a well-informed citizenry and leadership accountability been greater. *The Visual Media Age, the Fractal Era, has provided the breakthroughs in media technology and information processing that can expand what it means to be human. I look forward, along with John Naisbitt and Patricia Aburdene, as expressed in their* **Megatrends 2000** *(1990), to the final "triumph of the individual."*

GLOSSARY

CRITICAL THINKING
Thinking about what you are thinking while you are thinking, to know what you are thinking; reading between the lines.

EUPHEMISM
Inoffensive or positive word or phrase used to avoid a harsh, unpleasant or distasteful reality.

DOUBLESPEAK
Language that pretends to communicate but really doesn't.

DOUBLETHINK
The mental process that allows an individual to hold two contrasting ideas and believe in both.

FRACTAL ERA
A term coined by Professor Kirshner to refer to the modern multi-dimensional world of image processing.

GLOBAL VILLAGE
A borderless world in which the communications media transcend the boundaries of nations.

GOBBLEDYGOOK
Piling on words to overwhelm an audience.

INFLATED LANGUAGE
Designed to make the ordinary appear extraordinary; to make the simple appear complex.

INFOTAINMENT
Refers to how the entertainment industry provides information that mixes fact with fiction.

JARGON
Language of a trade or profession.

LUDDITES
A group of British workers who between 1811 and 1816 rioted and destroyed laborsaving textile machinery in the belief that such machinery would diminish employment.

MEDIA
Books, magazines, newspapers, movies, recordings and, above all, television, which convey facts and ideas through images.

MEDIA AGE
The recent era in which politics are increasingly intertwined with the media.

PHOTO OPS
Carefully staged photographic opportunities designed to promote stature.

POLITICAL SOCIALIZATION
The impact of society on the development of an individual's political views and values.

PUBLIC OPINION
Those views expressed by large groups of people who try to influence the political process.

SOLONS
Legislators.

SOUND BITES
Short catchy phrases that sound good and that may or may not convey insights into a political issue.

SPIN DOCTORS
Individuals retained by politicians as public relations people to speak with reporters and appear on the networks to favorably influence what the media presented.

VISUAL MEDIA AGE
> A world of media images that bombards our senses with emotions.

VIRTUAL REALITY
> An emerging three dimensional technology that provides the illusion of being physically surrounded by video images and interacting with them.

PART 2

HUMAN EVENTS, WHERE TO?

CHAPTER 5

Power Modules

Essay V

> *Power is the best aphrodisiac.*

> Henry Kissinger

Years ago I taught at a university in Florida. One of my students was a 24-year-old Vietnam War Veteran from Massachusetts. Vinnie (his name) received numerous military decorations. He joked that he moved to the South to avoid having his Mafia relatives use him as a hit man. Vinnie told many stories, and no one could tell which were true, which ones he embellished or which were just plain lies.

Students and faculty alike enjoyed associating with Vinnie, due to his affable personality and his great sense of humor. He had a unique quality that people call charisma. Please note that I am not defining this term. I cannot come up with a good definition of charisma. Perhaps the reason I have difficulty defining the word will become clear as I return to my tale of Vinnie.

One day Vinnie, driving home from college, cut off a pickup truck. The truck contained two "rednecks" with their requisite shotguns hanging on the racks in the rear of the cabin. The rednecks followed Vinnie to his trailer. They stepped out of the truck, shotguns pointed at Vinnie. They began cursing him with non-traditional southern language. [Aside—One reason I decided to leave the South was that I became tired of hearing, "gee-whiz," "dang-it," and "shucks."]

Vinnie looked straight at the two men and said: "I am going into my trailer and getting my shotgun. If you are not gone by the time I return, I am going to blow your fuckin' heads off." He turned around and headed for the trailer. They left! This is when I knew that I lacked charisma. If someone pointed a gun at me, my reaction would be simple, I would wet my pants—but, not Vinnie. He returned with his shotgun at the ready. I looked at him and said, "Vinnie, you're nuts, they could have shot you." Vinnie's response was characteristic, "Alan, if a redneck fails to shoot you right away, he won't, however, I am pissed at myself." I asked him what he meant. He smiled and said, "Well, I was so angry I forgot to load my shotgun and I couldn't have blown them away as I intended."

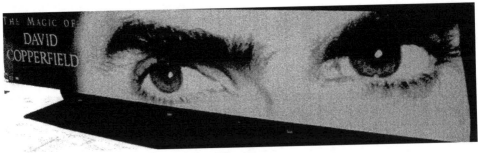

Charisma

Vinnie had charisma. This Greek word means gift of the gods. In a sense, the charismatic person functions as if s/he were immortal, like a god. Charismatic people seem to be able to do things that we mere mortals would never dare to imagine. They are usually beings of whom we say: "How could they have done that? I could never do something like that." Because of the uniqueness of their actions and of their magnetic personalities, people love the charismatic person. Many people also hate them. People are seldom apathetic about an individual with charisma.

Charismatic individuals project an aura that attracts or repels others. We all seem to have auras that attract or repel. I am sure you have met an individual that fit your list of the perfect person, yet you took an immediate dislike to the individual. In other cases, you ran into someone you knew you would dislike because they had every negative character you could list, but, you found yourself attracted to the person. The difference with charismatic individuals is that they move large masses of people through the power of their being. You seem to feel the strength of their personalities by a magnetic intensity emanating from their eyes.

Despite my technical ability to describe a charismatic personality, I still cannot define the term. I used to teach a course in the Women's Studies Program called, "A History of Masculinity." I researched charisma and leadership for a book I wrote based upon the course. I never found any material distinguishing charisma from leadership. Yet, I have little doubt that a vast difference exists between leadership and charisma. Leadership can be learned. Charisma appears to be inborn. An individual can lose charisma by failing to use the power. Charisma, when developed, is a unique form of leadership. Very few people, and even fewer politicians, have this inborn leadership attribute.

While we cannot define charisma, we seem to be able to agree on who has it and who does not. Great political leaders often lack charisma. During the early Democratic Party presidential primaries in 1972, George McGovern, seemed upset when the media described him as bland and lacking charisma. When he won the Democratic Party's nomination to run for President he remarked: "See, I do have charisma." No, George McGovern never had charisma. My photograph of him speaking, with a gentleman sound asleep behind him, symbolized to me his lack of charisma. George McGovern, however, was a respected political leader. He became the Democratic Party's standard bearer, losing the 1972 election to the equally non-charismatic Richard Nixon.

I have asked my students numerous times whom they would consider charismatic. Students are almost unanimous. John F. Kennedy is inevitably the first political name students blurt out. Richard Nixon has never made the charismatic list. Bobby Kennedy often appears on the list. When I ask about Ted Kennedy the students always respond with a loud, "No Way!"

Ted Kennedy, in his youth, was as handsome as his brothers. He certainly is a moving speaker and a great leader. Why do students and others feel that he lacks charisma? I am unable to answer that question. The example of the Kennedy brothers just underlines the amorphous nature of charisma.

Other presidents my students agreed had charisma include Franklin Delano Roosevelt, Teddy Roosevelt, Abraham Lincoln and Andrew Jackson. Obviously, none of my

George McGovern lacked charisma.

students lived during the terms of these presidents. Many of the students had never seen pictures of them, but somehow the being of these presidents, their presence, transcends the decades and centuries.

A few students name Bill Clinton, Ronald Reagan or Harry Truman as charismatic leaders. A borderline charisma may exist in these cases. The media called Ronald Reagan the "Teflon Man," implying that no matter what negatives the press or politicians threw at him, they never stuck. Harry Truman's "The Buck Stops Here!" sign on his oval office desk certainly appeals to our modern students, often frustrated by a perceived waffling and weaving found in many of our modern politicos.

I do believe it is difficult to stick negatives to charismatic leaders. Granted, those predisposed to dislike the individual might create negatives that adhere. Recent leaders, and especially presidents, seem to be made of fly paper. Every dust bunny clings to them, once the talk show hosts grab on to an issue.

Another individual whose name students always mention when I raise the topic of charisma is Martin Luther King, Jr. Jesse Jackson is often named along with, though not in the same breath, as Rush Limbaugh. There is near unanimity on Barack Obama's charisma. Most of my students viewed him as a modern day John F. Kennedy.

Charisma is not solely a male trait. Students who have heard of Eleanor Roosevelt, Indira Gandhi or Golda Meir add them to the list of people who exude charisma. The overwhelming sorrow and outpouring of sympathy throughout the world at the tragic death of Princess Diana underscored her charisma. The non-political Mother Teresa epitomized the charismatic woman. I continue to emphasize that charisma is not based upon looks, or speaking ability or success—it just is!

I never end the list of charismatic leaders without adding one or two names of individuals with "evil charisma." Inevitably the students mention Adolf Hitler's name. Students visualize Charles Manson as a charismatic devil.

Students name many charismatic individuals in the entertainment industry and among religious leaders. I do not find this surprising, as to achieve in these areas—to stand out—an individual needs that little extra something: charisma.

In a democracy, however, a charismatic person is not always the best leader. People rely on the charismatic politician to make the decisions. Democracy demands individual participation, responsibility and the ability to make reasonable decisions. A secular messiah is not what democracy needs. Charismatic leaders often create dictatorships in societies where people abdicate their power. Hitler, Stalin, Khadafy, Castro, Idi Amin are all examples of charismatic leaders who ignored the will of the people.

If a charismatic leader has the gift of god, is godlike, what better person to assassinate? If you kill a god, you inherit the power of that god—or so the nut believes. More charismatic leaders are targets for assassins than your run of the mill political leader. Andrew Jackson, perhaps our first charismatic president, was the first president anyone tried to shoot.

As president, Andrew Jackson vetoed more legislation than the total of all the preceding presidents. Charismatic people often see themselves as infallible. They are far less likely to compromise on issues, as they feel they know what is best for everyone else. A pluralistic democracy similar to the United States of America depends on political leaders able to reach compromise on a myriad of diverse positions. A democracy needs good leadership, not god-like directors.

Mighty Mouse once said, "Superheroes are good for getting free doughnuts." I am not sure what that means, but it sounds good. Voters often live vicariously through their charismatic heroes, so I guess they give them free doughnuts. Good leadership in a democracy does not require a charismatic hero. John Milton Cooper, Jr. in "The Presidency: Out of the Shadowlands" (*The Wall Street Journal*, May 22, 1995) wrote, "Nearly all the time, almost all of the problems of politics and government require wise, restrained human beings, not heroes, whether they work in the White House, the Capitol, or anywhere else that we conduct our public life." A democracy needs political leaders who spread awareness, frame solutions and offer a vision of a future we are able to create while providing a vision of the nightmares we need to avoid.

My purpose in this essay is to examine political leadership in a democracy and how politicians view and use their power. Since the President of the United States is considered the most powerful leader in the United States, I will complete the essay with a cursory look at the power of the presidency.

President Dwight Eisenhower (1953–1959) defined leadership as "the art of getting someone to do something you want done because he wants to do it." This definition is a bit too negative to suit my tastes. I would paraphrase General Eisenhower and propound the following definition: **leadership**—*the art of getting someone to do something that needs to be done.*

The power of symbols.

I suppose the requisite question is, "What constitutes good leadership?" I suspect the answer to this question can only come from those individuals being led. A leader provides leadership. Followers of the leader determine whether the leadership is effective, productive, or, in simplistic terms, good. Every situation requires a different form of leadership and, therefore, a distinct leader.

I do not believe that we have leaders and sheep as the pessimists would contend. I hold that all people become leaders at some point during their lives. Andy Warhol's famous statement about each individual receiving 15 minutes of fame might thus be rendered, "Every individual will be a leader for at least 15 minutes."

We generally perceive of leaders in the context of politics or business. Often we forget the unsung leaders who run our local Little Leagues and the Parent Teacher Associations. America is composed of a myriad of formal and informal organizations. Alexis de Tocqueville, the nineteenth century French observer of American life, as I wrote in a previous essay, said that America is a nation of joiners. It therefore follows that we are a nation of leaders. President Herbert Hoover (1929–1933) once said, "In the great mass of our people there are plenty individuals of intelligence from among whom leadership can be recruited." American groups and families recruit these leaders daily.

Few leaders, however, enter the political arena. The philosopher Bertrand Russell wrote in his essay, *Powers*, in 1938 that a leader will not likely be successful without enjoying the role of leader. According to Russell, the leader "will therefore be lead to a preference for the kind of situation, . . . that makes his success easy." Political leadership is never easy. The modern political leader has difficulty feeling successful. Politicos today have to confront numerous politicians who represent different clients, while attempting to fulfill the desires of their

Machine power.

own divided **constituents**—*residents of a district or members of a group represented by an elected official.* While the task of the political leader is more difficult, the same leadership traits apply to the Chief Executive Officer of a corporation or the President of the local Parent Teacher Association.

President Herbert Hoover, quoted earlier, seemed to believe that intelligence was the prime requirement for leadership. When I asked students in class to provide me with a list of leadership qualities they would want in a presidential candidate, they seldom mention intelligence. When I name intelligence as a factor of leadership, students always express wonderment why they failed to include the trait on their lists. I am also amazed, but have come to expect to find intelligence missing as a quality on the leadership lists. I am curious whether intelligence would have appeared on a student list of leadership traits during the era that Herbert Hoover served as president.

Perhaps my students, like many Americans, view an overtly intelligent politician as an **egghead**—*a highly intelligent individual whom some people view as lacking common sense.* In popular mythology the belief exists that individuals with high foreheads have a larger cerebrum and therefore are more intelligent. Many people used intellectual, highbrow and egghead as negative appellations toward Adlai Stevenson in his failed quest for the presidency in 1952 and 1956. They condemned his sophisticated vocabulary as snobbery and argued he was not suited to be president as he could not understand the needs of the common person. Adlai Stevenson lost both his bids for the presidency to the popular common man's hero of World War II, General Dwight Eisenhower.

Eggheads at UC Davis

Political candidates seldom state their academic accomplishments. Numerous members of Congress have advanced degrees, yet in their campaign literature they discuss their business and athletic experiences. President Gerald Ford, for example, always identified his All-American Football success at the University of Michigan and never mentioned graduating second in his class from Yale University Law School—no easy accomplishment. Bill Clinton was one of the few presidents to emphasize his academic qualifications and his intellect. The American public did not react negatively to his revelations. Perhaps because President Clinton gave the appearance of a "Good Ol' Boy." He certainly did not look like an intellectual—besides, who thinks of eggheads as coming from Arkansas.

In other parts of the world it is common for political leaders to list their academic achievements. I am often amazed at the diversity of academic publications that politicians from other nations have produced. I remember a former Chancellor of Germany discussing his many works on stoic philosophy. A number of years ago, the press informed us that a Japanese Prime Minister while traveling to meet with President Ronald Reagan had devoured a number of books on economics. President Reagan proudly identified to the press the western novel he had just read.

Ronald Reagan was a man of the people. No one described him as an intellectual. He obtained a C average at a small Iowa college. So he was not an intellectual, but he proved himself a great leader who exhibited signs of intelligence.

Yes, my students and Americans, generally, would accept intelligence as requisite to leadership even if they failed to include it on their list as a prime trait of leadership. Different leadership qualities abound and not all leaders have the same traits. Bertrand Russell said, "To acquire the position of leader he must excel in the qualities that confer authority: self-confidence, quick decisions, and skill in deciding upon the right measures."

Leaders must exude confidence to inspire confidence in their followers. *Time Magazine* in an article entitled "Barbara Bush: The Silver Fox" (January 23, 1989, p. 14) argued that much of Ronald Reagan's capacity to lead came from his belief in himself. *Time* wrote: "That Reagan believed in his *spiel,* and in himself, more fully than do most politicians enhanced his credibility." Bertrand Russell would have no difficulty accounting for Ronald Reagan's success as a leader. "Great leaders" he said, "have an exceptional self-confidence which is not only on the surface, but penetrates deep into the subconscious." Most individuals willing to take on leadership roles do so because they are convinced they can do the task better than someone else. We call that ego. There is nothing wrong with a leader having a strong ego—self-confidence—except if it is inflated beyond reality. In democracy, when leaders exhibit bloated egos and cannot deliver, the electorate soon removes them from their positions.

One of the complaints about today's American leaders is their inability to make a decision—forget a quick decision. This apparent inability to decide between issues stems from the numerous uncompromising factions that have appeared in American politics in recent years. The proliferation of interest groups has led to an unwieldy number of *Political Action Committees (PAC's)—the fundraising branches of interest groups that distribute money to candidates and, more recently, spend their cash in an attempt to secure the victory of their causes.* Some political scientists argue that the power of PAC's has come about since the 1970's specifically because of legislation Congress passed in 1974 legitimizing PAC's. The legitimization of PAC's and the expansion of their political power was tied to campaign reforms that included restrictions on the amounts of individual contributions to candidates and the public reporting of contributions. The number of national PAC's has grown from 600 in 1974 to over 4000 today. In their quest to be elected and re-elected politicians believe they need PAC money. They are careful not to offend any interest groups for fear of losing funding. This causes political leaders to be more hesitant about taking a stand on an issue or make quick decisions that just might offend an interest group.

I do not intend to give the impression that I believe that all quick decisions are good decisions. Leaders must contemplate the outcomes of their actions thoroughly. They must be able to listen to all sides of an argument and weigh the alternatives. Sometimes this search for the best decision must inevitably delay a decision. But, leaders must make decisions even if they are unpopular ones. Obviously, quick decisions could have unintended results. A leader must be able to admit a mistake and if possible rectify the error. In his book *Power! How to get it, How to use it*, (1975), Michael Korda wrote, "Nothing makes one seem more foolish or impotent than the inability to admit a mistake." He said that leaders must learn to accept their mistakes. He added: "Powerful people accept the necessity of taking risks and of being wrong. They don't waste time justifying their mistakes, either, or trying to transform them into correct decisions."

Leaders do have an uncanny way of coming up with solutions to problems that others miss. People often select a person to be their leader because that person finds what Bertrand Russell termed, "the right measure." Call it common sense or quick insight, this characteristic of leadership is difficult to develop. Other people often say of the leader's simple method of dealing with the problem, "How come I didn't see that solution? It was right in front of my nose."

At a conference a number of years back, the presenter handed out a chart on leadership qualities. The author postulated that leadership could be divided into five categories: Capacity, Achievement, Responsibility, Participation and Status. Almost all the traits he listed under these categories have appeared on my students' lists of desirable presidential leadership qualities. Under Capacity the creator of the chart included intelligence (I have already indicated that this trait has been noticeably absent from my students' lists), alertness, verbal facility, originality and judgment. The author of the chart divided Achievement into scholarship, knowledge, athletic, business or theatrical accomplishment. Under Responsibility appeared dependability, initiative, persistence, assertiveness, self-confidence and a desire to excel. The fourth criterion, Participation, included sociability, cooperation, adaptability and a sense of humor. In the last category, Status, the chart listed socioeconomic position and popularity.

Missing from this chart and from most scholarly works on leadership traits I have seen is a quality that very recently has appeared on the top of my student lists—honesty. My students often tie honesty to the more inclusive term character. Americans have always had a mistrust of government and those who administer it. Emphasis on the character and honesty of political leaders has also been part of the American political tradition. People today seem to have a morbid fixation on the morals of our politicians. Perhaps this new fascination started with the Watergate scandals of the Nixon Administration. I would hold that a prime cause of the new fascination comes about because our political leaders, similar to many people today, refuse to take responsibility for their blunders or mistakes. What could be sillier than presidential candidate Bill Clinton in 1992 admitting smoking pot in his youth and then adding, "But I didn't inhale!"?

Obviously, good character and its subdivision honesty, are important for leaders. Yet, people have to be careful of the pseudo-moral attention the media spends on some issues that really is out of proportion and fails in basic priorities. In an essay titled "Who Cares, Anyway" (*Time*, February 3, 1992, page 15) Lance Morrow implies that our present obsession with the sexual problems of politicians may be a way of avoiding dealing with the real sexual issues in America— abuse of children and spouses, rape and incest. He argues that "if the public is going to behave like an idiot on the subject of sex, the candidate will naturally do almost anything to avoid telling the truth about any behavior less than impeccable." When Alexander Hamilton, as Secretary of the Treasury during President George Washington's administration publicly admitted having an affair with the wife of a government contractor whom he had given favorable treatment, the scandal upset most Americans. However, they respected Hamilton's forthright-ness and his candor. He remained a powerful political figure.

The days are long past of a political candidate admitting to a peccadillo and apologizing without some excuse or doublespeak. I agree with Lance Morrow's assessment, "The issue of a candidate's sex life is essentially a phony, except when (as with Gary Hart, who recklessly dared reporters to find him out) it may reveal some troublesome trait of personality." Morrow concludes, "Collective judgments based on gossip are always crude, often stupid, and sometimes stir up a lynch mob. . . . Given the size of the job that needs to be done, it is time for America to get serious. At the very least, turn off the television set." Maybe then leaders will not fear being honest about their imperfections and allow us to judge their leadership capabilities based upon the sum of their accomplishments.

Do not misread me—I am not advocating electing an immoral and crooked politician who might get the job done. I agree that honesty as a part of good character is an important factor of leadership. I just feel that the media pander-ing to the escapist needs of a complex continuous flux society distorts the char-acter issue, making "it harder to judge a candidate on important questions—his or her stability, judgment, decency, intelligence, ethics, strength of will, experi-ence, truthfulness." (Morrow)

I have mentioned Ronald Reagan's exceptional leadership capabilities, despite his not being an intellectual. Ronald Reagan was our first divorced pres-ident. Some political analysts felt his divorce would hurt his support with the religious right. As I noted, however, the press referred to Ronald Reagan as the "Teflon Man" because negatives failed to stick. I believe a major reason for his success was a sense of humor that enabled him to make light of any negative accusations and charges. People laughed with him and the negatives rolled off.

I would argue that a sense of humor is an invaluable aid to leadership. Humor does appear as a leadership trait on the chart. Like intelligence, humor seldom appears on my student lists of leadership capabilities, nor did Bertrand Russell mention humor as a source of power.

I need to clarify my view as to humor as a leadership trait. I mean sponta-neous humor, not memorized jokes. The press portrayed the Nixon Adminis-tration as made up of very uptight individuals. Sure they told jokes, but they were canned—memorized. The Watergate tapes revealed that almost all the jokes told pertained to the can—the toilet. Please forgive my pun. Even the curse words Nixon's colleagues and close advisors used were toilet words. Four letter words pertaining to sex were noticeably absent from the discussions in the Oval Office.

The people in the Nixon White House were leaders. Yet, I would argue that their inability to react with spontaneous and emotional humor accelerated the fall of Nixon. They lacked the ability to joke "off-the-cuff," as the saying goes. I believe that spontaneous humor was President Reagan's strongest leadership trait. Sure, at times he had joke writers, and he delivered his lines in good Hol-lywood style, as if they were spontaneous, yet the extent of his spontaneity came through in his informal appearances. His humor was never mean spirited and if anything it tended to be self-degrading. Reagan's approach to humor was far different from his first Secretary of the Interior, James Watt. Secretary Watt used humor to put others down, often directing it against women, minorities and the handicapped. President Reagan first defended Secretary Watt's comments and his policies. When Secretary Watt refused to allow the Beach Boys, Nancy Reagan's favorite group, to perform at the Washington Mall on July 4—he felt their music was decadent and destructive to American life—Watt lost his favor with the White House and resigned.

Americans respect humor in their leaders, not only because it makes them laugh and thereby relax, but they feel that if leaders can laugh at themselves and at life they are less likely to break down under the pressures of holding office. Leadership demands a lot of responsibility. How a leader handles power dictates the effectiveness of leadership.

Of course, power is what leadership and politics is all about. Michael Korda in his book, *Power!: How to get it, How to use it* (1975), argues, "All life is a game of power. The object of the game is simple enough: to know what you want and get it." Bertrand Russell agrees: "Love of power, in various limited forms, is almost universal." However, the love of power, while one of the strongest of human motives, is unevenly distributed. "Those who most desire power," according to Russell, are "those most likely to acquire it."

I need to clarify that I am not discussing a Machiavellian sense of power—power that is selfish and amoral. True power is love of oneself. The ancient Roman philosopher Seneca wrote, "Most powerful is he who has himself in his own power." The individual who loves himself is more likely to use *neighborly power—altruistic power; power used to do something for someone else.*

Love of oneself and, in its widest sense, the love of power is part of a human's worst and best desires. If you love your neighbor, or your constituent as a politician, you will wish to make that person happy. Those who condemn the love of power may in a sense be damning the love of a person for self or an individual's love for a neighbor. Before censuring power and especially a politician's use of power, it is mandatory to examine the motivation and the results as an outcome of the use of power. In analyzing power an individual must be careful to differentiate between correlation and causation. "The truth is, you can make a correlation between almost anything," says Temple University mathematician John Allen Paulos, "Correlation doesn't tell anything about causation. . . . Indeed correlations may be nothing more telling than coincidence, or timing."

Jumping to conclusions about the use of power or the motives underlying the expression of power is a serious concern today with the expansion of conspiracy theories. The proponents of these theories, often using talk show programs, the Internet Usenet groups or militia movements, attack the elected politician's use of power. These paranoid conspirists, lacking peripheral vision, are unable to distinguish selfish power from neighborly power. They confuse correlation with causation and rationalize their misguided use of power against their perceived evil—and so we get an Oklahoma City bombing.

So far, I have not defined power. Candidly, I have never found a good definition of power. The Fremont Unified School District's *Report to the Board of Education* in May, 1994 defined power as "the capacity to alter something in the behavior or environment of another person." I have heard power defined in similar terms: "Power is the ability to have someone do something they would not normally do at that time." Silvano Arieti in *The Will To Be Human* (1972) provides, from my perspective, a useable and positive definition of *power—"the ability to bring about our desires."*

Coercive power (charity "hold up").

The core of politics, the heart of the politician, is power. Bertrand Russell recognized the politician's use of power in a democracy and identified its distinctiveness: "A politician, if he is to succeed, must be able to win the confidence of his machine (party), and then to arouse some degree of enthusiasm in a majority of the electorate." Once elected, the politician must be able to persuade his colleagues to go along with his platform. Power must be used to reconcile groups generally at odds with each other. To accomplish these tasks it is wiser to use *persuasive power—persuading someone to bring about one's desires without making them subservient*—rather than *coercive power—using fear to force someone to follow your will.*

Perhaps one way to distinguish between coercive and persuasive power is to examine the difference between aggression and assertion. An aggressive person tends to use coercive power. An assertive individual is more likely to use persuasive power. An aggressive person attacks and an assertive person stands up to the situation. If someone cuts in front of an aggressive person in line, the aggressive person is liable to strike out physically or orally. An assertive person would calmly explain how the cutting in line was wrong. Candidly, sometimes it is difficult to distinguish between aggressive power and assertive action. In the same manner coercive power and persuasive power can often overlap. An individual who uses manipulation as a means to gain an end can unconsciously be trying to make someone subservient, even though personally viewing the action as an attempt to persuade.

Sometimes people who manifest the outward signs of power feel powerless. A poem I read in high school, "Richard Cory" by Edward Arlington Robinson, always comes to mind when I think of people who seem powerful. Simon and Garfunkel adapted the poem into a song by the same name in the late 1960's. All the people Richard Cory encountered idealized him: "He had everything a man could want: power, grace and style." One night Richard Cory went home "and put a bullet through his head."

People who seem powerful are often, on closer examination, merely frightened and anxious. Asserting power while lacking a belief in your own power can cause ulcers, high blood pressure, tension headaches, mental breakdowns and even violence. An individual who senses a loss of power could abuse alcohol or drugs or engage in perverted sexual acts as escapism. I tell my students the apocryphal tale of a vice-president of a major corporation who forgot to send a contract proposal by Federal Express, and it arrived a day late. The CEO (Chief Executive Officer) of the company read him the riot act. The powerful executive, now feeling powerless, decides to have a few drinks on the way home. He arrives home and his dinner is not ready. He blows up at his wife and beats her as this seems to restore his power. The children arrive home and track mud into the house. The mother strikes out at the children. The children unable to retaliate, kick the dog. The dog bites the cat. Oh, well, you get the picture.

Power is only love of self when an individual feels powerful. True power is the ability to accomplish one's goals without making another person subservient.

I suspect that all politicians at sometime or other will use coercive power even when they do not feel insecure. As James Madison said, "The essence of Government is power; and power, lodged as it must be in human hands, will ever be

Persuasive or coercive power?

liable to abuse." Was Lord John Acton correct when he wrote, "Power tends to corrupt and absolute power corrupts absolutely"? Maybe, but I prefer playwright George Bernard Shaw's argument, "Power does not corrupt men; fools, however, if they get into a position of power, corrupt power." I hold that leaders who achieve absolute power become the real servants. They depend on their followers insofar as they need those they rule more than their victims need them. Michael Korda wrote, "The wise man soon learns that omnipotence is servitude." Politicians in a democracy, to avoid impotence, can best assert their power through persuasion.

The most common and successful form of persuasive power for the politician is what I call the ***power of obligation***—*achieving your desired objective because an individual believes in discharging a debt.* Humans seem to feel the need to return compliments or favors. If a person says, "What a beautiful pair of shoes," the individual who received the compliment seems compelled to find something to praise. So you might hear, "Thank you, and what beautiful socks you are wearing." If someone invites a person to dinner, that individual seems compelled to invite them to dinner in the future.

The power of the dollar.

Over the years, I have argued that most religions have gone astray. They have taught their parishioners how to give, but not how to take. True power—confidence—is the ability to say thank you and leave it at that. Individuals need to learn how to accept things from others because they are offered out of the goodness of their hearts. I would gladly start my own religion, but when my wife says, "I love you," I must reply, "I love you, too." Besides, no one, even my children, ever listens to my preaching, which is why I am writing these essays.

Since people seem determined to return favors, a politician's success depends on how well the power of obligation is used. To be elected, a politician must convince the electorate that something can be done for them. For the people to re-elect an individual, the politician must "bring home the bacon," and run a good constituent office. People have to feel that the politician's staff is really trying to accomplish something for them. Actually, more important is that the politician really do things for his or her constituents. Often the most simple favor can result in tremendous support from an individual. I once spoke to my congressman, whom I knew fairly well, about a young man who wanted an appointment to West Point. My congressman gave him that appointment. The young man was a Republican and my congressman a Democrat. Yet, this young man walked precincts to aid the re-election of the congressman. No one asked him to work in the campaign. He volunteered. He felt the power of obligation.

I had to lose $50 before I understood the power of obligation. In 1968, Richard Nixon announced that he would run for the Republican Presidential nomination. I knew he had little chance to win his party's support. I mean why would the Republican Party support a loser. Nixon had lost his Presidential bid to John F. Kennedy in 1960. He then ran for Governor of California and lost to Pat Brown. He left California for New York. I was sure that without a home state base his chance of obtaining his party's nomination was nil. I bet a colleague $50 that Nixon would not be the Republican candidate. Well, Richard Nixon became the Republican nominee and went on to win the presidency. Richard Nixon had spent the years between 1962 and 1968 helping other Republicans throughout the nation raise funds and win elections. In my hubris I failed to understand how much Nixon's fellow Republicans owed him. They wholeheartedly supported his campaign with financial aid and glowing endorsements. The loser became a winner due to the power of obligation.

Most *incumbents—the individual who currently holds the political office*—who switch political parties are re-elected. Their constituents are not voting for the party, but for the individual who has served them well.

Soothing power.

Politicians use the power of obligation to obtain support from their colleagues. At times the political use of the power of obligation is transparent. *Pork barrel legislation—legislation designed exclusively for a legislator's district*—is common. Politicians call in past favors and insist on their colleagues voting for the pork. At other times a legislator will use *log rolling—agreeing to vote for another politician's bill in return for a vote for his or her proposed legislation; "you scratch my back and I will scratch yours."*

In most cases the politician's use of the power of obligation is more translucent. Politicians help each other without linkage. Subconsciously they may know that whatever they can do for their colleagues will bring future premiums. Their actions, voting for a bill, helping to raise funds, sharing their campaign coffers, and socializing, are usually acts of friendship.

In recent years the concept of future premiums for supporting colleagues has reared its ugly head in an explosion of *earmarks—similar to pork as these are special projects and programs that a legislator adds to a bill that has little or no relevance to the specific piece of legislation and adds extra costs to legislation requested by the Executive Branch.* U.S. Congress' use of earmarks has become the focus of much controversy and little action.

The power of obligation takes on its own instinctive life. Colleagues, bureaucrats and voters who feel obligated to return the favor at some time provide future support for a politician's agenda.

Individuals, politicians, often obtain the image of power from the titles they receive. People hold them in awe due to their position. I tell people that before I obtained my Ph.D. I was viewed as a loud-mouthed, kneejerking troublemaker. Once I earned my Ph.D., people simply saw me as eccentric. The first time the faculty elected me President of the Senate, the administrators at the college treated me differently—with an indefinable respect. When I left my post a year later, one administrator said to me: "Alan, how does it feel not to have power any more?" The statement annoyed me a bit even if I did laugh. I felt just as powerful. But, power is perception and the Administration perceived me differently.

When Ronald Reagan became President of the United States, he insisted that his closest friends and everyone he met call him Mr. President. He felt that one reason Jimmy Carter appeared powerless as President was because he permitted people to call him "Jimmy." President Reagan knew that titles bring respect. "Ron, baby" might work in Hollywood, but not in the world of Washington politics.

Ronald Reagan also announced that he would always wear suits and ties when appearing before the public in his role as national leader. He felt that President Carter lost power because he wore leisure outfits during some of his public broadcasts. President Reagan did appear in his jeans and T-shirt while chopping wood on his ranch or horseback riding. His advisors considered these appearances photo-ops and not public appearances.

My brother, many years ago, took a managerial job in Washington. He dressed in leisurely California style. Those working for him failed to respond to his directions. Once my brother dressed in his three-piece suit and the requisite red power tie, people treated him with the respect he was due.

My brother had a little power problem with his short stature. Americans have this attraction to height. Companies often employ taller individuals, both male and female, for managerial and sales positions. I suspect that the tall person's allure is the ability to "one-up" others with height. The insecurity others may feel in the presence of a taller individual confers an immediate ability to push an agenda.

A person's perception of personal height may not match the reality and, therefore, the categorization of height as a power factor may be irrelevant. I grew to my full height at 12 years of age. Until that age, my schoolmates considered me tall. When friends grew taller than I had, I hardly noticed. I still feel tall despite the reality of the measuring stick. I have a friend who graduated high school at five feet four inches. He later grew to be six feet two inches. He still feels short.

Presidents of the United States have averaged two inches taller than the general male population. The taller candidate for President has been more successful in recent elections. Do Americans believe that the taller candidate will make a more powerful President? Candidates do not want to take the chance of people perceiving them as less potent due to their shorter stature. In presidential candidate's debates, when the disparity in height has been obvious, the shorter candidates have insisted on formats where the difference in their heights would not be as obvious. The televised presidential candidate debates between the short Jimmy Carter and the tall Gerald Ford were delayed until both sides agreed on a size equalizing format. The candidates would be on separate sides of the stage with their podiums at different heights to allow both candidates to appear to be the same height. In this 1976 election, the shorter candidate, Jimmy Carter, won the election.

Good looks, especially in our visual media age, provide a natural power conduit. Please do not misread me, I do not mean that a plain looking person cannot succeed in politics. Ross Perot, who probably fails the test of good looks, received a respectable amount of support in his independent presidential bids in 1992 and 1996. Perot's charisma and his anti-Washington-as-usual politics overcame the media's portrayal of him as a big-eared Ferengi.

Perot's billionaire status helped his campaign. I am not referring to his ability to spend 60 million dollars of his money, but rather the American people's fixation on wealth. A wealthy individual can influence the political process through campaign contributions—the power of obligation. Yet, the wealth alone makes others either envious or respectful, which provides the wealthy individual an immediate power platform.

My discussion of charisma, leadership and power in a political science book must inevitably lead to an examination of the President of the United States—albeit, a short one in this essay. I suspect that most people view the President as the pinnacle of leadership and power in our country. Granted, some individuals argued that the Speaker of the House of Representatives in 1995, Newt Gingrich, challenged the number one leadership and power spot. In 1985 Robert Weissberg wrote in his book, *Politics: A Handbook for Students*, "It is hard to imagine a president in an inferior position to the Speaker of the House or the Senate Majority Leader."

Some political scientists have argued that it was the original intent of the writers of our Constitution to have the Legislative Branch of government be the most powerful. They say that the Executive Branch has overshadowed the legislative branch only in the twentieth century. Weissberg wrote, "Perhaps no institution in American politics has undergone greater change than the presidency. While many people now see the president and the vast executive branch as the controlling force in government, this was not the expectation held by those who wrote the constitution. Many of the framers believed that Congress, because of its close electoral ties with the people, could very well dominate the national government. Through much of US political history, this vision has proved to be accurate. At times the president seemed so weak that some experts even proposed that the entire system of government be changed to give congressional leaders executive power both in name and in substance."

The major emphasis of the neo-Republican is on *devolution—empowering people in the local communities and destroying the federal bureaucracy that grew with the twentieth century.* A number of liberal writers agree that the federal bureaucracy has grown into a monster that the interest groups and PAC's alone have access to and they have suggested reducing the number of federal agencies and moving the headquarters of the remaining agencies from Washington to diverse locations in the United States. They believe that this distribution of federal agencies to other parts of the country would dramatically limit the ability of interest groups to dominate access to the federal bureaucracy, empowering people. Advocates of the dismantling of Washington argue that interest groups and their PAC's would have their resources scattered very thin, thereby dramatically weakening their power over how federal policy is determined. This call for decentralization parallels those leaders of industry recommending the elimination of hierarchical leadership by networking.

The anarchy of the Internet, creating unprecedented decentralization, will definitely have an impact on the future direction of our government.

With the explosion of government information on line such as *Thomas* (http://thomas.loc.gov)—*a project of House Speaker Newt Gingrich, named for President Thomas Jefferson, provides, among other things, information on bills in Congress and access to the Congressional Record*—the people's ability to have direct access to their government is being enhanced.

Sites on the Internet abound where private citizens have access to government information—and access is expanding every day. Individuals can learn the most mundane facts about what is happening in Washington. All the branches of government have their own Internet page and so do individual members of Congress.

I would argue that throughout our history there have been periods when Congress dominated the national government and other times when the Executive Branch held sway. The historic power of the presidency depended on the individual who served in the Executive Office as well as his charisma, leadership skills and how he asserted power.

The exact kind of figure the framers of the Constitution visualized for a Chief Executive is simply unknown. No matter what ultra-Conservatives might hold, the framers did not see the President as a lackey of Congress. *Article II of the Constitution*—*covers the Executive Branch of government and describes many of the powers of the presidency.*

According to the Constitution the President is the CEO (Chief Executive Officer) of the United States. He wields the executive power of government and sees that the laws are faithfully executed. Over the years presidents have developed extra-constitutional powers. Presidents often issue *executive orders*—*presidential orders that have the force of law.* An infamous example of the power of such a disposition was *Executive Order 9066*—*President Franklin Delano Roosevelt determined that Japanese living in the Western United States be placed in relocation camps.* Since the time of George Washington, although without a formal description, presidents have claimed *executive privilege*—*asserting executive branch confidentiality and the refusal to share information with the other branches of government.*

The President serves as Commander-in-Chief of the armed forces and the state militia. He appoints all commissioned officers with the approval of the Senate. However, while Americans have accepted the presidential Commander-in-Chief's right to protect American shores and American citizens, the Constitution says that only Congress can declare war. Congress has declared five wars, while Presidents have sent our armies into combat over 200 times. In 1973, because of the Korean and Vietnam Wars being undeclared, Congress passed, over President Nixon's veto, the *War Powers Resolution*—*an attempt by Congress to restore its war declaring power through setting statutory regulations and time limits on presidential war making.*

The Constitution provides that the President can grant reprieves and pardons for federal offenses except in cases of impeachment. Different from most state constitutions which indicate that governors cannot issue pardons before an individual has been charged and convicted of a crime, the President has no restrictions on his power to grant reprieves and pardons in criminal cases. Quite a stir occurred when President Ford provided former President Richard Nixon with a blanket pardon before federal prosecutors had even charged him with a crime. Many citizens felt betrayed by Ford's pardon of Nixon as they perceived

Who cares?

his action as another Watergate cover-up. Political pundits have argued that his pardon of Nixon caused Ford's defeat in the 1976 presidential election. Some individuals have even speculated that because of the vague wording of this provision of the Constitution, Richard Nixon could have pardoned himself. I honestly do not believe this would have happened. I just cannot visualize Richard Nixon saying, "Pardon me!"

The President can enter into treaties with other nations, but must obtain the consent of two thirds of the Senators present at a session. In recent years, presidents have played end runs on the Senate and increased their power through *Executive Accords—agreements between the President of the United States and the head of a foreign nation that at times have the legal base of a treaty even though they lack formal Senate approval.* As chief diplomat, the President receives ambassadors from other nations.

The President convenes Congress in special sessions. When Congress cannot agree on a time of adjournment, he may set the time of adjournment.

The President may appoint officials to lower offices. The Constitution provides that when appointing officials to higher posts—ambassadors, judges and high offices such as the cabinet—he must seek the advice and obtain the consent of the Senate.

The President usually sets forth his yearly legislative proposal in his constitutionally required State of the Union message. Presidents have used the State of the Union message to bolster their personal image as well. In 1998, President Bill Clinton won over a large part of his audience with an articulate and well delivered talk. People tuned in to observe how he might react to the tension and pressure of what some called Zippergate. After his speech, even though almost fifty percent of those polled felt he had an affair with Monica Lewinsky, almost 70 percent expressed satisfaction with the way he was doing his job as President.

He has a more vital role in his interaction with the Legislative Branch—his ability to approve legislation. His role as chief legislator derives from Article 1, Section 7 of the Constitution. He may sign a bill into law or refuse to sign the

The Original Airforce #1

legislation. If he refuses to sign a piece of legislation into law, it becomes law without his signature within ten days. The only exception to this is the **Pocket Veto**—*if Congress adjourns within ten days after the President received a bill thereby preventing its return, the bill cannot become law.* The Pocket Veto provides the President with absolute power, as it cannot be overridden as a normal veto—but, it occurs infrequently.

The President's veto power also stems from Article I, Section 7 of the Constitution: "Every Bill which shall have passed the House of Representatives and the Senate, shall, before it becomes a Law, be presented to the President of the United States; If he approve he shall sign it, but if not he shall return it, with his Objections to that House in which it shall have originated." The Congress can override a presidential veto by a two thirds vote in each house. However, only 4% of presidential vetoes have been overridden. The veto power of the President is a mainstay of his power. Simply the threat of a presidential veto sets off the movements for compromise. George Bush, the elder, even though saddled with a Democratic Congress, only saw one of his 36 vetoes overridden. The veto override came in the last hours of his term. He was a **Lame Duck**—*usually refers to an individual who is serving out a last term and will not return to power; other politicians have the impression that they need not fear anymore, since this individual will no longer have power, and often refuse their support.* In the case of George Bush's overturned veto it pertained to a bill restoring regulations on cable companies. Americans tend to hate their cable companies, and so the members of Congress had less to fear from the Lame Duck Bush than from their constituents.

The constitutional powers of the President provide for a Chief-of-State, a Chief Executive, a Commander-in-Chief, a Chief Legislator and a Chief Diplomat. The greatest source of presidential power is not found in the Constitution. *The real power of the President is the power of politics, leadership and public opinion, as I have tried to develop in this essay. Since the 1930's Congress has conferred upon the executive branch authority to achieve general goals. The personality and leadership capabilities of the person in the Oval Office will determine the delineation and outcome of these regulations and programs. Presidential power is a summation of the Constitutional authority, tradition, congressional legislation, party backing, popular support, leadership, the power of obligation and an office holder's ability to create in the art of politics.*

In concluding my discussion of the power of the presidency, I must note that presidential power can never be absolute. In the United States we have numerous forces that work to check presidential power. A good example of our system righting itself was the **Watergate scandals**—*while Watergate specifically refers to the break-in at the Democratic Headquarters on June 17, 1972 in the Watergate apartment complex, the term has come to mean any of the abuses of power during the Nixon administration culminating in his resignation.* Congress has in the past and will in the future keep checks on presidential power through the passage of legislation, refusing to approve treaties and appointments and by holding hearings on presidential actions that in extreme cases of the abuse of power could lead to impeachment. While not very common, the Supreme Court has checked presidential power by declaring its actions unconstitutional. Bureaucrats, as I wrote in my first essay, have power because of their tenure. They have checked presidential power by dragging their feet, going to their friends in Congress, or waiting for a new President. Relentless pursuit of presidential wrong-doing has been a role of the press in this country. Often fair exposure of presidential actions or inaction has turned into muckraking, but in cases like Watergate the press has helped to restore the balance of power in our democracy. And, finally, the voters can cast a President out of office after one term.

The framers of our Constitution favored a system of checks and balances, separation of powers and federalism to prevent the tyranny of one or the tyranny of the many. Yet, while creating strong controls on presidential power, they also favored an energetic Chief Executive. The framers provided the President with great power and created accountability. A powerless President, the writers of the Constitution understood, would lead to powerless government.

GLOSSARY

ARTICLE II OF THE CONSTITUTION
Covers the Executive Branch of government and describes many of the powers of the presidency.

COERCIVE POWER
Using fear to force someone to follow your will.

CONSTITUENT
A resident of a district or member of a group represented by an elected official.

DEVOLUTION
Empowering people in the local communities and destroying the federal bureaucracy that grew with the twentieth century.

EARMARKS
Similar to pork as these are special projects and programs that a legislator adds to a bill that has little or no relevance to the specific piece of legislation and adds extra costs to legislation requested by the Executive Branch.

EGGHEAD
A highly intelligent individual whom some people view as lacking common sense.

EXECUTIVE ACCORDS
Agreements between the President of the United States and the head of a foreign nation that at times have the legal base of a treaty even though they lack formal Senate approval.

EXECUTIVE ORDER 9066
President Franklin Delano Roosevelt determined that Japanese living in the Western United States be placed in relocation camps.

EXECUTIVE ORDERS
Presidential orders that have the force of law.

EXECUTIVE PRIVILEGE
Asserting executive branch confidentiality and the refusal to share information with the other branches of government.

INCUMBENT
The individual who currently holds the political office.

LAME DUCK
Usually refers to an individual who is serving out a last term and will not return to power; other politicians have the impression that they need not fear anymore, since this individual will no longer have power, and often refuse their support.

LEADERSHIP
The art of getting someone to do something that needs to be done.

LOG ROLLING
Agreeing to vote for another politician's bill in return for a vote for his or her proposed legislation, "you scratch my back and I will scratch yours."

NEIGHBORLY POWER
Altruistic power; power used to do something for someone else.

POWER OF OBLIGATION
Achieving your desired objective because an individual believes in discharging a debt.

PERSUASIVE POWER
Convincing someone to bring about one's desires without making them subservient.

PRESIDENTIAL LINE-ITEM VETO

This allows the president to eliminate sections of any budgetary bill subject to a possible 2/3 override of both house of Congress voting independently.

POLITICAL ACTION COMMITTEES (PAC'S)

The fund-raising branches of interest groups that distribute money to candidates and, more recently, spend their cash in an attempt to secure the victory of their causes.

PORK BARREL LEGISLATION

Legislation designed exclusively for a legislator's district.

POWER

The ability to bring about our desires.

THOMAS

A project of House Speaker Newt Gingrich, named for President Thomas Jefferson, provides, among other things, information on bills in Congress and access to the Congressional Record.

WAR POWERS RESOLUTION

An attempt by Congress to restore its war declaring power through setting statutory regulations and time limits on presidential war making.

WATERGATE SCANDALS

While Watergate specifically refers to the break-in at the Democratic Headquarters on June 17, 1972 in the Watergate apartment complex, the term has come to mean all of the abuses of power during the Nixon administration culminating in his resignation.

CHAPTER 6

Congress: That's The Wrong Question!

Essay VI

A number of years ago we had a bumper sticker war in my home town. Yes, back then cars sported bumpers. People seemed to create an identity through the sayings on their bumper stickers. Many of these had sexual overtones like "Teachers do it with class." An ultra-conservative political group allied with local Republicans organized a committee to try and defeat our Democratic congressman, Don Edwards. They titled their group ABCDE. The letters stood for "Anyone But Congressman Don Edwards." The anti-Edwards group distributed black and white ABCDE stickers for those large beautiful chromed bumpers. Well, the Congressman's campaign staff one-upped the ABCDE Committee. They retaliated with their own slogan: ABCDE. Their ABCDE bumper sticker shouted, "America's Best Congressman, Don Edwards." And, their coup de grace? They used the patriotic colors of red, white and blue.

The black and white ABCDE group even put out a drawing of a 45 record titled: "The Record of Don Edwards." Try to understand that CD's did not exist in those ancient times. They accused Congressman Edwards of aiding homosexuals, and, even more dastardly, of supporting funding for New York City. Their "Record" and the political commentary on the back of their leaflet won them the local newspaper's garbage award for dirty political campaigns.

While waiting for one of my son's Little League games to begin that Spring, I noticed his best friend's dad had a black and white ABCDE sticker on his car. Well, I could not resist congratulating him (I will call him Tom) on supporting "America's Best Congressman Don Edwards." Need I report that Tom blew. He said something like: "Me support that friend of homosexuals, that big money-spending, anti-gun, anti-defense, pro-busing, child-killing bastard. Don't tell me you would vote for that New York, International, Communist, Faggot, Pinko conspirator?"

I said, "Yes, I would." Tom, apparently unbelieving, mouthed, "What has Don Edwards ever done for you?" I replied: "I am afraid that is the wrong question." I went on, "Every year, Edwards sends me a Christmas card and a new

Congressman Don Edwards speaks at Ohlone

calendar. He provides me with commemorative books. He has created internships for a number of my students. But, most of all he provided his office manager with released time so she could coach my son's soccer team." Begrudgingly, Tom voiced, "OK, maybe he has done something for you, but what has he done for Fremont?" I retorted, "Once again, that is the wrong question. Don Edwards made sure that when the General Motors plant closed the workers received a stipend for retraining. He was also responsible for getting funding for a new post office. He pushed through Congress legislation to create a special computer training program for the blind and the deaf at Ohlone College." So, Tom uttered, "OK, maybe he did something for Fremont, but what has he done for America?" I told Tom that he finally had asked the right question. We would never agree on the Congressman's accomplishments for America. We had fundamental differences on what was good for America. Yes, I supported aid for New York. I was pro-busing and pro-choice. I believed in gun control and was opposed to state mandated prayer in the schools. Tom, hearing this, argued that the ultra-liberal Don Edwards, like myself, was out of touch with the views of the people of his district. Tom went on to assert that for that reason they would toss the bum out. I laughed and explained that even though I agreed that on national issues the congressman might be out of touch with the people in his district, Tom missed the point. I said that it was Tom's "wrong questions" that would get Don Edwards re-elected.

I tried my best to explain to Tom that Congress is really very local—that people vote based upon what a legislator does for them or their city. All the people in a district, I argued, expect a politician to bring home the *pork—government jobs, money grants, public works that politicians obtain for their constituents.* In their search for re-election, politicos know they must introduce *pork barrel legislation—custom legislation designed exclusively for a legislator's district.* This patronage frequently comes through *log rolling—agreeing to vote for another politician's bill in return for a vote for his or her proposed legislation; "you scratch my back and I will scratch yours."* Is it any wonder that when people are polled they state that they are unsatisfied with Congress, but believe their own congressman is doing a good job?

Don Edwards won re-election by his usual 66%. He may have been out of touch with the people in our congressional district on national issues, but, obviously he reached out to touch them on the issues that mattered most—personal and local.

All 435 members of the House of Representatives are elected every two years. The people who had founded the ABCDE, Any One But Congressman Don Edwards, committee mounted another campaign in the next election. I saw Tom's car parked down the street from my house. On his bumper, that year, was not a black and white ABCDE sticker, but a "Vote For Don Edwards" sign. Smiling, I went over to him. I, of course, proceeded to hassle him about his turn around. He said that he never really disliked Don Edwards. He only

Pork

had the anti-Edwards bumper sticker because he worked for a member of the ultra-conservative John Birch society. He felt it would help him keep his job. I retorted: "Come on now! Tell me the truth. What did Don Edwards do for you?" Tom admitted that he switched his position because of help he received from Don Edwards local congressional office. Tom had been on disability and was having trouble collecting his benefits. He went to the Congressman's office and they resolved the issue in a matter of days. Tom said: "How could I not vote for a person whose office can accomplish something for me that I was unable to do for six months?"

Yes, Congress is very local. If you can understand this you can understand the major purpose of a legislator. Legislators introduce large number of personal bills. When I taught at the University of West Florida, I had a weightlifting partner who was a professor of Political Science at the local junior college. He was married to a woman from Japan. He showed me a copy of a law that passed Congress and that President Truman signed specifically designed to allow his bride to enter the country.

Apparently, right after World War II, legislation prohibited American GI's from bringing their "War Brides" home. Many foreign nationals were enticing our lonely serviceman into marriage so they could enter the United States. Once legally in the country, they would leave their new spouses. This scenario happened to my mother's cousin. He married a woman in Germany at the end of the war. Once they returned to this country, she took off. I remember many years later his wanting to remarry and having to get a divorce for desertion.

Conrad, the name of my workout partner, went to his congressman in Oregon and asked for his help in bringing his Japanese wife into the United States. The congressman introduced legislation specific to Conrad's desire and pushed it through the House of Representatives. The bill then passed the Senate and was signed by the president.

Not all personal bills come out of a committee the way they are written. A few years back, members of the Ohlone College Board of Trustees wanted to change the election for Trustees from odd years to even years. California legislators had originally set aside even years for *partisan elections—elections where individuals run as a member of a political party*. They set odd years for *non-partisan elections—elections where an individual runs for an office that does not allow one to*

But for the jealous, anti-Olympic (spirit), paranoid, Cold War-prolonging, hypocritical, wilful, impolite & bad opposition of US Congress, China would have won its bid for the 2000 Olympics !!!

The difference was only one vote. If US hadn't sinned against God, China would've gotten more votes and won the bid — good reason for lots of indignation and .... rebuke !!!

Not everyone sees Congress as local.

run as a party candidate. The Ohlone Board felt they would save money if they held the election on even years. There would be more people and organizations dividing the cost of the ballot. The Board also argued that they would get a larger turn-out of voters in a year when there were state and federal candidates on the ballot.

Members of the Ohlone Board had the County Attorney draw up proposed legislation allowing them to change the election from odd to even years. They then requested that Bill Lockyer, the state senator from our district, introduce the legislation. I was told that Senator Lockyer opposed the legislation and, in fact, liked the odd-even year designations. However, he agreed to introduce the bill and push it through his Education Committee as a favor to his constituents on the Ohlone College Board of Trustees.

As with many bills that legislators introduce, this bill was changed in committee. The newly proposed legislation allowed the Board of Trustees of any community college in California to switch the election from odd to even years. *Private bills—legislation designed to help specific individuals or deal with narrow matters rather than general affairs—*are a major part of any legislator's agenda. Politicians know that to be reelected they must help their local constituents.

More than 90 percent of the *incumbents—the individual who currently holds the political office—*who run again are reelected. While pork barrel legislation and local staffs are major reasons for their reelection, they are not the only factors. Incumbents enjoy name recognition. They have *franking privileges—free mailings.* While these mailings are supposed to inform their constituents of the legislators' activities, they more often resemble campaign brochures. The incumbents can usually raise campaign funds more easily than challengers. Lobbyists and PACs (political action committees) seek their favor, and knowing that they are likely going to defeat a challenger, they prefer to contribute their money and lend their support to a winner. Incumbents also have the advantage of a paid staff who can research the wants of their constituents and service their needs.

Who are these legislators with whom we have a love-hate relationship? A former employee of the House of Representatives, William Mosley Miller, in his book *Fishbait* (1977), described them as "535 high-school class presidents with a few prom queens thrown in." The 535 stems from the 100 members of the Senate (two from each state) and the 435 members of the House of Representatives. The number of Representatives is fixed by law. If Congress added a new state to the union, the Senate would have 102 members, but the House would remain at 435. Since the number of Representatives is based upon the population of each state, the new state would have to have at least one Representative and some other state would lose one. A reason we take a census every ten years is due to the need to redistrict population changes. After the 2000 census the population of Texas officially surpassed New York. Texas became the second largest state in the union increasing its delegates in the House of Representatives as well as the electoral college. New York lost some Representatives, due to the proportion of its increased population in relation to the other states. California remains the largest state with 53 members out of the 435 in the House of Representatives.

The Constitution sets few criteria for election to Congress. Representatives must be at least 25 years old, a citizen of the United States for seven years, and a resident of their state. Representatives serve for two year terms. Senators must be at least 30 years old, citizens for nine years, and an inhabitant of their state. Senators serve six year terms. Senatorial elections are staggered. One-third of the 100 members are chosen every two years. Granted, you cannot have 33 1/3 people, so it is 33, 33, 34. Since we elect all Representatives every two years, we number the Congress based upon the two year terms. The 2009–2011 Congress is the 111th. Members of Congress received a salary of $169,300 per year in 2008. Those Senators or Representatives who take on leadership positions, such as Speaker of the House, receive a slightly higher salary.

Constitutional requirements provide us with little information about the characteristics of those who are supposed to serve us in our federal legislature. Unsurprisingly, the vast majority of the 535 members are, and have been, men and **WASP's**—*White, Anglo-Saxon Protestants*. Eighty-four percent of the Senators in the 110th Congress were men. The House of Representatives does not fare much better with 83 percent of its members having been men. More than 50 percent of the nation's population is female. The "high-school presidents" and "prom queens" also fail to reflect the diversity of occupations in our nation. The vast majority of the members of Congress start out their careers as lawyers. The number of attorneys in Congress has improved in the last 21 years. By improved, I mean there are fewer of them. In 1987, 63 percent of the Senators and 46 percent of the Representatives had been attorneys before entering Congress. In 2008, 56 percent of the Senators and 37 percent of the Representatives were originally attorneys. I write "originally" because once elected to Congress individuals generally remain, making a life-long career as a "Member of Congress." In 2008, the average number of years a Member of the House of Representatives had served was 10 (5 terms) and that of a Member of the Senate was 12.8 (a touch over 2 terms). As indicated earlier, over 90 percent of those members running for reelection were reelected. Is it any wonder that a national movement to limit the terms individuals can serve has sprung up throughout the nation?

Fin-de-siecle sentiment—*relating to an end of an era, usually with world-weariness and fashionable despair*—at the end of the 19th century introduced massive support for democratic reforms in the United States. This activity led to the introduction of primaries, recall, referendums and initiatives in many states and the direct election of United States Senators (see Essay 2). At the end of the 20th century a similar drive to advance American democracy has led to state initiatives for *term limits—where elected officials are limited to a set number of years in office.* Voters in the 1990's introduced term limits in over half the states through the initiative process. However, there is no federal initiative. A constitutional amendment would be necessary to term limit the members of Congress. While many federal legislators have expressed their support for term limits, they have not been willing to vote themselves out of office. Remember constitutional amendments require two-thirds of the Senators and the Representatives, voting separately, to begin the process. Then the legislators or a ratifying convention in three-quarters of the states must provide final approval.

The overwhelming support among the voters for term limits reflects their belief that political action committees and foreign governments have bought our legislators. To run for a congressional seat costs at least $300,000. And that usually is when the office is uncontested. Since politicians now see their position in Congress as a lifetime job, they spend a great deal of time fundraising. PAC's are more than willing to donate money to candidates whom they believe will be favorable to their cause. Political pundits believe that only the interests groups now have access to halls of power. Most telling is the failure of Congress to enact any meaningful campaign reform legislation.

I, personally, support term limits with the stipulation that after a set time out of office an individual can once again seek election. I think it is good to take a sabbatical every few years to refresh one's soul and to develop new ideas. After a few years in office, most legislators have accomplished their goals. I hold that a significant time away from the office allows the individual to reflect on what they have achieved and to aspire to greater heights the next time around.

Yes, I am aware of the arguments for and against term limits, and both sides have merit. Proponents of term limits hold that Congress will again become a people's legislature—individuals will give up their occupations for a short period of time to do public service and then return to their true professions. Meanwhile, these citizen-politicos will bring new vigor and ideas to Washington helping to reduce the undue influence of the vested interest groups. The citizen-politico will more accurately represent the wishes of the people.

Those who oppose term limits argue that we will be giving up experience for amateurs. Opponents believe that this will unbalance power in Washington towards the Executive Branch and its bureaucracy. They also contend that term limits are undemocratic and voters should have a right to vote for whomever they want. In *U.S. Term Limits vs. Thornton* (1995) the Supreme Court ruled that the states lack the power to restrict the number of terms a federal officer can serve.

Another impact of term limits might be the election of younger individuals. At the start of the 110th Congress (2007–2009), the average age of Senators was 61.73 years and 55.93 years for Representatives. Of the 535 members of the 110th Congress only 16 were between 30 & 39. Seventy-one were over the age of 70. The oldest Senator ever was Strom Thurmond from South Carolina. He was a spry 99 when he left the Senate a few years ago. Strom Thurmond had run for President as a candidate for the States Rights Party in 1948. He also holds the record for a single person *filibuster—"talking a bill to death," or attempting to do so; the Senate, not the House, allows a member or members to prevent any action on a bill through marathon uninterrupted speeches.* Strom Thurmond's filibuster, against civil rights legislation, lasted for a little over 24 hours. I will discuss filibustering more thoroughly later in this chapter.

As I have indicated, members of Congress do not match the profile of average citizens, not only in age and in original occupations, but also in gender. Despite a a record number of women serving in the 110th Congress with 74 in the House and 16 in the Senate, these numbers fall far short of the 51 percent of the American population that is female. Two of the women in the 110th Senate are from California, Diane Feinstein and Barbara Boxer. Interestingly, both these women are Jewish.

Religion does not play as much of a factor in the election to Congress as it seems to for the President. Only one President has not been a Protestant. John F. Kennedy (1961–1963) was Catholic. While, presently, the religious preferences of the Congress match the three main religious groupings in the United States—Protestant, Catholic and Jewish—it will be awhile before, if ever, we can say the same for Hindus, Muslims, Buddhists or atheists. The talk show circuit was a booming when the first ever Muslim, Keith Ellison of Minnesota, asked to be sworn in with the Koran in 2007. He was joined in March 2008 after a special election by another Muslim, Andre Carson of Indiana. Two Buddhists entered the 110th Congress, the first ever: Mazie Hirono of Hawaii and Hank Johnson of Georgia. Perhaps, the new religious diversity in the 110th Congress, albeit, minimal, encouraged Representative Pete Stark of California to be the first to announce he was an Atheist.

While member's religions closely represent a cross section of the American populace, this is not true for race. Whites constituted the vast majority of our federal legislature. The Senate has one African American. The House boasts 42 African-Americans. The number of Hispanics in the 110th Congress was also low with 26 in the House and three in the Senate. There are five Asian-Americans in the House and two in the Senate. One Representative is of Native-American origin.

I might argue that all of the above statistics are irrelevant. While diversity and *proportional representation—an electoral system that allocates seats in a legislative body to each group approximately equal to their numbers in society*—would be nice, it does not guarantee that the representatives would accurately portray the feelings of their group. Ethnic, racial and gender groups do not have uniform needs and demands. Legislators have proven they can understand and represent diverse groups. Granted, enough differences exist among the pluralistic groups in our society to justify some diversity in our legislative body. This would enable at least segments of these groups to be heard in the halls of power in Washington.

Diversity, or lack thereof, might have minimal impact on the workings of Congress. The organization of Congress along party lines is vital to an understanding of how this national, via local, body functions. The party that has the most members controls its respective house. Any *independents—members of neither the Republican or the Democrat party*—must ally themselves with one of the two parties to obtain their committee and seating assignments.

The organization of both houses of Congress is similar. Almost everything is done through the political parties. Both houses have what are termed a *minority party—the party, between the Republicans and Democrats, that has the lesser number of elected members—*and a *majority party—the party, between the Republicans and Democrats, that has the greater number of elected members.* At this writing, the Democrats have a majority in both the House of Representatives and the Senate. Therefore, they are the majority party and their leader in each house is called the

Capitol Hill

majority leader—*the head of the majority party selected through a caucus or confer-ence of the members of the party.* The leader of the Republican Party is known as the *minority leader*—*the head of the minority party selected through a caucus or con-ference of the members of the party.* The minority and majority leaders help to frame party strategy and to keep their respective members in line—to get them to vote correctly. The leaders of both parties help to determine the legislative agendas and they have strong influence over committee assignments. Another name for these posts is minority or majority floor leaders. The majority and minority leaders in both houses are aided by *whips*—*assistant party leaders in Congress.* The name whip derives from the whippet, a dog used in fox hunts in England. Whips must round up the members of their party to get out to vote on pending legislation. The whips also keep party members informed on party-sponsored bills and often do special fund raising. Party loyalists benefit the most from the money the whips raise—one way to get out the vote.

The majority leader in the House of Representatives does not have as much power as the Senate majority leader. The House has an elected chair known as the *Speaker of the House of Representatives—the presiding officer in the House of Representatives*. The Speaker and the majority leader are from the same party and that dilutes the power of both. The majority party nominates the Speaker who is formally elected by a vote of all the members. The Speaker runs all the meetings. The Speaker decides who shall speak and how the House rules shall be interpreted. The power of the Speaker has varied from era to era.

After a strong Republican victory, in 1994, where Republicans became the majority party in both Houses for the first time since 1956, Newt Gingrich as Speaker moved to create a very powerful office. The media speculated that the new Speaker would replace the President as the symbol of American democracy. The press and the public showered attention on the Speaker for about a year. Newt Gingrich's abrasive uncompromising style and his bloated ego soon turned his image from one of extreme popularity to one of the most unpopular politicians in Washington. The House issued a mild rebuke to Newt Gingrich after learning he used a tax-exempt organization for his own political purposes. Finally, when he cried about being mistreated by the President and he demanded absolute conformity to his budget demands, looking like a selfish egoist, Newt Gingrich was forced by his own party to give up some of his power and, finally, removed.

The presiding officer of the Senate, according to the Constitution, is the Vice-president of the United States. He receives the title, *President of the Senate—the presiding officer of the Senate who is also the Vice-president*. The President of the Senate has little power besides running the meetings and ruling on Senate procedures. The Vice-president, as President of the Senate, does get to vote when there is a tie vote. Although tie votes are not very common, they do occur.

Since the Vice-president at times functions as America's ceremonial leader and sits in on Cabinet meetings, he can be expected to be absent from the Senate a fair amount of time. The majority party elects a *President pro tempore—whose job it is to preside over the Senate when the President of the Senate is absent*. The President pro tempore must be a Senator. The honor usually goes to the member of the majority party who has been in the Senate the longest.

To aid the House Speaker and the President of the Senate to decide on the rules for running a meeting, both houses have a parliamentarian. A *parliamentarian— is an individual who is well versed in the procedures for running a meeting*. Parliamentarians are not elected members of Congress. They are hired to provide advice on the parliamentary laws as described in the procedures each house established at the beginning of each session and *Robert's Rules of Order, Revised—the traditional standards set forth for running a formal meeting*. The presiding officer does not have to follow the advice provided by the parliamentarian. Other appointed officials of Congress that do not have a vote include congressional aids (lots of them), historians and sergeants-at-arms.

The major task of the legislative branch is to legislate. I have already discussed the local flavor of Congress. While feeding pork to their constituents, members of Congress also introduce national legislation. Congress also holds hearings on the need for new legislation. Congressional investigations often go beyond the stated purpose, legislative hearings, and become educational forums and even trials. The hearings are supposed to be fact-finding, but they often become accusatory and have a circus air. Perhaps the most notorious example of the trial by Congress approach was the so-called McCarthy hearings in the early 1950's. Although Senator Joseph McCarthy was not the head of the committee investigating alleged communist infiltration of the United States government, his aggressive style caused the media and the public, and now the history books, to give his name to the hearings and the era. His questioning of witnesses trampled on individual rights. His methods gave rise to the term *McCarthyism—using innuendo and smear tactics to defame innocent people and to pry into their personal lives.* These hearings and McCarthy's style helped add to the paranoia sweeping America of communist plots and conspiracies. Many left-wing individuals and liberals lost their jobs due to fears that they were harboring pro-Soviet positions. People began to refer to left-wing individuals, the vast majority of whom had no sympathy with communism, as *pinkos—individuals who were not quite red (the color of the Marxist flag)—*or *fellow-travelers—individuals, although not communists, who aided and abetted their cause.* I was in high school during this era when people were even afraid to mouth the word communist for fear that someone would accuse them of being a communist. I had a history teacher who told us he was going to teach us about communism because we could then protect ourselves from that evil. He prefaced his remarks by telling us that he was doing so at a risk to his job. Well, he did not lose his job like many others. In the end Joseph McCarthy was discredited with the help of a number of brave souls in government and in the media.

Not all Senate or House hearings are invasive of individual privacy or attempts by members of Congress to grandstand for the television cameras. Hearings often serve as conduit for information to reach the general public. Congressional investigations provide experts an opportunity to submit their opinions and important facts. Ideally members of Congress can vote more knowledgeably on pending legislation.

Another function of Congress is to oversee the Executive Branch. The oversight function of Congress allows it to be sure that the Executive Branch is enforcing legislation and carrying out its programs efficiently.

I would sum up the role of Congress as having to examine bills that members introduce, hold hearings to see if new legislation is needed and to be sure the Executive Branch is fulfilling congressional wishes. Almost all of this work is done in committees. Former President Woodrow Wilson (1913–1919) wrote, "Congress in committee is Congress at work."

Members of Congress usually serve on two *standing committees—permanent committees in the House of Representatives or the Senate that exist from session to session.* Every now and then a "reform" movement increases or decreases the number of standing committees. In 1995, the new Republican majority in the House eliminated three standing committees. There are presently 19 standing committees in the House and 16 in the Senate. They range in tasks from Agriculture to the Budget. They may also serve on *select committees—also known as special committees, formed to examine particular or narrow issues.* Select committees are temporary and most cease to exist after one term of Congress. While on a committee the members are assigned to subcommittees. Subcommittees deal with specialized areas of the mother committee's responsibility.

At times Congress creates *joint committees—formed with members of the Senate and House to deal with issues that require a coordinated effort.* Joint committees

Congress provides support to bunny keepers?

are usually permanent and are used almost exclusively for investigative purposes. They seldom pass legislation on to one of the houses for a vote.

Members of Congress attempt to serve on a committee that will benefit their reelection. Freshman members of Congress will try to be appointed to a committee that deals with issues important to their constituents. They want to bring home the bacon. For example, if a legislator came from a farming community, service on the Agriculture Committee would make the most sense. A select group of party members in each House decides committee assignments. Individuals who previously served on a committee generally are allowed to return to that committee in the next session. This is part of the seniority principle in Congress. The *seniority principle—refers to those who are in Congress the longest receiving preference.* In the case of committee chairs, the individual from the majority party who has been on the committee the longest usually becomes the chair. Before 1973, this was automatic. Today, party caucuses select committee chairs with approval of the full House or Senate. In reality, the post goes to the senior member of the majority party. The same is true for subcommittee chairs.

These chairs have tremendous power over the affairs of Congress. A few years ago, Jesse Helms, ultra-conservative Senator from North Carolina and chair of the powerful Senate Foreign Relations Committee, refused to allow his committee to even discuss President Clinton's nomination for an ambassador to Mexico. The individual was a Republican like Mr. Helms, but was a moderate. With the committee not being able to vote on the nomination, it could never reach the floor of the Senate for a vote. Well, yes, the Senate could vote to override a committee chair, but this is very unlikely based upon some strange principle of mutual respect.

The same kind of non-action can occur with proposed legislation. Committee chairs at times had the right to *pigeonhole*—*to keep legislation from being discussed in a committee by never submitting the bill to the committee.* Today, it is more common for a chair to simply ask that a bill be *tabled*—*put aside so it will never be discussed.* Once tabled the bill is considered dead. In the House this could be overcome through a *discharge petition*—*a device used to take a bill out of the jurisdiction of a committee with a petition signed by 218 members and approved by a majority of the House so the bill can be discussed and voted on by the whole House.* Discharge petitions are rarely used. Once again members of these august bodies do not believe in unnecessarily stepping on each others toes. They know such an action might come back to haunt them in the future. Members of Congress have long memories and the "get even" principle does prevail.

Actually, committee chairs are only one factor in the death of a bill. The system is set up in such a way that bills are killed along a myriad of places. Of course, most of you are familiar with how a bill becomes a law. Every Saturday morning you watched School House Rock and "I'm a Bill on Capitol Hill." Recently, the little ditties have been revised into a Broadway production. While the cartoon with the character singing "I'm a Bill on Capitol Hill" was a fairly simple rendering of how a bill becomes a law, it set down the fundamental path. What it did not identify was how few bills become law. In 1997, of the more than 5,000 bills introduced into the House and Senate, only 1.7 percent become legislation.

Members of Congress are the only individuals who can introduce a bill and they must do so in their respective house. You or I or even the President cannot introduce legislation. A member of Congress can present a bill for us or the President. In reality, the Executive Branch drafts a large portion of the major bills introduced. Members of Congress often agree to introduce bills in both houses simultaneously. There is one exception. The Constitution provides that all *appropriation bills*—*revenue raising bills*—must originate in the House of Representatives.

Legislators, introducing bills, often try to get as many other members of Congress as possible to support their proposed legislation. If they can get *bipartisan support*—*when members of both parties support the issue*—they have a better chance of the bill becoming a law. Bills are often known by the name of the chief sponsors or by the bill's number. The clerk who receives the bill assigns it a number according to when it was introduced in a specific session of Congress. For example, HB 705, 105th, would be the 705th bill introduced in 105th Congress in the House of Representatives. S705, 105th, would be the 705th bill introduced in the Senate in the 105th Congress.

Once a bill is introduced, the clerk of the house along with its leadership assigns the bill to a committee. The Chair of the committee then generally sends the bill to a subcommittee. The subcommittee holds hearings on about ten percent of the bills it receives. The remainder die in subcommittee. When the subcommittee has finished its investigation of the bill and recommended changes, it goes back to the full committee. The standing committee then votes yea or nay. If yea, the bill is sent on to the full House or the Senate, depending on the status of the committee. If nay, the bill is dead. Once in a while, on major pieces of proposed legislation, the standing committee will send a bill from committee with a recommendation to defeat.

The bill is then placed on the respective house's calendar for debate and a vote. Members of the House have a limited amount of time to debate and vote on a bill. The Senate has an unlimited amount of time, which gives rise to the filibuster. Members of the Senate can stop a filibuster with a 3/5ths vote. Since, once again, they do not like stepping on each others toes, they usually try to compromise an issue when a filibuster is threatened. Filibusters were much more common in the days when southern Senators wanted to prevent any civil rights legislation. The vote to end debate is known as *cloture—the procedure that ends debate in order to obtain a vote on the bill.* The Senate established the original cloture rule in 1917 at which time it required two-thirds of the entire Senate to end a filibuster. In 1975, the Senate changed to the present three-fifths of the entire Senate (60 Senators) being needed to terminate a filibuster.

Both houses allow members to amend a bill; however, it is much more common in the Senate to add **riders**—*provisions that are added to a bill that have little relationship to the proposed legislation.* For example, a bill might provide aid to Israel and a rider added to the bill makes prayer in the schools legal. Senators often use riders to force presidential action on legislation that he may oppose, but for which there is public support. The President is forced either to accept the rider or to veto the whole bill, which perhaps included something the President desired.

If the bill passes both houses of Congress, but has different wording, the bill must go to a **conference committee**—*a joint committee of a few members of Congress who are supportive of the specific legislation, whose task it is to create a compromise version of the bill that both houses will accept.* If the conference committee cannot agree on a compromise, the bill is said to have died in conference. If they come up with a compromise, both houses must once again approve the bill. If one house fails to do so, the bill is dead. If the bill finally passes both houses in identical form, it goes to the President.

The President has four constitutional actions he may take. The first action a President can take is non-action. He can refuse to sign a bill. If he does so, the bill becomes a law automatically without his signature, either immediately or according to a date established in the bill. There is one exception, the **pocket veto**—*if Congress adjourns within ten days after the President received a bill, thereby preventing its return, the bill cannot become law.* Congress cannot override a pocket veto. This second option is a President's most powerful, because Congress must wait until the next session and try to re-introduce the bill.

The third action a President has is to veto the legislation. The President must indicate his reasons for vetoing the bill and then send it back to the house it originated in. The original house and the other house of Congress can override a presidential veto with a two-thirds vote. To get a two-thirds vote in both houses is quite difficult. Congress has only overridden about four percent of presidential vetoes. Just the threat of a presidential veto gets Congress scrambling to create a compromise. The final action a President can take is to sign the bill into law. The bill becomes a law immediately upon signing or based upon a date given in the legislation. The bill, now a law, can still wind up on the trash heap. If someone, breaks the law and challenges it as unconstitutional in the courts, the legislation could reach the Supreme Court. If the Court decides the law or just a part of the law is unconstitutional, then it is bye-bye to that legislation.

It is the economy, stupid!

Congress could now introduce a new bill minus the unconstitutional segment or attempt to amend the constitution. A constitutional amendment requires two-thirds of both houses voting approval and then three-fifths of the state legislatures (38 states). Obviously, very few Congressional attempts to amend the constitution to override the Supreme Court have succeeded. The best known amendment overriding a Supreme Court decision was the 16th amendment creating an income tax.

I have attempted to show you that "Bill on Capitol Hill" becoming a law was unusual. Bills fall into jeopardy at any number of places in the law-making process. This complex system provides us with the checks and balances so vital to creating reasonable and reasoned laws. Of course, partisan bickering can lead to *gridlock—where everything becomes tied up in partisan squabbling and nothing is passed*. And, in more recent years this has led to what some political scientists have referred to as a nasty atmosphere in Congress. Yet, for all the gridlock and all the nastiness, laws do get passed and people work together more often than not.

Of course, the working together for personal gain, the pork barrel legislation, the log-rolling accounts for a good portion of the bills enacted into law. So, "all politics is local," except, as in 1994, when a combination of national moods and of national issues brought the Republicans to power in Congress. Anomalies do occur and if Tom had asked me the wrong questions in 1994, they would have been the right questions, albeit, not in our district. For in our district like so many others, the right questions were and are "what has my representative in Congress done for me and my locality." This may be the selfish question, but, from my perspective, it is the major question. Why else have a people's legislature?

GLOSSARY

APPROPRIATION BILLS
Revenue raising bills.

BI-PARTISAN SUPPORT
When members of both parties support the issue.

CLOTURE
The procedure that ends debate in order to obtain a vote on the bill.

CONFERENCE COMMITTEE
A joint committee of a few members of Congress who are supportive of the specific legislation, whose task it is to create a compromise version of the bill that both houses will accept.

DISCHARGE PETITION
A device used to take a bill out of the jurisdiction of a committee with a petition signed by 218 members and approved by a majority of the House so that the bill can be discussed and voted on by the whole House.

FELLOW TRAVELERS
Individuals, although not communists, who aided and abetted their cause.

FILIBUSTER
"Talking a bill to death," or attempting to do so; the Senate, not the House, allows a member or members to prevent any action on a bill through marathon uninterrupted speeches.

FIN-DE-SIECLE SENTIMENT
Relating to an end of an era, usually with world-weariness and fashionable despair.

FRANKING PRIVILEGES
Free mailings.

GRIDLOCK
Where everything becomes tied up in partisan squabbling and nothing is passed.

INCUMBENTS
The individual who currently holds the political office.

INDEPENDENTS
Members of neither the Republican nor the Democratic party.

JOINT COMMITTEES
Formed with members of the Senate and House to deal with issues that require a coordinated effort.

LOG ROLLING
Agreeing to vote for another politician's bill in return for a vote for his or her proposed legislation: "you scratch my back and I will scratch yours."

McCARTHYISM
Using innuendo and smear tactics to defame innocent people and to pry into their personal lives.

MAJORITY LEADER
The head of the majority party selected through a caucus or conference of the members of the party.

MAJORITY PARTY
The party, between the Republicans and Democrats, that has the greater number of elected members.

MINORITY LEADER
The head of the minority party selected through a caucus or conference of the members of the party.

MINORITY PARTY
The party, between the Republicans and Democrats, that has the fewer number of elected members.

NON-PARTISAN ELECTIONS
Elections where an individual runs for an office that does not allow one to run as a party candidate.

PARLIAMENTARIAN
Is an individual who is well versed in the procedures for running a meeting.

PARTISAN ELECTIONS
Elections where individuals run as a member of a political party.

PIGEONHOLE
To keep legislation from being discussed in a committee by never submitting the bill to the committee.

PINKOS
Individuals who were not quite red (the color of the Marxist flag).

POCKET VETO
If Congress adjourns within ten days after the President received a bill thereby preventing its return, the bill cannot become law.

PORK
Government jobs, money grants and public works that politicians obtain for their constituents.

PORK BARREL LEGISLATION
Custom legislation designed exclusively for a legislator's district.

PRESIDENTIAL LINE-ITEM VETO
This allows the President to eliminate sections of any budgetary bill subject to a possible 2/3 override of both houses of Congress voting independently.

PRESIDENT OF THE SENATE
The presiding officer of the Senate who is also the Vice-president of the United States.

PRESIDENT PRO TEMPORE
Whose job it is to preside over the Senate when the President of the Senate is absent.

PRIVATE BILLS
Legislation designed to help specific individuals or deal with narrow matters rather than general affairs.

PROPORTIONAL REPRESENTATION
An electoral system that allocates seats in a legislative body to each group approximately equal to their numbers in society.

RIDER
Provisions that are added to a bill that have little relationship to the proposed legislation.

ROBERT'S RULES OF ORDER, REVISED
The traditional standards set forth for running a formal meeting.

SELECT COMMITTEE
Also known as special committees; they are formed to examine particular or narrow issues.

SENIORITY PRINCIPLE
Refers to those who are in Congress the longest receiving preference.

SPEAKER OF THE HOUSE OF REPRESENTATIVES
The presiding officer in the House of Representatives.

STANDING COMMITTEE
Permanent committees in the House of Representatives or the Senate that exist from session to session.

TABLE
Put a bill aside so it will never be discussed.

TERM LIMITS
Where elected officials are limited to a set number of years in office.

WASP's
White, Anglo-Saxon Protestants.

WHIP
Assistant party leaders in Congress.

CHAPTER 7

The Judicial System: Truth, Justice, and the American Way?

Essay VII

"I feel strongly that there ought to be fair justice."

George Bush, the Younger 9/20/07

At 6 AM on August 20, 1993, my phone woke me to one of the most tragic events in my life. Patricia Smith, a very close friend, cried out that the local police had murdered her husband and my best friend, John.[1] Both Patricia and John worked at local hospitals as registered nurses. John had been one of my house-mates during my single years. A short while after I married, he decided to follow suit. He became the father to Patricia's nine year old daughter, as my new wife became the mother to my nine year old son. We went most places together and the Smith's became the godparents to my second son.

As Patricia wept uncontrollably on the telephone, the ugly story unfolded. The Smith's had come over during the early afternoon of August 19 to take my son number two out to a movie matinee for his twelfth birthday along with son number three, then ten. After the movie and the obligatory ice cream, the Smith's headed to Patricia's parent's house. John never got along with his in-laws. Apparently, he did some drinking while there. John never handled his liquor well. Sadly, he was one of those drinkers who became aggressive and negative. His aggression always turned inward.

Patricia told me that when they returned home John immediately headed for their bedroom and got his pistol. He then secluded himself in a closet. Neither Patricia nor her daughter, Tina, could coax him out. Finally, he screamed at them to leave him alone and fired his pistol into the floor of the closet. Tina, then 23, made a decision that I am sure will haunt her for the remainder of her life. She called the local police for help to try and prevent what she feared would be his suicide.

---

[1]I have changed the names to protect the people involved, as well as to cover any inaccuracies that may unintentionally appear in my account of events.

Is the truth out there?

I guess it was a slow night for law enforcement as four patrol cars arrived along with a police dog and a novice negotiator. By this time John had gotten into their petite back yard in his underwear and took refuge behind a fairly large lemon tree. Patricia told me that she asked the police to have them call me to come over and try to persuade him to put down his weapon and exit the yard. The police refused, informing her that this was not their procedure.

In the next few minutes the negotiator tried to do his thing as the dog barked and John shouted for the police to leave. My understanding is that John finally yelled out that he knew how to get them to leave. A gunshot occurred and the police reported that they saw a flash convincing them that they were being fired upon. They expended nearly 50 rounds. Twenty plus bullets entered John and a few went into the lemon tree and the houses behind the yard. The coroner reported that the bullet that killed John came from his own gun.

A few days later, Patricia and Tina retained a San Francisco law firm that specialized in wrongful death suits. The attorneys agreed to handle the case at a 40 percent **consignment fee**—*lawyers will, at times, cover all the costs of handling a suit with the stipulation that they will receive a percent of the settlement, if awarded.* The vast majority of lawsuits are settled out of court due to the high cost of pursuing what both sides—the plaintiff and the defendant—might term justice. Many argue today that in our legal system, justice is no longer sought after and that both sides simply try to resolve conflict. The ultimate question for those of us raised on Superman comics, Superman movies or Superman TV shows "truth, justice and the American way" is can truth be learned within a process that is designed to resolve conflict? Is the truth really out there anymore? Perhaps expanding this system of the resolution of conflict is what George Bush, the Younger, meant when he said he felt strongly "that there ought to be fair justice."

Some argue that the drive for compromise rather than justice has always been the case once lawyers became involved. I read many years ago, during my graduate studies, that the Spanish crown forbade lawyers from going to colonial Mexico for the first fifty years of its existence in order to preserve justice. If a **civil suit**—*all cases brought to court that are not categorized as criminal law; a dispute between two parties over such issues as injury or business problems*—such as Patricia's, cannot be settled out of court, it is not uncommon for it to drag on for many years before a trial date is set. While the delays may be due to an overcrowded court system, some argue they are mainly due to the parties in the lawsuit postponing litigation in hopes that a voluntary agreement can eventually be reached. Another reason critics cite for civil cases not reaching the courts in a timely manner is judge shopping. Since judges have a lot of *discretionary power—the law is often written loosely, providing judges with the ability to interpret what the law says and, often, to determine sentencing*—attorneys can, at times, try to delay when a case is heard based upon who is sitting on the bench at a specific time. In many localities, concerns for the perceived arbitrariness of judicial decisions, especially in *criminal cases—where the agent of a government entity accuses a person or persons of a crime*, has led to the establishment of *mandatory sentencing laws—where the law limits judicial discretion by establishing a minimum sentence*. Patricia's wrongful death suit filed in the early Fall, 1993 against the police and the city they worked for finally landed in a California Superior Court in March of 1996.

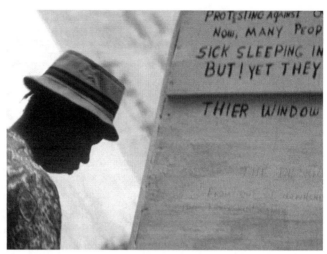

"Fair Justice?"

In California, *Superior Courts—are trial courts where most civil and criminal cases are heard*. Each of California's 58 counties has a Superior Court. Until June 1998, California also had *Municipal Courts—local courts that usually covered misdemeanors, traffic matters and some criminal matters*. A constitutional amendment the people of California passed in that year allowed for the merger of the Municipal Courts with the Superior Courts. Each California Superior Court has a number of courthouses throughout their county with many judges and courtrooms within each building. The Superior Court of my county, Alameda, in 2008, had 66 judges to hear thousands of civil and criminal cases. Superior Court judges are elected by county voters and serve six year terms. The Governor fills any vacancies. In our *adversary legal system—where opposing sides (plaintiff versus defendant in civil proceedings or prosecution versus defendant in criminal cases) dispute each others findings of fact*—judges often encourage attorneys to settle out of court in civil cases. In criminal cases, judges prefer in most instances to see a *plea bargain—an agreement where a defendant agrees to plead guilty to a lesser charge or reveals other information found beneficial to the prosecution to receive a lesser penalty or to get some special considerations*. Settling out of court or plea bargaining may allow parties in a civil or criminal dispute to feel that the issue has been resolved, yet this approach may not arrive at truth, achieve justice or obtain the sense of fairness the American way expects.

Studies estimate that 80% of both civil and criminal cases are settled before reaching trial. My local newspaper, *The Argus*, reported on December 7, 1992 that in the previous year 94% of all felonies, or 5402 cases, in Alameda County were resolved through plea bargaining. In the State of California that year plea bargaining ended 96% of felony cases. Plea bargaining historically provides an effective tool in resolving conflict. The question at hand is whether it is an effective tool for achieving justice. Critics of plea bargaining argue that this system perverts justice by allowing people to plead to lesser charges or achieve reductions in sentences for dispensing information. They say that the system encourages individuals to commit crimes when they know that all they have to do if caught is to cop a plea to obtain a reduced sentence.

The vast majority of lawyers and judges support plea bargaining as a method of reducing legal costs as well as obtaining information. If we eliminated plea bargaining, they argue, the courts would be overcrowded and trial delays extended near indefinitely. While the vast majority of pleas end with reduced penalties, those opposed to the process argue that the same results would be achieved without compromising the actual charge. Alaska banned plea bargaining from 1975 until 1993. The Alaska Judicial Council found that prosecutors heeded the ban resulting in longer sentences as many had hoped. Interestingly, a backlog in criminal cases failed to occur.[2] Many defendants accepted the penalty for the actual crime rather than face a trial.

Statistics indicate that going to trial tends to produce longer sentences. The statistics from Alameda County showed that in cases where criminals pleaded guilty to forcible rape the average sentence was ten years. However, if convicted in a court of law, the sentences for the same offense averaged 25 years. The study found that results were similar in charges of lewd acts with children—6.9 years for accepting the charges and an average of 15.3 years at trial.

The argument to maintain plea bargaining does not revolve around justice, but revolves around the concept of a necessary evil. Prosecutors find themselves in the driver's seat, according to Maricopa County (Arizona) Attorney Charles Hyder, asserts "usually the defendant is not aware of any weaknesses in a case." Attorneys for the defense can enhance their status through obtaining deals for their clients. Judges can rapidly clear very heavy caseloads. Harvard Law School Professor and iconoclast Alan Dershowitz argued "that bargaining is often born not of necessity but of 'laziness'—or of judges competing for the cleanest docket, prosecutors aiming for high conviction rates or defense lawyers who find it more profitable to make quick deals than go through long trials."[3]

District Courts—*are the trial courts in the federal judicial system.* They are similar to the Superior Courts in California. As the Superior Courts have jurisdiction over all criminal and civil law in California, the District Courts serve the same role in relation to federal law. Due to our *federal system*—*a sharing of power between the central government and the subdivisions*—the United States has both a state and a federal judicial system. At times, jurisdictional disputes occur, but in the vast majority of times state law is decided in state courts and federal law in federal courts. In rare occasions a case originating in a state court will travel to the federal courts when an issue of federal or constitutional law pertains.

---

[2]For further information go to: http://www.time.com/time/magazine/article/0,9171,916340-1,00.html

[3]http://www.time.com/time/magazine/article/0,9171,916340-2,00.html

There are 94 District Courts in the United States. Each state has at least one federal District Court as does Washington, D.C. and Puerto Rico. Another District Court hears cases within our other territories. There are 674 District Court judges. The President appoints federal judges with the "advice and consent" of the United States Senate. While the United States Constitution sets the basics for our judicial system in Article III, the appointment of all federal judges is covered in Article II, Section 2, paragraph 2. Article II specifies that the President shall nominate judges and the Senate, not Congress for it includes both the House of Representatives and the Senate, will confirm these appointments by a majority vote. Since the same article and subsection allows Congress to set standards for the appointment of sub-officers, District Court judges have the authority to appoint for eight year terms

Anti-War demonstration in front of Federal District Court Building in New York City

magistrate judges—*judges who can perform some of the tasks of the District Judges, such as supervising pre-trial motions, supervise discovery proceedings and provide preliminary consideration of petitions for post conviction relief.* Congress created the system of magistrate judges in 1968 to ease the workload of the district court judges.

A separate section of the District Courts are bankruptcy courts. According to Article I, Section 8, of the U.S. Constitution, states cannot regulate bankruptcy. People must file for all bankruptcies in one of the 94 federal judicial districts. The judges in the Court of Appeals, by a simple majority, appoint the judges in the bankruptcy courts for a term of 14 years. Congress determines the number of bankruptcy courts. Since 2005, before filing for bankruptcy, most debtors must go through a special briefing from an approved credit-counseling agency. The 2005 amendment to the bankruptcy code seems to have fulfilled Congress's intent to reduce the number of bankruptcy filings, especially those that might be designed to avoid paying debts.

Since Patricia Smith's wrongful death suit pertained to a police force within California, the trial took place in the Alameda County courthouse in Oakland in March of 1996. Patricia's attorney called me as a witness for the plaintiff. As noted before, I had not been at the site of the shooting. In a civil case it is up to the plaintiff to establish the value of the loss involved, *compensatory damages—money awarded beyond costs to cover what was lost, and nothing more.* These compensatory damages are considered remedial rather than preventive or punitive. However, a jury may also award in particular types of wrongful conduct *punitive*

The American Way?

damages—monetary awards to punish the defendant for harm imposed on the plaintiff or society and perhaps to ward off a similar action in the future.

My testimony began the process of establishing the kind of person John was and would have been if the police had not caused his death. The jury, if it decided that the police killed John, or forced him to commit suicide, or added to his desire to commit suicide, would then determine his future worth. In the case where the jury might decide that the police were only partially responsible for John committing suicide, they would have to decide the final monetary value of his future life and divide that by the percentage of fault that lay with the police. So, if the jury decided that John's life would have produced an income of 10 million dollars and he was 90% responsible for his own death while the local police must take 10% of the responsibility, they would owe his widow one million dollars.

A civil case does not require proof beyond a reasonable doubt, but only a presumption of guilt. A few years back, a judge explained to a potential panel of jurors that I sat on, that if the scales of justice are used in a criminal case, one guilty side must be all the way down to achieve a verdict, i.e., beyond a reasonable doubt. In a civil case the scales must only tip somewhat in one direction for a decision to be reached.

Upon completion of my testimony, I had to leave the courtroom. I went home and encountered my number two son's chess instructor. He asked me how the Smith case was proceeding. As we talked I realized he knew many details of the case that had never appeared in the papers or in our conversations. I queried him on how he had learned so much about the case. He replied that he really should not tell me, but he would anyway. Like a fair number of chess people I know, Tom (his name), was a bit eccentric. He made much of his living as a test subject. That is to say that he had his name listed in a number of agencies that send people out to test products or participate in research projects. Tom informed me that a number of months back he served on a mock jury. Similar to the movie "Runaway Jury" (2003), attorneys in high profile cases or where a lot of money is at stake have jury consultants and even hold mock trials to test their case. Some companies now advertise their services on the web that include focus groups for witness research, trial simulations, witness preparation, jury selection and trial monitoring.

Tom told me how he was selected from a panel of potential mock jurors. Patricia's law firm had a psychologist on their staff who examined the background of the potential mock jurors and provided advice to the attorney who would be presenting the case as to which jurors might be favorable to the plaintiff's case. Depending on the type of case and the statute, attorneys for the plaintiff (prosecution) or defendant (defense) are allocated a number of *peremptory challenges*—*the right to challenge a juror without stating a reason for the challenge*. If they should use up their peremptory challenges or do not care to use one, the attorneys have the option to try a *challenge for cause*—*to challenge prospective jurors for a lack of impartiality*. Attorneys have an unlimited number of challenges based upon cause. However, judges determine whether a person should be dismissed. In the cases I have observed, a judge has asked if the potential jurors felt they could be impartial and the vast majority said, "yes." Translation, judges are not prone to dismiss jurors via challenges for cause.

Tom informed me that in the mock trial held in a mock courtroom in the law firm's office, one of the partners played the attorney for the defendants. Both the plaintiff's attorney and the mock attorney for the defendants questioned a few of the plaintiff's witness. The mock jury then retired to a meeting room. Patricia's attorney asked the mock jury members to inform him on what they felt worked well in the mock trial and which elements hurt the plaintiff's case. Members of the mock jury, Tom related, informed Patricia's attorney that the issue that hurt the demand for damages the most stemmed from her having remarried in only two years after John's death. They questioned the grief John's death brought on plus the continued hurt she claimed. Attorneys can request that a judge prohibit certain testimony or information. During pre-trial motions, the judge in Patricia's wrongful death suit, granted the plaintiff's attorney's request that he, the judge, prohibit any testimony or information pertaining to her remarriage. The conundrum: is the end result justice when in high profile cases, or those with large monetary stakes, no expense is spared to try to directly or indirectly manipulate jury selection and the information introduced into a courtroom?

Certainly, Patricia felt righted when a jury awarded her and Tina combined compensatory and punitive damages of $5,288,804. What she soon learned was that the legal process had just begun.

The attorney acting for the city and its police force filed an appeal with the trial judge to overturn the jury verdict. Yes, trial judges can overturn a jury verdict although they seldom will as this would seem to negate the value of the jury system. An appeal to the trial judge to overturn a verdict is usually done on procedure—whether there was an error of law. Although I never saw the brief the defendants' attorney filed, I suspect it claimed something to the effect that the police could not be held responsible for John's committing suicide and, therefore, the jury could not assess damages.

I clearly remember Patricia's concern during the week she awaited the trial judge's decision. She informed me that the judge had a son who was a police officer and her attorneys felt that this might bias his decision on the defendants' appeal. When the judge finally read his response, he apparently expressed certain misgivings with the jury's verdict and stated his opinion that the damages were much too high. He urged the plaintiff and the defendant to accept a settlement of $1,500,000. Patricia and her attorney decided to forgo any negotiations on that sum and insisted on the jury's award.

The attorney for the defendants now filed an appeal with the California appellate court. In California there are six *Courts of Appeal*—*an intermediate court to review the procedure in a civil or criminal case to try and ensure that the law is interpreted and applied uniformly.* The Governor and a Commission of Judicial Appointments name the 105 judges on the six Courts of Appeal. The voters must confirm the appointments at the next general election. They serve for 12 years at which time the voters must once again confirm them. Unlike a Superior Court judge who can face opposition on confirmation the people may only vote to confirm or to retain an appellate court judge.

The federal system also has an intermediate system of courts for appeals. The 13 Courts of Appeal are often known as the *Circuit Courts*—*courts in the federal system that hear appeals from the district courts in their circuit, as well as appeals from administrative agencies.* As noted earlier, the President with the advice and consent of the Senate appoints the judges who serve on the circuit courts of appeal. Some specialized courts of appeal also exist such as the Court of Appeals for the Armed Services. Twelve of the Circuit Courts of Appeal are geographically defined; however, the thirteenth court, the Court of Appeals for the Federal Circuit, covers appeals from throughout the nation based upon specific subject matter. The number of judges on each circuit court varies from nine for the first circuit to 28 for the ninth circuit.

California's First District Court of Appeal centered in San Francisco heard the city's appeal of the jury's damages awarded in Patricia's wrongful death suit in 1998. Three judges normally sit in civil or criminal proceeding to hear an appeal in both state and federal appellate cases. The main difference in civil and criminal cases is that in civil cases either side can appeal a verdict and in criminal cases only a defendant may appeal if declared guilty. *Appellants*—*those who file an appeal*—must show that an error in procedure/law occurred that impacted the decision in the case. The three-judge panel makes its decision mainly on the written record of the case although they will question the attorneys for both sides on the issues and *case law*—*published court decisions and interpretations of the law that can be cited as precedents*—presented in their *briefs*—*documents that provide legal arguments.* Each attorney is usually allocated about 15 minutes to make arguments and judges will interject questions. Patricia informed me that her contract with her law firm indicated that the consignment percentage went from 40% to 50% after the case entered the appeals process. Apparently, the need to bring in an attorney who was qualified to practice before the California Court of Appeals and the California Supreme Court necessitated the increase in the percent of the award the law firm would receive for its services.

At least two of the three judges must vote in the same manner for an appeals court decision. Obviously, a three to nothing vote would be more definitive. When the court rendered the decision, two judges felt that the police cannot be held responsible for a suicide. The two judges in the majority also found that the charges against the defendants must be dismissed due to a lack of evidence that would allow the jury to find in favor of the plaintiff. My interpretation from the press reports of the case was that the third judge wrote that he believed that John had been forced into a corner through poor police procedure and that attributed to his decision to shoot himself.

The three judge panel in the courts of appeal is usually the final word. In a very few cases, an appeal court may decide to review the next appeal *en blanc*—*a hearing by a large group of judges (usually all) within the specific court of appeal.* Now it was Patricia's turn to appeal. The next and final level of appeal in California is to our Supreme Court. The highest court of appeal in the federal system is also called the ***Supreme Court***—*the court of last resort on questions of law.* We differentiate the two by designating the federal court as the U.S. Supreme Court and in many writings you will simply read, The Court.

Security!

Patricia's attorney filed a ***writ of certiorari***—*a document asking the Supreme Court to review a case.* The Supreme Court, neither in California nor in federal jurisdiction, does not have to grant a review. In California there is one exception where an appeal must be heard—when a trial court has imposed the death penalty. Four of the seven *justices*—*a title often reserved for judges on a Supreme Court*—of the California Supreme Court must decide as to whether the full court should review a case. The same is true of the federal Supreme Court even though there are nine justices rather than seven as in California. The decision to hear a case does not mean that any of the judges agrees with a petition. I might note here that in all states but Maryland and New York the ultimate court of appeal is called the Supreme Court. My home state of New York for some strange reason calls its trial courts Supreme Courts and its highest appellate court is known simply as the Court of Appeals. Maryland's highest court is also referred to as the Court of Appeals, while the trial courts are known as District and Circuit Courts.

The California Supreme Court receives thousands of appeals each year, but only reviews about 5% of them. They are most likely to review cases where California Courts of Appeal have published conflicting opinions and where the legal question at hand is so important as to demand the high court's resolution. Any decision of the California Supreme Court is published and the Superior Courts and Courts of Appeal in the state must adhere to the precedent.

The U.S. Supreme Court Building

When an issue in a case decided by the California Supreme Court pertains as well to federal statute or the United States Constitution, the losing party may try appealing to the United States Supreme Court.

The United States Supreme Court will decide on fewer than 100 of the 9,000 or so cases that come to them each year. Usually, the Court picks those cases to hear that they hold are compelling issues of law. Like the California high court these compelling reasons will include conflicts of opinions from the Circuit Courts of Appeal and where an issue of federal and constitutional law is so important that they feel they must resolve any conflict in interpretation. While the Constitution established the Supreme Court as the appellate court of last resort, it also provided that in a few cases it was to have ***original jurisdiction***—*cases brought before a court in the first instance*—*starting out in that court.* The Court hears cases in the first instance that pertain to ambassadors, to other public ministers and consuls, to maritime jurisdiction and to where states are a party. The eleventh amendment modified this somewhat by forbidding the federal courts from dealing with suits "commenced or prosecuted against [a State] by Citizens of another State, or by Citizens or Subjects of any Foreign State." States may waive this prohibition. A 1996 law provided that suits under $75,000 between citizens of different states must be brought in the state courts. Any suit over $75,000 will be heard in the federal courts. Most states have established a process to settle smaller claims between citizens from within the state and from those between states known as ***Small Claims Courts***—*civil courts that have jurisdiction over monetary judgments where an individual is seeking compensation of a modest sum for a financial or property claim.* In California, individuals can ask for up to $7500 and corporations or other business can sue for a maximum of $5000. Lawyers are not permitted in Small Claims Courts; however, they are permitted in an appeal. There are no federal small claim procedures except in Federal Tax Court.

Article III of the United States Constitution lays out the basic structure of the federal judicial system. And, candidly, there is not a lot there—hardly a guideline compared to the articles of the Constitution that established the legislative and executive branches. Section I of Article III states: "The judicial Power of the United States, shall be vested in one Supreme Court, and in such inferior Courts as the Congress may from time to time ordain and establish." Obviously, the three-tiered court structure I have laid out in this essay is not delineated in this article. Congress created the layered approach under the authority that Article III provided. In 1789, after the first Congress met, they created a judiciary act that set the basic structure of the federal judicial system. Yet, in 1803, in a precedent setting decision, the Supreme Court under Chief Justice John Marshall, declared the Judiciary Act of 1789 unconstitutional taking upon itself the power of *judicial review—a court's authority to examine an executive or legislative act and to declare on the constitutionality of that act. Marbury v. Madison—was the name of the case under which the 1803 Court rendered this landmark decision establishing judicial review.*[4]

Naysayers have argued that judicial review was simply another example of the U. S. courts establishing themselves as law making bodies, violating the principle of the separation of powers between the legislative, executive and judicial branches of government. Nothing exists in the Constitution authorizing judicial review. Yet, the power of the courts to nullify a law had its roots in the English system since early in the 17 century and colonial courts had at times declared laws in violation of Royal charters. In issue number 78 of the *Federalist Papers—a*

Protest in front of U.S. Supreme Court building.

*series of essays written in 1787 and 1788 under the pseudonym Publius by James Madison, Alexander Hamilton and John Jay to try to persuade New Yorkers to ratify the Constitution—*Alexander Hamilton wrote: "The interpretation of the laws is the proper and peculiar province of the courts. A constitution is, in fact, and must be regarded by the judges, as a fundamental law. It, therefore, belongs to them to ascertain its meaning, as well as the meaning of any particular act proceeding from the legislative body." Most legal scholars argue that not only is judicial review an integral and historical part of our judicial system, but it was also something so basic to English law that the framers saw no need to spell it out in the Constitution.

The fundamental dispute today is no longer over judicial review, but over whether judges should act with restraint or should be active in interpreting the Constitution. *Judicial restraint (judicial self-restraint)—is the concept that judges should hesitate to use judicial review or strike down laws unless they find them to be in direct violation of the words of the Constitution and/or the intent of the framers.* Another term applied to those judges and individuals who support restraint in the courts

---

[4]Details of Marbury v. Madison: http://caselaw.lp.findlaw.com/scripts/getcase.pl?court=US&vol=5&invol=137

ruling on legislative actions is ***strict constructionism***—*a term usually applied to conservatives who hold that judges must apply the text of a law as written.* Some judicial restraint judges like U.S. Supreme Court Justice Anthony Scalia reject strict constructionism, a term often attributed to his philosophy, arguing that judges should look at the ordinary meaning of a word, not its "strict" meaning.

Political commentators often describe the opposite of judicial restraint as ***judicial activism***—*the concept that judges can use judicial review in considering the Constitution and law in the context of existing societal standards and needs.* Those who argue against judicial activism believe that judges who adhere to this interpretation are too willing to ignore precedent and to promote their own agendas. They see judicial activists as usurping the power of the legislature and of diminishing the natural order established in the concept of separation of powers. The so-called activist judges are more likely to hold that the Constitution is a living document and even if the intent of the framers could be known, and the exact words of the Constitution agreed upon, today's society's view of these terms and ideas must be taken into account. Personally, I feel that those who banter around these terms over use and even abuse them to justify their own narrow political perspectives and agendas. Most judges do not see themselves as judicial activists or judicial restraintists, but simply upholders and purveyors of the rule of law. Granted, this may not always mean attempting to achieve truth, justice and the American way, but rather to resolve conflict within the context of the law.

Article III, Section 1 of the United States Constitution, which I quoted earlier, continues: "The Judges, both of the supreme and inferior Courts, shall hold their Offices during good Behavior, and shall, at stated Times, receive for their Services a Compensation which shall not be diminished during their Continuance in Office." No, the Constitution does not provide that federal judges shall serve for life, but only "for good behavior." OK, so that really does mean life, but it might be argued that if the article said life instead of good behavior, congress would not be able to impeach and remove federal judges. Since the inception of the Constitution, the House of Representatives impeached only sixteen federal officials—two presidents, a cabinet member, a senator and twelve federal judges. Of the twelve judges only one sat on the Supreme Court—Associate Justice Samuel Chase. The Senate, which tries the impeachment, acquitted him in 1805. The Senate historically found seven of the remaining eleven federal judges guilty and removed them from office. The last conviction and removal of a federal judge occurred in 1989.

William Blount of Tennessee was the Senator that the House of Representatives impeached in 1799. The Senate had expelled Blount earlier and so the trial never took place. The decision not to try him may have been based on the wording that allows the House of Representatives to only impeach civil officers. The U.S. Constitutions states that "The President, Vice President, and all other civil Officers of the United States shall be removed from Office on Impeachment for, and Conviction of, Treason, Bribery, or other High Crimes and Misdemeanors." The argument that members of the legislature are not civil officers has prevailed since that time. The Constitution does provide authority for the legislators of either house to expel its own members.

The principle underlining the security provided federal judges—"serving for life," receiving a salary and not allowing that salary to be reduced during their term of office—is to protect them from any political retribution for their decisions. The idea was simply that they should render their decisions without pressure from the executive or legislative branches of government and not fear retaliation. As noted in my Essay II, the framers of the Constitution did not believe in the democratic principle of equality. They established a government under a written constitution that would provide for representative government that could preserve liberty, or as the Declaration of Independence indicates—life, liberty and the pursuit of happiness. Granted, today many people hold that these god-given inalienable rights can only be achieved through providing for equality. Some demand that courts and their judges be responsive to the will of the people. This would include the election of judges and removal if necessary through a political process that allows the masses to determine what truth, justice and the American way is at a specific point in time. Yet, the wisdom of our framers in their goal of preserving liberty through an independent judiciary also sowed the seeds for a judicial system that protects the equality fundamental to the people's inalienable rights of life, liberty and the pursuit of happiness. Aliens like Kal-El of Krypton (Superman) arrive in America to enjoy liberty and equality and are often the strongest defenders of truth, justice and the American way.

Alex de Tocqueville, whom I mentioned (pp. 10, 37, 97) along with his two volume study, *Democracy in America,* published in 1835 and 1840, reported that any political question arising in the United States failing resolution will eventually become a judicial question. I am sure this explains why both liberals and conservatives have attacked the federal courts as politically biased when decisions failed to meet their ideological needs. Only a few weeks separate two Court decisions in 2008 that brought angry rants from the right in one case and the left in the other. Yet, it was the same court and both were narrow 5-4 decisions.

On June 12, 2008, the Supreme Court raised the ire of most conservatives by deciding in Boumediene v. Bush that the detainees at the Guantanamo Bay detention camps maintained their right to the constitutionally guaranteed habeas corpus review. Basically, the decision held that detainees had the right to appear before an American court to challenge their imprisonment. Liberals cheered the decision while conservatives jeered it. President Bush, the Younger, expressed his strong disagreement with the decision and, like other conservatives, questioned the strength of the ruling from a deeply divided court. He echoed the right wing cries that the decision would foster further terrorism. United States Senator Jeff Stevens (Republican, Alabama) mouthed the words of many conservative talk show hosts, commentators and political pundits arguing that the Court had no right to tell Congress or the military how to handle enemy combatants. Besides, it was only 5 to 4, and that really cannot be seen as any mandate or meaningful precedent. Representative Stevens went on to point out how even Chief Justice John Roberts, voting with the minority, referred to it as a judicial activist decision. That is the catch phrase I wrote of earlier that conservatives love to use to negate any court decision they disagree with as violating the rule of law.

Two weeks later, on June 26, 2008, the conservatives smiled as the liberals frowned when the same Supreme Court ruled that the people in Washington D.C. had a right to keep and bear arms. For the first time in its history the Supreme Court in the District of Columbia v. Heller, once again in a 5-4 decision, directly addressed whether the Second Amendment provided for an individual right to bear arms or a collective right under a state regulated militia. I discussed this issue in greater detail in my Essay III and described how, after the 1939 Court decision in the United States v. Miller, many liberals argued that only those who belong to a "well-regulated Militia" had the right to keep and bear arms. Conservatives now talked up how the D.C. v. Heller case finally set an unchallengeable precedent and they made no comments about a deeply divided court due to a 5 to 4 vote. Liberals found solace, as the conservatives had in Boumediene v. Bush, that only five of the nine justices argued for an individual right to bear arms. They saved face by identifying that the Court dealt only with a law pertaining to a federal district and said nothing about whether it could or would be incorporated under the Fourteenth Amendment into the states. The decision also failed to extend to other federal gun laws. Conservatives looking forward to future litigation on the gun control issue quoted Justice Anthony Scalia: "it (the decision) surely elevates above all other interests the right of law-abiding responsible citizens to use arms in defense of hearth and home." Now, the liberal talk show hosts, commentators and political pundits did the name-calling by referring to the justices in the majority as simply strict construction-ists whom ultra-conservative presidents elevated to the high court.

With all the rhetoric that explodes in the public media and around dinner tables after a controversial court decision, the vast majority of Americans defend the concept of an independent judiciary. Neither politicos nor the public want anyone messing with this tradition. The strength of belief in the need for the courts to act independently and without outside interference is best exemplified in what has been called President Franklin Delano Roosevelt's "court packing scheme." President Roosevelt and others in his administration became frustrated in the 1930's as the Supreme Court justices declared much of the New Deal legislation unconstitutional. Republican presidents had appointed most of the members of the Court before President Roosevelt, a Democrat, took office in 1933. Early in 1937, President Roosevelt introduced a plan to add a maximum of six more justices to the Supreme Court that could bring the total to fifteen. While the Constitution fails to specify how many justices should serve on the Supreme Court, the tradition since 1869 has been nine—one Chief Justice and eight Associate Justices. Actually, the constitution does not even mention the make-up of the Court directly except for an indirect reference in Article I, Section 3 pertaining to impeachment that "when the President of the United States is tried, the Chief Justice shall preside." President Roosevelt's proposal advanced the concept that as each current justice reached the age of 70, the chief executive could appoint, with the advice and consent of the Senate, another judge to the high court. Few bought his argument that he was concerned for the heavy workload of the older justices. Later, in one of his fireside radio talks to the American people, he admitted that his true intention was to create a Supreme Court that understood present needs. The public and members of his own party rejected his arguments and attempts to compromise. The Senate Judiciary Committee's report released on June 14, 1937, best expresses the sentiment of Americans toward tampering with the independent judiciary, even when proposed by a very popular president: "a needless, futile and utterly dangerous abandonment of constitutional principle . . . without precedent or justification." Historians debate whether President Roosevelt's plan to "pack the court" hurt his credibility and his New Deal, yet one thing is certain, the American way of truth and justice supports a separation of powers that includes an independent judiciary.

They march for justice.

Oh, and what about Patricia Smith's *writ of certiorari* that appealed to the California Supreme Court to reinstate the jury verdict that declared that the local police had caused a wrongful death to her husband, John Smith, and had awarded a combination of compensatory and punitive damages of $5,288,804? They denied a hearing on the writ. This meant that the Appeals Court verdict stood—Patricia and her attorneys would receive nothing, not one cent. She could take a bit of solace in that a jury had placed on the record that the local police were at fault for John's death.

The story is not over yet! The local city's attorney soon brought Patricia out of the stoic demeanor that she had adopted due to the events of the last six years. He filed papers against her for the city's costs charging she had brought into the courts a *frivolous lawsuit*—*a case filed that the claimant (or defense) knew had no merit.* Since the brief argued that Patricia's legal counsel would have known her suit had no merit, they became a party to the action. In fact, a judge could have sanctioned and held Patricia, her lawyer and his law firm in contempt for filing the wrongful death suit. A fair number of months passed before a trial judge declared that Patricia and her law firm had filed the original suit in good faith and dismissed the counter action.

Finally, the legal processes ended. Neither Patricia Smith nor the local city authorities felt that truth or justice had been achieved. Perhaps a conflict had been resolved in that the city felt vindicated through an appeals process that threw out the jury's verdict and Patricia could always look to the support she received from the twelve jurors. And, just maybe, President George Bush, the Younger, could have maintained his faith in an American way that did, after seven years and the expenditure of tens of thousands of dollars, achieve "fair justice." *I, however, will continue to believe that the truth is out there and justice, without qualification, can be achieved if Americans continue the tradition of fighting to right unrightable wrongs.*

GLOSSARY

ADVERSARY LEGAL SYSTEM
Where opposing sides (plaintiff versus defendant in civil proceedings or prosecution versus defendant in criminal cases) dispute each others findings of fact.

APPELLANTS
Those who file an appeal.

BRIEFS
Documents that provide legal arguments.

CASE LAW
Published court decisions and interpretations of the law that can be cited as precedents.

CHALLENGE FOR CAUSE
To challenge prospective jurors for a lack of impartiality.

CIRCUIT COURTS
Courts in the federal system that hear appeals from the district courts in their circuit as well as appeals from administrative agencies.

CIVIL SUIT
All cases brought to court that are not categorized as criminal law; a dispute between two parties over such issues as injury or business problems.

COMPENSATORY DAMAGES
Money awarded beyond costs to cover what was lost, and nothing more.

CONSIGNMENT FEE
Lawyers will, at times, cover all the costs of handling a suit with the stipulation that they will receive a percent of the settlement, if awarded.

COURTS OF APPEAL
An intermediate court to review the procedure in a civil or criminal case to try and ensure that the law is interpreted and applied uniformly.

CRIMINAL CASES
Where the agent of a government entity accuses a person or persons of a crime.

DISCRETIONARY POWER
The law is often written loosely, providing judges with the ability to interpret what the law says and, often, to determine sentencing.

DISTRICT COURTS
The trial courts in the federal judicial system.

EN BLANC
A hearing by a large group of judges (usually all) within the specific court of appeal.

FEDERAL SYSTEM
A sharing of power between the central government and the subdivisions.

FEDERALIST PAPERS
A series of essays written in 1787 and 1788 under the pseudonym Publius by James Madison, Alexander Hamilton and John Jay to try to persuade New Yorkers to ratify the Constitution.

FRIVOLOUS LAWSUIT
A case filed that the claimant (or defense) knew had no merit.

JUDICIAL ACTIVISM
The concept that judges can use judicial review in considering the Constitution and law in the context of existing societal standards and needs.

JUDICIAL RESTRAINT (JUDICIAL SELF-RESTRAINT)
    The concept that judges should hesitate to use judicial review or strike down laws unless they find them to be in direct violation of the words of the Constitution and/or the intent of the framers.

JUDICIAL REVIEW
    A court's authority to examine an executive or legislative act and to declare on the constitutionality of that act.

JUSTICES
    A title often reserved for judges on a Supreme Court.

MAGISTRATE JUDGES
    Judges who can perform some of the tasks of the District Judges, such as supervising pre-trial motions, supervise discovery proceedings and provide preliminary consideration of petitions for post conviction relief.

MANDATORY SENTENCING LAWS
    Where the law limits judicial discretion by establishing a minimum sentence.

MARBURY V. MADISON
    The name of the case under which the 1803 Court rendered this landmark decision establishing judicial review.

MUNICIPAL COURTS
    Local courts that usually covered misdemeanors, traffic matters and some criminal matters.

ORIGINAL JURISDICTION
    Cases brought before a court in the first instance—starting out in that court.

PEREMPTORY CHALLENGES
    The right to challenge a juror without stating a reason for the challenge.

PLEA BARGAIN
    An agreement where a defendant agrees to plead guilty to a lesser charge or reveals other information found beneficial to the prosecution to receive a lesser penalty or to get some special consideration.

PUNITIVE DAMAGES
    Monetary awards to punish the defendant for harm imposed on the plaintiff or society and perhaps to ward off a similar action in the future.

SMALL CLAIMS COURTS
    Civil courts that have jurisdiction over monetary judgments where an individual is seeking compensation of a modest sum for a financial or property claim.

STRICT CONSTRUCTIONISM
    A term usually applied to conservatives who hold that judges must apply the text of a law as written.

SUPERIOR COURTS
    Trial courts where most civil and criminal cases are heard.

SUPREME COURT
    The court of last resort on questions of law.

WRIT OF CERTIORARI
    A document asking the Supreme Court to review a case.

CHAPTER 8

The Unicorn vs. The Lion: Foreign Affairs

Essay VIII

A strange title for an essay on foreign affairs, n'est-ce pas? Not if you are a student of heraldry; or an individual like myself who enjoys playing with ideas to help people better to comprehend the nuances of political issues.

During the Medieval era, unicorns became popular as the symbol of purity and goodness. People believed that ground unicorn horns could ward off evil, provide luck, and even remove poison from beverages.

Unicorns, in the popular mythology, could only be seen by a female virgin, as she symbolized purity. The cult of the virgin dominated Medieval life, including the worship, in some places, of Mary mother of the Christ. The unicorn often became identified with the Virgin Mary and even symbolized the Christ.

The unicorn embodied a universal church, a one world government under God—of purity, piousness, peace and finally salvation. On the other hand, the heraldic symbol of royal sovereignty was the lion.

Fables describe the lion as noble—the king of beasts. The lion, usually portrayed on heraldic shields as rearing up with forepaws in the air, clearly stood for the interests of the landed princes and not the King of the heavens. The lion in its aggressive posture represented strength and power. Animosity between the unicorn and the lion, as found in the popular mythology, symbolized the selfish interests of the princes versus the attempts to create a universal church of peace.

A third creature entered the fables—the eagle. The noble lion was king of the beasts, but not of the birds, over whom it had no control. The eagle symbolized a different kind of universal government, that of imperial power.

Any relationship between the unicorn and the eagle is obscure. Odell Shepard in his *Lore of the Unicorn* (Harper Colophon Books, 1979, p. 148) does discuss an eagle-stone—a poisonous stone an eagle placed in her nest to guard her young. Taking a bit of liberty with the lore, apparently the eagle, in creating a world government, followed the aggressive interests of the lion, but guarded her off-spring with poison. The unicorn's internationalism was dependent upon passiveness and peace.

Our world today is the world of the lion—of nation-states. The unicorn perhaps became invisible with the division of Christianity into many nation-churches. In 1517, Martin Luther's protestations against Catholic doctrines shattered a universal Christian church.

Four years earlier, *Niccolo Machiavelli—authored* The Prince *(1513) in which he advocated political expediency above morality.* Machiavelli believed in the unification of Italy and his philosophy soon became the creed of the newly emerging nation-states. He told the prince to be strong as a lion. He never mentioned unicorns, nor eagles.

Previous political works, written by clergymen, advocated moral politics and debated the relationship of ethics to politics. Political advisors before Machiavelli told a prince to be pure and just. Machiavelli, whom some call a realist, provided leaders with a practical guide on how to fulfill their drive for power. The Christian tone of universality gave way to *amorality—neither moral nor immoral, simply not to be judged by the criteria of morality.* Machiavelli created state morality and in this sense the rationale of the *nation-state—a political entity bound by defined borders and usually having a common language, customs, traditions, and experiences.*

The purpose of this essay is to examine the relationship between these nation-states. In examining how the nation-states interact, I will develop the impact of nationalism on these associations. Since this is a book on American government, the general discussion of international politics will center around the United States' foreign affairs. Having a preoccupation with unicorns, I will briefly examine international movements for universal peace. I will give special attention to those scholars who believe we are in a transition period from nationalism to internationalism.

Nation-states have certain goals when they engage in *foreign affairs—those matters pertaining to the policy of one country in its relations with other countries.* The prime goal, to which the nation-state will sacrifice all others if necessary, is the security of its political community. This translates to the preservation of the nation's sovereignty in an atmosphere relatively free of any fear for its survival.

Countries also have this irresistible impulse—need—to expand their territory, a manifest destiny. If it is not territory they covet, then it is a desire to spread their religion or *ideology—an integrated system of ideas that provides people with rationalizations for a way of life, guides for evaluating right and wrong in public affairs, and impulses to action.* Least of the national cravings is the expansion of its trade. All nations choose between their goals, techniques, and capabilities to create a *foreign policy—the nation's general and specific goals in international politics.*

Actually, international politics is the only true anarchistic political system. Philosophical *anarchy—means the absence of government.* And, despite the United Nations or the International Court of Justice, there is no world legislature and no executive or judicial system that creates or enforces binding laws.

Philosophical anarchy holds that governments are unnecessary because people will function altruistically—unselfishly. Anarchy, as it works in our interna-

Can humans redirect their aggression to productive recreational activities?

tional system, is based on the selfish needs of nations. Each state accepts international law because it benefits that state's existence.

A nation can also violate international law with little fear of punishment. In 1980 and 1981, Iran permitted terrorists to occupy the American Embassy and to hold hostages for 444 days.

With the demise of the Soviet Union, a bit of trepidation exists among the outlaw nations. Who will they get support from? In 1991, the United States and its allies, with the United Nations' sanction, pushed Iraq from Kuwait in 100 hours. A world order may be blooming. Or, anarchy may continue to prevail with the United States acting only on its own selfish interests as some feel it did with its invasion of Iraq in 2003.

International politics differ significantly from domestic politics. Relations between nation-states tend easily to conflict because of the lack of a formal, legal or political framework. All politics involve conflict, but nations moderate domestic politics by some common interests. In nation-states people see themselves as members of a political community. Individuals in a political community differ in power and values. They are perpetually struggling over "who gets what, when, and how."

A government cannot satisfy all groups equally. Domestic politics can lead to resolutions because people have common interests. When a nation-state fails to resolve a domestic issue, the outcome is seldom violent.

On the international scene, no authoritative power exists to determine "who gets what, when, and how." Each nation must compete with other nations. Nation must confront nation to convince the other to act as it wishes. Success depends upon how well a nation succeeds in influencing world policy in a world without policy.

Stakes are high for the losers in the *international arena*, as national servitude or the extinction of the country may result. Since national survival is the prime goal, actions to this end can be ruthless.

In a world where people's identities have become tied to the nation, they are willing to accept actions externally that they would regard as abominable if carried out within their own nation. Lying, espionage, subversion, and massive violence have become the survival weapons of nationalism.

Nationalism is a modern phenomena. Before the American Revolution, nationalism failed to arouse deep emotions. What is nationalism? Hans Kohn, a prolific writer on the subject, in his *Nationalism: Its Meaning and History* (Princeton, N.J.: D. Van Nostrand Co., 1965) defines **nationalism**—as *"a state of mind in which the supreme loyalty of the individual is felt to be due the nation-state."*

Conceptually, nationalism embodies the masses of individuals in an area. Some people professed sentiments akin to nationalism before the eighteenth century. The difference in pre-eighteenth-century sentiments was that the masses never felt their life dependent upon the existence of the nation-state.

Today, the basic loyalty of the individual is to the nation. In the past it had been to a church, race or economic class. To get a better understanding of the component parts of nationalism, I would recommend Boyd C. Shafer's *Nationalism: Myth and Reality* (New York: Harcourt, Brace and World, Inc., 1955).

For this essay, however, simply understand that nationalism is a deep emotional commitment to the existence of a political community that believes it shares common bonds. Comprehending the principle of nationalism will better enable you to penetrate the complexity of America's position in the modern state system.

Welcome to the Third World.

Most history books study nationalism as a phenomena of the nineteenth and early twentieth centuries. However, most of the nations in the world today received their independence after World War II. Over 190 countries are members of the United Nations. In a visit to the U.S. Post Office, recently, I noticed a chart of a little over 200 nations.

Most of the polities that joined the United Nations did so to advance their own principles and try influencing "who gets what, when, and how" in a world of scarce resources. The first principle of every member of the United Nations is to defend their **nation's sovereignty**—*the ability of a nation to create and enforce their own laws and only voluntarily accept any external limitations.*

Right after World War II, with only 50 nations, the United States found it a bit easier to convince most other sovereign states that our view of the

"Fight CommUNism; "Let's Win in Vietnam"; "One Nation Under God."

world had some merit. America's posture in world affairs had reached its peak. Our making the world safe for democracy seemed to have been fulfilled. Even in Vietnam the devout Marxist Ho Chi Minh, in declaring his nation's independence from France in 1946, presented his people with a constitution. He took his constitution almost verbatim from our Declaration of Independence and Constitution.

After the communist take over of China in 1949 we began to fear a threat to the free world from the East. The newly emerging nations soon refused to buy our vision of the world situation. Even our allies began to question the unfair distribution of the earth's resources—"the who gets what, when, and how."

Although estimates vary, economists believe that Americans, who constitute about six percent of the world's population, use fifty-five percent of the world's resources. While most of us enjoy a decent standard of living as we bitch about deficit spending, ghetto unemployment, over-taxation, and crime, fifty percent of the world's population is suffering from malnutrition and eighty percent live in substandard housing.

Is it any wonder that we feel threatened? Other nations demand their fair share. They ignore our insistence that they continue to accept our democratic mission? They only want to maintain their sovereignty and get a piece of the pie.

Until the recent demise of the Soviet Union and its satellite nations in Eastern Europe, we viewed the world in **East-West terms**—*the concept that the basic struggle in the world is between the freedom-loving nations of the West and the communist tyranny of the East.*

Perhaps now we will better understand the viewpoint of the developing nations. They have always felt that the battle was in **North-South terms**—*the concept that the basic struggle in the world is between the have and have not nations; the have nations represented by the former colonial powers and their ally the United States.*

The United States, in its drive to maintain its world preeminence, has traditionally allied itself with Western Europe. Like any nation, the U.S. governs the game of power politics by our permanent interests—we are eurocentric. Up until 1991, we interpreted our agenda to be with any country that sided with us against the "monolithic communist menace."

American presidents often advocated human rights policies and support for democracy. We allied ourselves, however, with dictators and tyrants in the name of freedom. This hypocrisy became evident to the **Third World Nations**—*nations with developing economies which have usually asserted their political neutrality in the capitalist-communist competition.* America's selective enforcement of human rights policies depended upon our vital interests. This usually boiled down to how we viewed the Third World nations' positions in the East-West conflict.

Historically, America has faced what Seyom Brown calls, "The Trilemma of U.S. Foreign Policy," *(AEI Foreign Policy and Defense Review,* Vol. 2, No. 5, 1980). Different presidential administrations have advanced a foreign policy that would fit into one of Brown's three categories.

President Ronald Reagan (1981–1989) believed in **Realpolitik**—*practical politics: a euphemism for amoral politics that work for the advantage of the nation-state.* Brown describes this view in his first trilemma.

In simple terms, the idea of Realpolitik was to support friendly regimes—those that were anti-communist. We were to enable them to secure themselves against external and internal Marxist threats.

The United States would look to a country's international alignment in the East-West conflict to determine whether to send aid to that nation. The ideology of the state was not at issue. Realpolitik inclined American's foreign policy toward rightist governments, as we suspected leftist governments of leaning toward the Soviet Union. We also believed that leftist nations must by definition be hostile to our capitalist economic system.

President Reagan's foreign policy advisors, therefore, used doublespeak to rationalize our support for select third-world countries. They found it fashionable to distinguish between authoritarian and totalitarian regimes. They argued that we could provide aid to authoritarian regimes, but not to totalitarian countries. Any country accepting aid from a communist nation they called totalitarian. Nations like the Republic of South Africa, despite its racist ideology, they called authoritarian.

In Essay II, I defined **totalitarian governments**—*where the state has total control of the institutions of the society and maintains command with a political ideology.* **Authoritarian governments**—*are governments that demand unquestioning obedience to the authority while limiting, if not eliminating, freedom of judgment and action.*

If totalitarian and authoritarian sound very similar to you, do not feel alone. The only distinction I see is that a totalitarian regime demands adherence to an ideology, while an authoritarian regime requires unquestioned obedience to the individual or group in power.

"Sister" Boom Boom protests President Reagan's aid to Nicaraguan Contras.
(Photo courtesy of Tom O'Neill)

President Reagan and his foreign policy advisors found authoritarianism to be a mild evil while they saw totalitarianism as a virulent evil. They held that the United States should be tolerant of "merely" authoritarian governments and resolutely opposed to totalitarian regimes. They argued that authoritarian regimes could evolve into democratic governments, whereas war was necessary to overturn a totalitarian system. Their policy was convenient, for those governments they classified as totalitarian they felt opposed our position in world politics. Those they listed as authoritarian they viewed as allies.

Advocates of this semantic debate took their lead from Hannah Arendt's classic study, *The Origins of Totalitarianism* (1951). She argued that people living in an authoritarian regime can live relatively free from fear. A despot may create laws according to his/her whims, but an individual can survive by obeying these impulses.

Totalitarianism, she wrote, created a rule of "consistent arbitrariness." No distinction could be made between the friends or enemies of the system. Both are subject to universal terror.

Hannah Arendt's original study shed light on the atrocious practices of fascism and communism. However, I believe that excusing any atrocity committed by a so-called friendly regime termed authoritarian avoided the issue and detached words from reality—murder is murder whoever commits the crime.

Hannah Arendt's view that totalitarianism was irreversible and that no totalitarian regime could ever transform itself without external force may become nothing but a footnote to the history of the twentieth century. In 1991, the Eastern European communist nations along with Russia transformed themselves without external force from totalitarian to democratic or authoritarian regimes.

As I identified in Essay IV, the Fractal Era, the Visual Media Age, permits individual access to information and, therefore, power. Dictators can no longer control people's wants and their minds.

We have lived through the dismantling of the Soviet Empire. The Republic of South Africa has gone through a transformation. *Apartheid*—*state ordered racial segregation*—is a thing of the past. Nor would it surprise me that the vestiges of Marxism found in Cuba and China will soon be relegated to a history of the second half of the twentieth century. In February 1998 Fidel Castro, Cuba's communist leader at the time, invited the Pope to visit. The Pope did. I personally feel that Hong Kong, which rejoined the People's Republic of China on July 1, 1997, has planted the seeds for the end of communism in that nation.

Realpolitik will continue, however. Modern nations protecting their survival will justify their actions through euphemisms.

For the United States, the Cold War's end has brought an enemy gap. John Updike's aging Everyman hero laments this closure of an era in *Rabbit at Rest* (1990): "I miss it, the Cold War. It gave you a reason to get up in the morning."

A new reason to get up in the morning is emerging. Nations often need external threats to unify their people. We now tune in the television to learn about some Japanese politico's most recent obnoxious remark about Americans, or how the Japanese are ripping us off. Then there are those crazy Muslim fundamentalist terrorists. And, of course, we must wake and go to bed with the daily media alarm of the threat directed to modern civilization from the terrorists of al-Qaeda and their fellow-travelers. Islamist terrorists do not represent a specific nation or regime. They desire to create a world Islamic government that they will claim is the true unicorn. If their concept of purity prevails they will in fact establish a totalitarian eagle—various nations and people who will be oppressed by their wings. Their ideology will be their brand of Islam and they will demand total adherence or death.

We must have an enemy—real or imagined. That is Realpolitik!

The danger, as Seyom Brown noted, of Realpolitik as the motivating force in foreign policy is that yesterday's friend might be tomorrow's enemy. The past isn't what it used to be.

President Jimmy Carter (1977–1981) advocated a human rights policy. This would fit Brown's second trilemma. The second trilemma's focus is on the United States as the champion of liberty and equality. In a world without the Soviet Union, following the second trilemma should endear us to Third World nations. We would identify with our revolutionary past now that the Marxist revolutions appear to have failed. Instead of seeing us as an ally of the former colonial powers, the Southern nations would, as right after World War II, follow our lead.

Proponents of the second trilemma believe that providing hope and aid to the progressive democratic forces will enable the United States to become the patron of the reformers and revolutionaries of the Third World.

President Carter's human rights policy failed due to inconsistency and maybe a bit of incompetence. However, I feel that we should return to a foreign policy that promotes liberty and equality—human rights.

Seyom Brown, on the contrary, believes the United States must follow his third trilemma. He holds we must remain neutral towards rivals for power. He feels we can provide support and aid for projects but not for personalities and parties.

The United States, according to Brown, should object to policies that would harm our interests or values. He believes in using *linkage*—*tying our monetary aid to political concessions.*

Despite his willingness to accept linkage, Brown argues for non-intervention in the affairs of other nations. He recognizes the inherent danger in his stance— the temptation of a major adversary to intervene. Brown believes this unlikely. He feels our adversaries would not want to risk provoking us.

With the demise of our major adversary, the Soviet Union, a quadlemma appears to have emerged. The new foreign policy advocated by the Pentagon is to prevent the emergence of any rival. The *New York Times* revealed, in early March 1992, the existence of a 46 page Defense Department document which advocates the U.S. preventing any new superpower from emerging.

In the post–Cold War era, the American mission, according to this broad new policy statement, will be "convincing potential competitors that they need not aspire to a greater role or pursue a more aggressive posture to protect their vital interests." The document made a case "for a world dominated by one super power whose position can be perpetuated by constructive behavior and sufficient military might to deter any nation or group of nations from challenging American primacy."

I believe that Brown echoes the direction of American foreign policy. The United States State Department and Brown still view the world as lions. They fail to understand the new eagle masquerading as a unicorn. Al Qaeda is an organization composed of a myriad of nationalities wanting to restore the eighth century Islamic world.

As with Brown's trilemmas, this new foreign policy direction rejects collective internationalism—an active United Nations that could mediate disputes and police outbreaks of violence.

Brown advocated "the integration of Germany and Japan into a U.S.-led system of collective security and the creation of a democratic zone of peace." More specifically, the strategic goal of the U.S. must be to check nuclear proliferation by removing any temptation Japan and Germany might have to acquire nuclear weapons. The document expressed the fear that if Japan and Germany developed a nuclear arsenal, it would start them down the road to global competition with the United States. The possibility would arise that in a crisis over national interests, they would become a military rival. Of course, in recent years we are more concerned about the nuclear capabilities of North Korea and Iran and the awakening giant, China.

I believe the United States must avoid becoming a victim of *hubris*—*the Ancient Greek concept of excessive pride.* We must avoid the belief that our system and our leading a "New World Order" will be best for everyone. We must create a world *detente*—*a maximizing of cooperation, originally used to refer to the relaxation of strained relations between the Union of Soviet Socialist Republics and the United States.*

World War II Memorial

No matter which foreign policy stance the United States takes, I believe we must always remember the adage that "war is too important to leave to generals." This is why in all nations that are not military dictatorships, ***national security**—is determined by civilian leaders analyzing both foreign policy and defense policy.* To paraphrase the above adage, it should also be said that "defense is too important to leave to generals."

The framers of the United States Constitution insisted on safeguards against military control of our foreign affairs by making the President Commander-in-Chief of the armed forces. Certainly, we must expect military leaders, the Pentagon bosses, to push their cause.

Shakespeare wrote in Henry V: "In case of defense, 'tis best to weight the enemy more might than he seems." A civilian commander, the President of the United States, must balance the exaggerated claims and demands of the generals against the real capabilities of the enemy. Both the President and Congress must decide how to judge another nation's true military capacity.

Some political scientists and students of military affairs have applied game theory to international politics. They feed computers with data in elaborate mathematical scenarios to develop model conflict situations. Rather than get into the complexity of this approach, let me simply identify the type of capability components that these military affairs experts use for analyzing the potential power of a competing state.

The ingredients usually studied include such elements as geography (geographic opportunity—location, natural resources, and even the size and shape of a country), population (productive vs. unproductive—age brackets, male-female ratios, education levels, distribution), national self-image (public sup-

A world apart!

port and cohesion), industrial capacity, military preparedness, cost-tolerance (willingness to suffer, as expressed in the Mexican Revolutionary General Emiliano Zapata's famous maxim: "It is better to die on your feet than to live on your knees.") and the personality of policy-makers.

The United States, like most nations today, functions under Julius Caesar's advice set forth 2,000 years ago: "If you want peace, prepare for war." Contemporary history preoccupies its existence with war.

The causes of war have always intrigued theorists. Marxists present one reason—capitalism. According to their argument, domestic markets cannot absorb the surplus produced under the capitalist system. So, entrepreneurs who own the governments direct them to embark on the conquest of other nations. Therefore, international wars occur when various capitalist-imperialist states try to conquer the same region. Marxists argue that they do not cause war, but they are forced into them for liberation or self-defense. Back to semantics—doublespeak!

Non-Marxist writers are more eclectic. Steven J. Rosen and Walter S. Jones in their *The Logic of International Relations* (Cambridge, Mass.: Winthrop Publishers, Inc., 1980, pp. 307–339) develop twelve causes of war. I will try and paraphrase their list in understandable terms: unfavorable distribution of power, nationalism, survival of the fittest theories, failures in communications, arms races, external aggression to promote internal cohesion, want of power, promotion of economic or scientific advancement, vested economic interests with an ideology of conflict, unequal distribution of resources, genetic reasons, a lack of a device to resolve conflict.

John G. Stoessinger, in his *Might of Nations: World Politics in Our Time* (New York: Random House, 7th edition, 1982, pp. 224–232), rejects most of these reasons and places the blame on a single factor—leaders, their perceptions, or better said, their misperception of another's power or by accident. He holds that war occurs because of one nation's misperception of another's power or by accident. He concludes his chapter on a note of hope, viewing "a slow dawning of compassion and of global consciousness over humanity's bleak skies in our generation."

Perhaps Stoessinger's optimism will prove correct and all we will face are what, for lack of a better term, can be called ***brush fire wars***—*conflicts that erupt suddenly, but end rapidly before a full scale war occurs.* The words of the eighteenth-century

Nuclear madness rally.

English poet William Cowper come to mind: "War lays a burden on the reeling state and peace does nothing to relieve the weight."

The cost of preparing for peace, or war if you prefer, is enormous. Defense contractors like the preparation better than war itself. George E. Berkeley in a *New Republic* article (December 20–27, 1969, p. 16) called "The Myth of War Profiteering," provided some impressive data. He argued that Vietnam, like other wars, could not be blamed on the munitions manufacturers.

George Berkeley provided data to support his position that the war industry has done better financially in times of peace. The United States government paid cost overruns in peace time and denied them during war. Of course, Berkeley's data depends on the supposition that defense contractors always act rationally.

The cost of peacefare takes a huge portion out of the gross world product. Israel's defense budget eats up 18% of its gross national product. During the height of the Soviet military establishment, experts estimated that the defense budget took 25% of that nation's gross national product. The United States spends proportionally less. About 6% of our gross national product goes to defense.

The question for the future is how to balance military and non-military spending. The United States must respond to economic conditions and free up financial resources that have been going into the arms race to benefit human needs.

One of the capability components for success in conflict I mentioned earlier was the support of the people for their homeland. If the government places a heavy tax burden on citizens who question its validity, and if people feel they are in colloquial terms "being ripped off," there will be little societal support for any conflict.

Worse, if people believe their survival threatened more by their own government because of the lack of interest in domestic programs, social disorientation and voter discontent could result. It is for this reason, some senators argue, that the question should not be "How much should be spent for defense?" Instead, they say, we should ask: "How should we be spending the allocations for defense?" Perhaps, in an era of intense competition for resources, the answers to the latter question is far more valuable.

A difficulty of a democratic system like ours is who is to decide the answer to such questions. Democracy places many restraints on national security decisions. Citizens debate strategic and technical assumptions in the open marketplace of ideas.

A wide range of people enlist in political battles over these issues. Each group, with its own lobbyist, argues its assumptions about the size of the Pentagon's budget or what they feel should be emphasized in domestic spending.

Neither our President nor the State Department has an unrestrained monopoly on policy decisions. They make judgments within the very real limits imposed by public opinion. In a democracy, leaders cannot make foreign policy decisions in isolation. They must listen to the demands of the citizenry.

The United States Constitution creates a federal government monopoly over the conduct of foreign affairs. The Constitution denies states the power to negotiate treaties, form alliances, support troops or engage in war.

In practice, foreign policy decisions are in the hands of the President, the State Department headed by the Secretary of State, the members of the National Security Council, the Joint Chiefs of Staff, the Department of Defense, and the Senate Foreign Relations Committee. However, the public is the undeniable force behind many of the national security issues.

U.S. Defense Policy: Weapons, Strategy and Commitments (1980, 2nd edition, p. 1) identified how "base closings and weapons production schedules are linked to primary election timetables and congressional committee memberships."

R. Erie Weise and Alfred de Grazia, in the *Eight Branches: American Government Today* (Columbus, Ohio: Collegiate Publishing, Inc., 1975, p. 369) stated: "Since many people cast their votes according to their mood about world affairs, the leaders adjust their foreign goals to the limits set by this mood."

Karl A. Lamb in his *The People Maybe* (Belmont, CA: Duxbury Press, 1971, p. 270) showed how "the party in power has been punished for the results of its foreign policies, whether those results could have been avoided or not."

A new perception of America's role in the post–Cold War era scares some students of public opinion and foreign policy. They believe that on the home front, many people fail to view the United States through the "arrogance of power," a concept coined in the late sixties by J.W. Fulbright, Senate Foreign Relations Committee Chair. Demonstrators against the Vietnam War protested this "arrogance of power."

Many Americans supported President George H. W. Bush's call for a "New World Order" directed by the United States. They looked forward to the Americanization of the globe. They held that our McWorld image is far superior to that of our chief economic rivals, Japan and the European Community.

Luckily, the American citizenry does not speak in one voice. We are a nation of religious, cultural, and racial diversity. All of these groups bring pressure to bear on Washington to advance their own interests or perceptions. For example, large numbers of Jews exhorted Washington foreign policymakers to support the right of Soviet Jews to emigrate. African-Americans demanded that the United States ban all trade to the Republic of South Africa until they ended *apartheid— racial segregation.* Irish-Americans wanted Great Britain to exit North Ireland.

Many people of Latin-American descent protested the U.S. aid to Great Britain in her conflict with Argentina over the Falkland/Malvina Islands (1982). They received the backing of Jean Kirkpatrick, then ambassador to the United Nations, a recognized authority on Latin-American affairs. However, the Reagan administration continued its support for our Anglo-Saxon mother.

Demonstrators against the Vietnam War.

If there seems to be confusion, especially in recent years, in America's foreign policy, you can often blame it on the pluralism of our society and the diversity of interests.

Yes, I recognize that our leadership selectively hears public opinion. And, this particular listening worries me. It leads me back to John G. Stoessinger's comment about the role of the policy-maker's misperception in causing a war. Can the "dawning of compassion and of global consciousness over humanity's bleak skies" ever break through the thick clouds of the nation-states?

Benjamin R. Barber, writing in the March, 1992 edition of *The Atlantic* ("Jihad Vs. McWorld," pp. 53–65), fears the retribalization of humankind. He warns that international institutions that reflect globalization "often appear as ineffective reactors to the world's real actors: national states and, to an even greater degree, subnational factions in permanent rebellion against uniformity and integration."

The Soviet Union split into fifteen separate nations. Yugoslavia is no more and tribalism reigns in the Balkans.

Benjamin Barber, in his discussion of what he calls "the Lebanonization of the World," says:

> The headlines feature these players regularly: they are cultures, not countries; parts, not wholes; sects, not religions; rebellious factions and dissenting minorities at war not just with globalism but with the traditional nation-state. Kurds, Basques, Puerto Ricans, Ossetians, East Timoreans, Quebecois, the Catholics of Northern Ireland,

Anti-Israel demonstration at Ohlone College.

> Abkhasians, Kurile Island Japanese, the Zulus of Inkatha, Cataloni-
> ans, Tamils, and of course, Palestinians—people without countries,
> inhabiting nations not their own, seeking smaller worlds within bor-
> ders that will seal them off from modernity.

Benjamin Barber feels "international relations have sometimes taken on the aspect of gang war—cultural turf battles featuring tribal factions that were supposed to be sublimated as integral parts of large national, economic, postcolonial, and constitutional entities."

Will we return to the tribal state? Will hyperdisintegration of the former Soviet Union continue? Will the world become a place of nano-nations—miniature entities—with kittens that roar like lions?

Nation-states, even nano-nations, must confront a more terrifying reality at the turn of the twenty-first century—Third Wave Terrorism. The futurist Alvin Toffler predicted a "third wave" replacing the agricultural "first wave" and the industrial "second wave." The "third wave" provides a decentralized information processing society with a broad dispersion of power and communications. As the state lost control of the media in this devolution process, it is now losing its monopoly over lethal knowledge. Nathan Gardels, editor of *New Perspectives Quarterly* (Summer, 1995) writes: "No sooner were non-proliferation policies fairly succeeding in stemming the spread of nuclear, chemical and biological weapons to rogue *states* than such weapons have begun falling into the hands of rogue *groups* beyond the reach of the deterrence strategies, sanctions and treaties of the nation-state era."

Today the Internet serves as a conduit for unemployed post–Cold War scientists who provide a large pool of tappable nuclear, chemical and biological knowledge. Hans Magnus Enzensberger has called this new peculiar form of nihilistic violence that has arisen from the post-modem fragmentation of societies "molecular civil war." (*NPQ*)

Nathan Gardels fears that the likes of the Aum Supreme Truth sect (gas attack in Tokyo subway), or the fanatic right-wing Muslims of al-Qaeda or a Unabomber can "drive us sooner rather than later toward a new and forbidding social model: a police state on the streets with freedom confined to virtual reality." I would argue that the lions (nation-states) and the eagles (the empires) must give up their selfish tribalism to the unicorn (a world government). A political effort can then, and only then, be made to integrate the pariahs and provide inclusion rather than exclusion, thereby eliminating the most dangerous sources of terrorism.

Harold J. Laski, the renowned British political scientist, wrote in the 1920's: "If men are to live in the great society, they must learn the habits of cooperative intercourse. They must learn to think of their platoon as a part of the great regiment of mankind." (*A Grammar of Politics,* London: George Allen and Unwin, Ltd., 5th edition, 1967, first published in 1925, p. 66).

Professor Laski argued emphatically that the "territorial character of the sovereign nation-state enables a small section of its members to utilize its power for their own ends, even against the interests of their fellow-citizens. Against such a danger, international government represents the most solid protection we have." (p. 234).

Professor Laski placed his hope for global peace in the League of Nations. As most of you know, World War II occurred despite the League.

After World War II, the most ambitious experiment to create world order came into being—the United Nations. Article I of the United Nation's charter sets forth the purposes of the organization:

> Section 1. To maintain internal peace and security. . . .
>
> Section 2. To develop friendly relations among nations based on respect for the principle of equal rights and self-determination of peoples, and to take other appropriate measures to strengthen universal peace;
>
> Section 3. To achieve international cooperation in solving international problems of an economic, social, cultural, or humanitarian character, and in promoting and encouraging respect for human rights and for fundamental freedoms for all without distinction as to race, sex, language, or religion, and
>
> Section 4. To be a center for harmonizing the actions of nations in the attainment of these common ends.

To achieve its purpose, the Charter established six permanent organs: The General Assembly (legislative), The Security Council (peace-keeping), The International Court of Justice (judicial), The Trusteeship Council, The Economic and Social Council, and the Secretariat (executive). I will not detail the functions of these UN organs.

As far as the success in meeting its stated purposes under Article I, I do not feel the United Nations has been able to maintain international peace and security. In the past, the inability of the UN to maintain peace and security was due to the East-West conflict. In the present, the failure to maintain world peace is due to the continued selfish direction of the Security Council members.

As I wrote on the margins of the textbook I used in a graduate course in International Organizations, the United Nations' success in meeting its purpose in being "a center for harmonizing the actions of nations" would depend upon the willingness of the sovereign states to move towards this goal. The textbook I used in the course was Inis L. Claude, Jr.'s *Swords Into Plowshares*, (New York: Random House, 1961). I have yet to read a textbook that provided me with more insight into international relations.

Neither the United States, nor the former Soviet Union had been willing to use the United Nations as a true peace-keeping forum when it opposed their interests. They preferred to work out their differences between their foreign ministers or at summit meetings. The United Nations, however, did obtain some measure of success in eliminating trusteeships and providing for human, economic, and social needs.

The world federalist movement is floundering. International cooperation in many other areas, however, is blooming. *The Yearbook of International Organizations* (Brussels: Union of International Associations) in 1978 reported that non-government international organizations grew between 1909 and 1976 from 176 to 2381. While the number of international organizations remained fairly stable during the nineteenth century, they have doubled in number in the last twenty years. The *Yearbook* listed many categories of international organizations such as education, arts, health and medicine, social welfare, trade unions, humanistic studies, religion, and sports and recreation.

I once had the honor of being an official at one of the new international sporting organizations—The World Games. The World Games held its first competition in Santa Clara, California, in 1981. These games were designed to permit international competition in non-Olympic sports between Olympic games.

At the World Games, national teams competed. They did so under the banner of their home federation and the organizers banned national flags. They hoped that, lacking displays of nationalism, they could create a true international competition. They felt if they prohibited the flying of national flags, the playing of national anthems and an unofficial accounting of national medals, they would end much of the discontent that has plagued the Olympics.

I use the World Games as just one example of transnational movements that some people hold will ultimately reduce world tension. Whether such schemes are utopian and will falter depends once again on the nation-state and its perceptions. Some observers are arguing that we are in a transitional era. They see nationalism waning and believe people will owe their loyalty to some new system that has not yet emerged. Their hope is that it will be an international order that can provide tranquility and freedom.

Technology and global economics has introduced an integrated world. Every person on earth has the potential, due to the vast interactive communications and information network, to be interactive with every other person. The Internet is truly a world superhighway.

The spread of American popular culture seems to have brought on the first stage of this emerging global society. A headline in my local newspaper (*The Argus*, March 12, 1992, p. 1) for an Associated Press story read: "Madonna, Batman and blue jeans won war." The idea some scholars advanced at a recent conference was "that American popular culture—from Madonna to the Super Bowl, from Stephen King to the Reader's Digest—helped conquer communism and now, for better or worse, is overrunning the world."

Conservative scholar Irving Kristol, while deploring the spread of American culture, saw the positive traits to this new Americanization of the world: "American popular music, like American popular culture generally, has a wonderfully corrosive effect on all totalitarian and strongly authoritarian regimes. . . . The spirit of this culture is profoundly individualist, almost anarchic in fact, and crosses the grain of all collectivist societies."

Evidence for the pervasiveness of American pop culture abounded as scholars ticked off the facts: "Pretty Woman," the 1990 hit film in the U.S., was the No. 1 film in five European countries; U.S. television accounts for almost half of the 50 highest rated shows in Italy and Spain; CNN is seen in 122 countries; Mary Higgins Clark, Danielle Steel and Stephen King recently made the best-seller list in France; 300 million Chinese watched the Super Bowl on television; 49ers caps are fashionable in Europe; and American fast food places are shooting up in almost every part of the world.

American popular culture is intermingling with an emerging international youth culture. A new international lifestyle reigns in Tokyo, Madrid and San Francisco as we enthusiastically swap food, music and fashion. John Naisbitt and Patricia Aburdene in their *Megatrends 2000* comment on this new global lifestyle seeded with American popular culture: "It is consumer-driven: drinking cappuccino and Perrier; furnishing the apartment with IKEA; eating sushi; dressing in the United Colors of Bennetton; listening to U.S.-British rock while driving the Hyundai over to McDonald's."

Benjamin R. Barber, whose view on the danger of the Lebanonization of the world I discussed earlier, recognizes this globalization of lifestyles and views it more positively. He identifies four imperatives that make up the dynamics of a global lifestyle, "a market imperative, a resource imperative, an information-technology imperative, and an ecological imperative." He continues: "By shrinking the world and diminishing the salience of national borders, these imperatives have in combination achieved a considerable victory over factiousness and particularism, and not least of all over their most virulent traditional form—nationalism."

Benjamin R. Barber echoes John Naisbitt and Patricia Aburdene in *Megatrends 2000* when he argues "the pursuit of science and technology asks for, or even compels, open societies." We are seeing a global acceptance of the principles of human rights.

Time magazine (January 6, 1992, p. 26) found recent developments to be "prime evidence for the evolution of McLuhan's borderless world." *Time* continued: "As corporations become multinational and free trade transcends tariffs, as Europe develops a single currency and other regions build spheres of economic cooperation, as pop culture and air travel and migration and, yes, television make the world psychologically smaller, these theorists contend that the concept of nationalism recedes."

In the last twenty years, many writers have argued that the next stage of world development will be under the scrutiny of multinational corporations (MNC's) and not directed from nation-states. C.P. Kindleberger, in his book *American Business Abroad* (New Haven: Yale University Press, 1969, p. 207), saw the nation-state as "just about through as an economic unit." A two and one-half day conference on multinational enterprise in 1969 produced the first major work on the subject, a series of papers and commentaries edited by John H. Dunning (*The Multinational Enterprise*, New York: Praeger Publishers, 1971).

Global Reach by Richard J. Barnet and Ronald Miller (1974) is perhaps the most thorough study on multinational corporations. The work describes multinational corporations as a transition from the nation-state to planetary enterprise.

The World Games: International cooperation.

Over the past years, the influential American Marxist publication, *The Monthly Review*, edited by Paul Sweezy, has built on Lenin's view that finance capital caused imperialism. Included in this modern analysis is the impact of multinational corporations on Third World countries.

The argument holds that the MNC's have created a new type of vicious exploitation. Sweezy and his fellow travelers ignore the data that show most of the MNC's investments take place in developed nations.

Definitions of multinational corporations vary. MNC's, by any definition, differ from the former ***international corporations***—*business centered in one nation with subsidiaries in other countries and usually involved in the same kind of enterprise.* I would say that ***multinational corporations***—*are businesses with interests and stockholders in many countries and whose boards of directors and managers come from all of the areas where the corporations do business: these businesses are involved in many different kinds of enterprise.*

Many large international corporations are also diversifying their holdings, but nationals of one country still own and operate them. Stockholders and managers in MNC's are from many countries.

In previous years, international corporations would be interested in, let us say, the dairy business and so they would have milk, butter and ice cream subsidiaries throughout the world. The multinational corporation, on the other hand, may own dairy interests along with drug companies, wineries, and transportation networks.

With MNC's, it is almost impossible to figure out who runs what, with the complicated interlocking of boards of directors. The system is as complicated as feudalism used to be when lords were vassals and vassals were lords and some claimed to be liege lords. Some MNC's are not even businesses in the true sense of the word, but holding companies who own majority or controlling stock in diverse corporations.

Most people in this country talk about American business. Multinationals, originally based in the United States, fail to see their allegiance to this country or any country. Names with American or U.S. in them are quietly disappearing from what we used to consider our prestigious firms. U.S. Rubber has become Uniroyal; American Metal Climax now calls itself Amax; and, even BankAmeri-card changed its name to Visa.

The multinational corporations can no longer owe loyalty to one country. They have no country which they will call home. *Global Reach* quoted a Union Carbide spokesperson as saying: "It is not proper for an international corpora-tion [read MNC] to put the welfare of any country in which it does business above that of any other" (my notation).

The April 19, 1973 *Wall Street Journal*, in an article entitled "Many Critics Charge Multinational Firms Create Money Crises," (pp. 1, 20) explained how so-called American firms speculated in various currencies. Lacking concern for the changes in the dollar, for example, the article identified how the MNC offsets its losses in one currency by purchasing another. Such dumping of the dollar weak-ened it further and contributed to the double devaluation of our currency dur-ing the Nixon presidency.

The U.S. Department of Commerce's extensive study in 1972 on MNC's said:

> The most significant impact of multinational enterprise is in the internationalization of production and in the incipient development of a world economy. In this process, the investment decisions and operations of companies are increasingly viewed in terms of world allocations of resources and of maximizing world welfare.
>
> The [*multinational corporation*] has become the most important vehicle for developing a world system based on a more rational allocation of resources than has been the case in the past. . . . What is called into question by this development—which is likely to continue—is the whole concept of the traditional nation-state with its politics, sociol-ogy and economics. (p. 16, my italics)

MNC's can transcend international boundaries. If a nation-state burdens the MNC with too much taxation or restrictions, that MNC simply goes to another nation and ships the product back. The same movement occurs if an MNC con-fronts a labor problem in one country—off they go to a place like Singapore which promises them five years of no labor problems, no taxation, and free land.

Nation-states have developed a fear that an MNC will leave and, therefore, often permit them free reign of operation. With the increased articulation of peo-ple for health, education and welfare benefits, the nation-state must increase the taxes on its people, rather than threaten the profits of the MNC (if they could even calculate the profits considering the size of today's MNC's and their diversity).

Heavily taxed populations receiving few benefits might lose their allegiance to the nation-state because of its inability to meet their demands. People might turn to the only power left with the resources to provide a domestic program—the multinational corporations.

A Global Village!

Citizens of the nation-state must also confront the reality of future clashes to preserve the scant resources of the nation. *Global Reach* said: "It is true of course, that the state can no longer provide a high level of security either . . . (as) territory, any territory, is indefensible in the nuclear age. Moreover, . . . the nation-state does not seem to be able to provide much security even within its own borders." (p. 95)

MNC's have developed their own security systems to protect their employees. Rather than call in the Marines as the old international corporations did, the MNC hires mercenaries. I heard one MNC soldier of fortune brag on television about his operations for Coca-Cola and how that company's executives were never threatened again. Some have asked if these same mercenaries that are under contract with the U.S. in places like Iraq really support the long range interests of the MNCs.

To protect their investments, the MNC's want the United States to provide a low military profile. MNC's are, in fact, developing their own foreign policy (see P.G. Block, "The Transnational Corporation and Private Foreign Policy," *Society*, January/February, 1974, pp. 44–49).

MNC managers talk about building an integrated global system incorporating the Commonwealth of Independent States and China into a "belt of capitalism." In a sense, the MNC's executives have become "peacemongers." They feel that empires or nation-states cannot run the world. They believe that for the first time in history, with the MNC's organization, technology, money, and even ideology, they can try to create an integrated world.

Orville L. Freeman and William Persen, writing for *The Futurist* (December, 1980) supported the contention that the MNC's are the most powerful force for peace today. The authors hold that the selfish interests of the nation-state and their restrictions are anathema to the multinational corporation.

The renowned sociologist Irving Louis Horowitz, in his "Capitalism, Communism and Multinationalism" (*Society*, January/February, 1974, pp. 32–43) foresaw all countries sharing the capitalist goals for material goods. He called for a study of a new economic model to understand the MNC's role in the global village, as capitalism and communism were outdated. Back in 1974 he predicted that the unending demand for consumer goods in the global market place would end the *cold war—the conflict (ideological, political, and economic) between East and West that brought clashes in every fashion short of all out war.*

And what do I feel? The idyllic, utopian, peaceful world that the advocates of the global shopping center portray disturbs me. I remember the movie "Rollerball." A world of MNC's providing a game designed to keep the populous happy. A future world similar to the old Roman bread and circuses where the emperors pacified the people with free food and entertained them with gladiator fights. In the film, the MNC's demanded the submergence of the individual within the anonymity of the corporate personality.

Benjamin R. Barber ("Jihad Vs. McWorld," *The Atlantic*, March, 1992, p. 64) expresses my fear:

> For McWorld [*read MNC's*], it is the antipolitics of globalism: bureaucratic, technocratic, and metrocratic, focused . . . on the administration of things—with people, however, among the chief things to be administered. In its political-economic imperatives McWorld has been guided by laissez-faire market principles that privilege efficiency, productivity, and beneficence at the expense of civic liberty and self-government. (my italics)

As a believer in individuality and an advocate of democracy, it scares me to read that the Council of the Americas suggested as a good slogan for its corporate members: "consumer democracy is more important than political democracy." People voting with their pocketbook or with their stock proxies fall short of my concept of democracy.

Individuals must be able to determine their preferences, signify their preferences and have their preferences weighted equally in the conduct of government. I cannot see where the MNC intends to permit this option. I also fail to believe the glowing words from supporters who claim that it is in the best interest of maximizing profits for the MNC's to work together to bring peace to the world. "Tech Scam," where our government indicted representatives of Japanese firms for industrial theft, and "insider trading" where American investors went to prison, symbolize to me the real competitive nature of the corporate world.

I cannot forget the numerous apologists for capitalism, in the time before MNC's, who claimed it would end war. Joseph Schumpeter, who died in 1950, argued that capitalism was helping to build a just world legal order. The Austrian born Harvard professor held, in books like his *Imperialism and Social Classes* (N.Y.: Augustus M. Kelley, 1951), that capitalism's penetration of the Third World brought peace parties and a fundamental opposition to war and its trappings.

A Global Market Place!

Schumpeter believed imperialism caused war but was atavistic—a throw back to the past. Imperialism continued to exist due to a sociological and psychological hang-up. Within a short time, imperialism would fade away and capitalism would unite the globe. To date, imperialism has not ceased to exist and capitalism has not brought an end to war.

I am skeptical about MNC's bringing peace and purity to the world and I definitely prefer the unicorn of world federalism. My curiosity is peaked as to what the next step in world evolution will be. Marxist states are disintegrating; eagles (empires) are spawning lions (nation-states); and lions are producing litters of runts (nano-nations).

I am convinced we live in a transitional era. Nationalism, despite the tribalism we read about in the paper every day, is in transformation. People living during the hundreds of years it took for feudalism to change to the nation-state and the emergence of nationalism lacked awareness of the specific changes.

Any such evolution is slow and unpredictable. Well, maybe not unpredictable, but I have the feeling that the more one predicts something the greater the chance there is for something different to emerge. Sort of a quantum approach. Your observation can never tell you what actually was occurring because as soon as you observe, you change the direction of movement.

Perhaps multinational corporation societies are the world of the future. My optimism leads me to feel that the more writers who observe and predict this

Symbols of peace, love, and sharing.

MNC phenomenon, the greater the likelihood that it will never occur. A few words from *Global Reach* (p. 96) sum up my feelings toward the predictions of the multinational corporation world in a global village: "But of course, reality is less neat than college course catalogs."

This essay should have provided you with an overview of how the United States must function in a world of political anarchy. It should have become clear that American foreign policy, like that of any nation-state, is dependent on its own perception of itself and its determination to survive. International politics and international law only work when a nation-state determines it will accept the outcome as it works to its own best advantage.

The United States, I identified, similar to other democracies, faces a pluralistic society that places strains on foreign policy decisions. We have had a general mission to advance the cause of democracy which succeeded beyond our wildest hopes. We now feel the need to preserve our position and status in world affairs.

I explained that the United States viewed the world as an East-West conflict. Now, with the demise of the Soviet Union, we must examine the North-South conflict. How our foreign policy-makers respond depends upon their interpretation of the American mission.

In the last section of the essay, I examined the hopeful visions of those writers who believe we are in a transitional era from nationalism to another sovereign force. I felt unable to state with any certainty that it will be a global market place of multinational corporations. I expressed my trepidation toward this possible change. In the end I remained a world federalist, as idealistic and utopian as this might be.

Scholars often study the differences between humans and cultures. More emphasis on the similarities of Homo Sapiens as a species, I believe, would lead the world toward some resolution of conflict. East versus West, North versus

South, nation-state versus nation-state, fundamentalist Christian versus fundamentalist Muslim, fail to recognize that we are all human and the Earth is our common home.

Internationalism, be it an empire, the thousand years of God on Earth, the return of our extraterrestrial foreparents, a global marketplace, world federalism, or a system still not delineated, remains, from my perspective, the only salvation of humankind. Of the known systems, I prefer world federalism, where each nation-state gives up some selfish sovereignty to avoid the political anarchy of the present international relations which all too often turns to chaos.

I am not overly optimistic. I am aware that the task of creating a world government is formidable. Boyd Shafer in his book *Faces of Nationalism* (New York: Harcourt Brace Jovanovich, Inc., 1972, pp. 373–374) puts it succinctly:

Look in the mirror!

> If the history of nationalism contains meaning for the future, men will move beyond their present nationalism to internationalism only when this internationalism offers more security and hope than nationalism does at present. And if new international groups, whatever they are, are to become established, they will have to (1) penetrate the consciousness of individuals—at least those of elites, (2) encourage individuals to participate in the larger group's affairs—thus afford them a sense of belonging; and (3) enable individuals to relate their interests to those of the international community and thereby give them a sense of significance and identification. Otherwise, they will not be or feel secure or dare to hope.

My optimism remains rooted in the hope projected in the ancient Greek myth of Sisyphus. In a book by the same title, the existential philosopher, Albert Camus, years ago identified that Sisyphus reflected the true nature of humankind. Condemned by the gods for his refusal to die, Sisyphus had to push a boulder up a hill for eternity. As the boulder reached the peak it would roll back down and Sisyphus had to begin the endless task all over.

For centuries philosophers argued that Sisyphus exemplified the hopeless and meaningless conditions of human existence—getting nowhere. Camus set them straight. We create our own existence. That is the moral of the *Myth of Sisyphus—in Greek mythology Sisyphus had to roll a boulder up a hill for eternity. At first the myth seemed to symbolize the hopelessness of life, but today many see the myth as a reflection of humankind's everlasting hope and determination.* Humans never give up even against hopeless odds. Humans continue to strive for success even when every action looks meaningless. For without such optimism, such hope, such drive, then life truly becomes hopeless and meaningless. Who knows, maybe someday the gods will relent and Sisyphus' boulder will roll down the opposite side of the hill. In the meantime, it has not rolled back and crushed him.

My vision, the other side of the hill, is a democratic world federation where communities work together while maintaining their distinctive identities—maybe even a United Federation of Planets. Again it takes me back to the symbolism of the unicorn and the lion—internationalism versus nationalism. We must locate the unicorn and prevent its destruction by the teeth of the lion or its new born runts. The outcome cannot be, must not be, the one related in Edward Topsell's *History of Four-Footed Beasts* (London, 1607):

> He (a unicorn) is an enemy of Lions, wherefore as soon as ever a Lion seeth a Unicorn, he runneth to a tree for succor, that so when the Unicorn maketh force at him, he may not only avoid his horn but also destroy him; for the Unicorn in the swiftness of his course runneth against the tree, wherein his sharp horn sticketh fast. Then when the Lion seeth the Unicorn fastened by the horn, without all danger he falleth upon him and killeth him.

GLOSSARY

AMORALITY
Neither moral nor immoral; simply not to be judged by the criteria of morality.

ANARCHY
Means the absence of government.

APARTHEID
Racial segregation in the Republic of South Africa.

AUTHORITARIAN GOVERNMENTS
Demand unquestioning obedience to the authority while limiting, if not eliminating, freedom of judgment and action.

BRUSH FIRE WARS
Conflicts that erupt suddenly but end rapidly before a full scale war occurs.

COLD WAR
The conflict (ideological, political and economic) between East and West that brought clashes in every fashion short of war.

DETENTE
A maximizing of cooperation, originally used to refer to the relaxation of strained relations between the Union of Soviet Socialist Republics and the United States.

EAST-WEST TERMS
The concept that the basic struggle in the world was between the freedom-loving nations of the West and the communist tyranny of the East.

FOREIGN AFFAIRS
Those matters pertaining to the policy of one country in its relations with other countries.

FOREIGN POLICY
The nation's general and specific goals in international politics.

HUBRIS
The Ancient Greek concept of excessive pride.

IDEOLOGY
An integrated system of ideas that provides people with rationalizations for a way of life, guides for evaluating right and wrong in public affairs, and impulses to action.

INTERNATIONAL CORPORATION
Business centered in one nation with subsidiaries in other countries which are usually involved in the same kind of enterprise.

LINKAGE
Tying our monetary aid to political concessions.

MACHIAVELLI, NICCOLO
Authored *The Prince* (1513) in which he advocated political expediency above morality.

MULTINATIONAL CORPORATIONS
Are businesses with interests and stockholders in many countries and whose boards of directors and managers come from all the areas where the corporations do businesses; these businesses are involved in many different kinds of enterprises.

MYTH OF SISYPHUS
In Greek mythology Sisyphus had to roll a boulder up a hill for eternity.

NATIONALISM
Is a state of mind in which the supreme loyalty of the individual is felt to be due the nation-state.

NATIONAL SECURITY
Civilian leaders and military leaders analyzing both foreign and defense policy.

NATION'S SOVEREIGNTY
The ability of the nation to create and enforce its own laws and only voluntarily accept any external limitations.

NATION-STATE
A political entity bound by defined borders and usually having a common language, customs, traditions, and experience.

NORTH-SOUTH TERM
The concept that the basic struggle in the world is between the have and have not nations; the have nations represented by the former colonial powers and their ally, the United States.

REALPOLITIK
Practical politics: a euphemism for amoral politics that work to the advantage of the nation-state.

THIRD WORLD NATIONS
Nations whose economies are underdeveloped and usually asserted their political neutrality in the capitalist-communist competition.

TOTALITARIAN GOVERNMENTS
Where the state has total control of the institutions of the society and maintains command with a political ideology.

CHAPTER 9

Dream On, America!

Essay IX

On the evening news, a number of years ago, I listened to a Reagan Administration spokesperson defending an evacuation plan in case of a pending nuclear attack. Each target area would have a designated evacuation site less likely to be bombed. People would drive there in an orderly fashion and presumably watch the fireworks. Meanwhile, the President and his staff would be flying high in the Doomsday Plane. When asked about the realism of this program, the spokesperson expressed his firm belief in its effectiveness because, despite the impact of a nuclear war on other nations, Americans would be, as always, survivors. And, to my dismay, he insisted that perhaps ninety percent of us would persevere to rebuild our great culture, once again validating the American work ethic.

Americans have been survivors, in a way, and our work ethic built a great nation. In this respect I agree with the spokesperson from the Reagan Administration. I feel, however, that if a nuclear war occurred, even with one of the former Soviet Republics, with a major Third World power, or the Islamic extremists, it would be the end of life on this planet as we presently know and revere it.

My purpose in this essay is to examine the historical development of the American work ethic and describe its impact on politics. I also intend to show how the work ethic created a spiritualistic American Dream in our early history, which over the years evolved into a materialistic American Dream. I will examine how the spiritual and material values produced a people who survived and grew into a great nation based upon their belief in merited success; throughout most of America's history, the society could be called a **meritocracy**—a nation where people are rewarded and honored for their achievements and excellence.

I will discuss how America could become an **egalitocracy**—a nation where people receive awards and honors, not for their achievements or excellence, but because they are simply people; equality of condition rather than equality of opportunity. *I will argue that the new immigration from Asia and Eastern Europe of scientists and*

181

business people is resurrecting the old American Dream of merited success—an **Immigrant Work Ethic**—immigrants to the United States have traditionally worked hard to succeed and to partake of the American Dream. *Previously settled Americans are forced to compete for their fair share of the pie. Tragically, many Americans cannot or do not have the inclination to be retrained for an information processing society. The gap between the haves and the have nots seems to be growing, as exemplified by the hundreds of thousands of homeless Americans.*

I will attempt, finally, to relate these value changes to the present and future of the American political system, showing how in a meritocracy individuals exist within a political community and compromise on issues for the betterment of society, while in an egalitocracy, with its attempt to restrict individualism leads to the disintegration of a political community because of **factionalism**—a conflict within a country between individuals or groups producing dissension rather than the resolution of problems.

I must now put on my historian's cap and go back to October 31, 1517, to begin my development of the American Dream. No, I do not intend to discuss Halloween in that year, but to explain the significance of Martin Luther posting 95 theses on a church door in the city of Wittenberg, Saxony. This action led to what historians call the ***Protestant Reformation***—*when Christianity in Western Europe split into numerous groups and the Catholic Church was forced to coexist with other churches, especially the Lutheran, Calvinist, and Anglican.*

Martin Luther, upset by a cleric named Tetzel selling indulgences (a remission of worldly or purgatorial punishment still due after the sin has been forgiven through the sacrament of penance) as a representative of the German banking house of the Fuggers, questioned the principles and practices advanced by the Catholic Church on the attainment of salvation. Luther contended that salvation did not occur because of good works and good deeds, as set forth in the accepted Christian dogma of the time, but through faith. His principle of salvation by faith alone held that through reading the Bible, people developed faith in Jesus, thereby entering a state of grace and then performed good works and good deeds.

Max Weber, a German sociologist, theorized in his book *The Protestant Ethic and the Spirit of Capitalism* that protestantism led to capitalism and Luther's break with Catholicism began what has become known as the Protestant Work Ethic. Other sociologists and historians have turned Weber's position on its head, arguing that in reality capitalism had been developing much earlier and demanded a new religious faith to promote its advance. For Max Weber, protestantism led to capitalism, while for his critics, capitalism produced protestantism.

I refuse to become involved in this controversy over which came first, the chicken or the egg. I do need, however, to examine this Protestant Work Ethic and analyze its impact upon the values of the people of the United States. Before I do, I would prefer to turn to the theories of another author, Erik H. Erikson, as presented in his book *Young Man Luther.*

Erik H. Erikson was a Freudian psychologist and, in a sense, an historian. His intent in writing *Young Man Luther* was to examine the historical record of Martin Luther's formative years and in Freudian terms explain why Luther succeeded in his break with Catholicism where others had failed. Basically he concluded that Martin Luther had an anal retentive personality (compulsive, dogmatic, somber, humorless, uptight, and toilet oriented). Because of his early development, Erikson argued, Luther had little choice but to refuse any compromises with the Catholic Church and fanatically advanced his interpretation of God's word as revealed in the Bible.

Forgive me, but I must take this digression on Erik Erikson's views and play with it. Many sociologists see the American personality, at least before the 1960's, as anal retentive. Did the United States, a predominantly Protestant nation, inherit Luther's personality as a character trait, or was there just something about the descendants of Northern Europeans that produced anal retentive people lending that personality to the nation? Translation—we have been a nation of compulsive loners, somber rugged individualists who struggle in silence without humor to survive and carve a country out of the wilderness.

Americans, traditionally, held it all in. As anal retentive people they worked hard to release their internal tensions. Work was an outlet for their constipation. Feeling and emotion were limited and could only be expressed through formalized rituals with fixed smiles. Americans lacked spontaneity.

The lone cowboy riding into town symbolized our hero, the John Wayne image. The frontiersman staking out an isolated home in the wilderness, produced the Daniel Boone image. The captain of industry building a business empire created the Andrew Carnegie image. These traits were embodied in presidents like Andrew Jackson and Theodore Roosevelt. Our political candidates had little choice but to exhibit such behavior and present the image of being trustworthy, loyal, helpful, friendly, courteous, kind, obedient, cheerful, thrifty, brave, clean, and reverent.

A candidate who laughed too much, showed emotion, cried, or even touched another man by embracing or hugging, caused fear and trepidation in the voters. A politician who cried committed the worst sin. This was exemplified by the defeat of Edmund Muskie in the 1972 Democratic primaries. In his presidential bid, Muskie broke down in tears while defending his wife against a vicious attack at the hands of a New Hampshire newspaper editor. Most political observers attribute his loss of the nomination to his honest emotions.

Such was our society which demanded that people get no closer than 18 inches apart. Note how Southern Europeans, generally Catholic, can talk right next to a person even while chewing garlic.

In our society, the gun predominates—violence from a distance. Our hero is the lone gunslinger, an analogy Henry Kissinger, Secretary of State in the early 1970's, used about himself in a famous interview. Southern Europeans often prefer the closeness of a knife.

To complete the examination of our distant uptight personality, one has only to compare our bathrooms with those in the rest of the world. Where else can you find colored and perfumed toilet paper, padded toilet seats, fancy tile, soap balls in fancy dishes and bowls, cabinets full of underarm deodorants and mouth washes, designer shower curtains, special commode joke books, and even telephones?

This somber, controlled, structured, intellectual, orderly, striving American personality probably reached its political apex in the administration of Richard

Nixon (1969–1974). The Watergate Tapes, which finally forced Nixon's resignation, revealed that he and his staff did have some humor, but could only tell canned jokes (pun intended). They lacked spontaneity in their humor and only repeated memorized toilet jokes, never telling jokes referring to sex. The same proved true of their curse words.

The expletives deleted, so often found in the transcripts of the Watergate Tapes, were toilet four-letter words, never sexual. Richard Nixon, a man driven by his compulsiveness, worked hard, but destroyed himself because of his isolation, ambition and *hubris—a Greek word meaning excessive pride*. He, like so many American politicians before him, reflected in part the heritage of Martin Luther and a later Protestant theologian, John Calvin.

Perhaps Martin Luther's alleged anal retentive personality helped form the attitude of Americans because of his theology, and perhaps he set the seeds for capitalism to blossom, but there is little disagreement among scholars that our spiritual work ethic came to fruition due to the theology of *John Calvin—a French theologian who after 1541 took control of Geneva, Switzerland, and introduced a theocracy based upon his concept of only the elect being saved.*

The basic concept underlining Calvin's religious doctrine is called *predestination— God foreordained all souls either for salvation or damnation*. The belief that people were predestined to be saints or sinners infiltrated American values through the Pilgrims and Puritans. Although these early settlers of New England failed to follow a rigid Calvinistic line like the Presbyterians in Scotland, they adhered to the basic concepts of predestination. Their settlement in New England lacked the large number of colonists of other regions. They, however, created an educational elite and their values permeated all areas of American society and culture.

To the Puritans, universal literacy became mandatory, for the saints needed to read the Bible. In a very few years after their settlement, they created educational institutions like Harvard and Yale.

The Southern Colonies, made up mostly of Anglicans (Henry VIII broke with the Catholic Church in 1532 and established what in reality might be called an English Catholic Church), still functioned under the theology of good works and good deeds and thereby failed to develop major educational institutions to influence America until many years after the first settlements.

The Puritan society and culture brought to America a value system that demanded rigid control of one's life and personality. The Saints feared that any little sin, or any action that might be interpreted as leading to sin, would mean that they were among the damned. So they held it all in—well, at least they tried to.

The Puritans created a political democracy where all the Saints could vote on the issues of the day, either in their congregational churches or in town meetings. In respect to religious issues, the church leaders in Boston announced their directives after hearing the local input. Once decreed from Boston, all the Saints had to adhere to the dogma. A sort of native American *democratic centralism— a concept usually associated with Marxist groups and attributed to Lenin, where the various local party assemblies vote on issues and then introduce them at a general meeting of the Central Committee; after a final decision is arrived at, the local party members must adhere to it, no matter what their original vote.*

Pennsylvania Amish community today—modern-day Puritans.

The Puritans, through their cultural and religious centers, had an important impact on the development of the American democratic creed. Democracy in America, in a sense, came to mean respect for the individual as long as that individual remained within the community. The individual needed to be one of the Saints, otherwise, s/he could not be accorded the full duties, responsibilities, and privileges of citizenship. One way of identifying the sainthood of an individual derived from how well he or she adhered to leadership decisions. Compromise at the congregational assemblies and town meetings brought about a position to be advocated and voted on at the highest level of leadership and then all obeyed or left the settlement—America, love her or leave her. Another way to identify sainthood stemmed from how hard the individual worked for the community, which, in a sense, translated to how hard they worked for themselves, not concerned with the material rewards—the spiritual work ethic.

Generations of American children memorized adages developed from Puritan values: "Empty hands are the devil's workshop"; "A stitch in time saves nine"; "A penny saved is a penny earned"; "Neither a borrower, nor a lender be"; "A bird in the hand is worth two in the bush"; "Cleanliness is next to godliness." These are just a few examples which most of us have heard but no longer recite as gospel truth. Hymns sung in American churches glorified the doctrine of work, even when the religions had little if any relationship to Calvinist doctrine. New England's culture prevailed.

Politicians emphasized their hard work, their frugality and their humble beginnings. I grant that exceptions existed, especially in the early years of our Republic when the Virginia dynasty controlled the presidency—George Washington, Thomas Jefferson, James Madison, James Monroe. But early in the nineteenth century, the myth of birth in a log cabin soon enveloped the political atmosphere as our leaders pointed to their humble beginnings and identified their sainthood.

U.S. Post Office honors Horatio Alger.

Yes, an egalitarian ethic developed as politicians claimed their affinity with the common person, but the meritocracy still prevailed. For the politician let the voter know that he had stood alone to confront his destiny and carved out his own unique identity, obviously predestined by God for sainthood in the next life and to be rewarded for his success in this life.

The politician, reflecting the Puritan seriousness of purpose, often quoted the adages memorized in school, and humbly identified how he embodied that lifestyle. He could not directly say so, but he indirectly pointed to his perfection, his inability to err—a true saint. He could never admit a mistake or a weakness for this would, he thought, raise questions about his meriting an office. A political leader was human like anyone else, but a superior human. To paraphrase George Orwell's *Animal Farm*—all humans are created equal, but some are created more equal than others. In an expanding commercial and agricultural America, these political saints preached the spiritual work ethic to a receptive audience. I am not saying that materialism did not exist, but it failed to become the prevalent cultural value until after the Civil War and particularly after 1900.

Spiritual fulfillment did give way to material success. The Puritan values, the Protestant Work Ethic continued, but as the critic Harold Clurman identified in his *Lies Like Truth* (New York: Macmillan, 1958), the American dream, by the second half of the nineteenth century, became distorted into a drive for material success. The spiritual dream lived on in the works of *Horatio Alger (1834–1899)— who wrote over 100 books and became the most popular author of the last thirty years of the nineteenth century; his heroes maintained their morality and work ethic and were rewarded with success, usually material; the values presented in his books exerted one of the most powerful influences on American culture as they reinforced the Puritan ethic.* The Horatio Alger stories kept alive the ideas of enterprise, courage, and hard work for numerous generations of American youth.

By the end of the century, the new heroes were the Andrew Carnegies (1835–1919; born in Scotland and became one of the wealthiest American industrialists), the John D. Rockefellers (1839–1937; made his fortune through Standard Oil and developed a banking empire) and the William Randolph Hearsts (1863–1951; multi-millionaire newspaper and magazine publisher). These were the so-called "Barons of Industry."

Being trustworthy, loyal, helpful, friendly, courteous, kind, obedient, cheerful, thrifty, brave, clean, and reverent still identified the select few, the elite whose reward would come in the next life, but for now the Saints could flaunt their position and status. The simple abode and clothing of the Puritan gave way to San Simeon (Hearst's Castle) and tuxedos and mink coats for the elite to attend the opera. Millions of Americans worshipped the 400 (a listing of the wealthiest Americans) and hoped some day to achieve similar status and material rewards.

Tug-of-war at traditional July 4th picnic.

When they made a little money, the new rich purchased season tickets to the opera, the ballet, or the symphony. They bought classical art and decorated their stylish homes with the culture of the 400. It mattered little whether they appreciated the opera, ballet, symphony, or classical art. Status, position, proof of their sainthood demanded their conspicuous consumption. Politicians, of course, joined the bandwagon. They still could emphasize their humble beginnings, but they needed to show their success by being seen with the best—in this case defined by material rewards.

The political leaders got their constituents jobs when necessary and held Fourth of July picnics, but they also campaigned for monuments to themselves. Every small urban area constructed theaters, opera houses, art museums, symphony halls and lots of statues in classical style, all with the blessing of political leaders.

And, those who failed to achieve the material success, what about their position in society? In simple, direct terms, they could only be viewed as sinners to be damned in the next life, explaining their damned life now. Maybe the Saints never said this directly, but it was implied. At times the attitude of society and political leaders would simply be—well, God has determined their destiny, so the faster they go to hell the better.

Government's role was not to change God's will. Of course, some people did feel a desire to promote the general welfare, but this meant the minimum of charity and a sort of hope the problem would go away. John D. Rockefeller had no difficulty in giving dimes to beggars, but that reached the peak of his generosity and I might add that of government as well.

Since history is written by elites, it is always difficult to know how the common people accepted their fate as sinners. I can only assume that they had little time to think about it as they fought simply to survive. Perhaps they felt their reward for the perseverance would come sooner or later: the old myth of a pie in the sky when they died, or a rich uncle somewhere who would leave them a fortune as in a Horatio Alger parable.

As the idealization of the 400 reached its peak, the **Progressive Movement**—*a reform movement from around 1900 to the U.S. entry into World War I, aiming to correct abuses which had accompanied the growth of big business*—began to chop away at their sainthood. Books like Upton Sinclair's *The Jungle* (1906) and Ida Tarbell's *History of the Standard Oil Company* (1904), showed the Barons of Industry to be Robber Barons. With the **muckrakers**—*a term coined by President Theodore Roosevelt in 1906 to characterize those writers he felt were arousing discontent by uncovering corruption in business and politics during the early 1900's*—came a demand for reform. The average American began to feel that his or her sainthood had been denied by wealthy sinners.

Politicians nationally, and especially in Western states, began to pass legislation designed to equalize opportunities for all Americans to become the saints they deserved to be. Lost, almost forever, was the Calvinist idea that only a select few were saved.

Americans expanded their egalitarian ethic, viewing most Americans, at least those who fit into the political community, as being among the saved, while only a few individuals were damned. This translated into a subliminal belief for

Saint or sinner?

many that the Sinners consisted of those racial and ethnic groups who looked, acted, or functioned differently than the White, Anglo-Saxon Protestant.

Since these pariahs also tended to be identified with manual labor, hard work became redefined. The materialistic work ethic continued under a sales ethic. As Harold Clurman identified in the aforementioned book, *Lies Like Truth*, the salesman works hard but sells his personality. This became the prevalent drive after the First World War. The intrinsic value of the work is no longer an issue. In fact, salesmanship carries with it a touch of fraud—the selling of a product no matter its worth, even if the product is the individual's personality.

The sales ethic became necessary in the assembly line society. American industry began to turn out products in abundance. Business people needed to create a market. They did this through slick advertising and salesmanship.

Politicians soon capitalized on the new sophisticated methods of sales and advertising. By the 1920's, American industry boomed and political leaders reaped the profit.

A trickle-down economy developed which provided a greater number of people with leisure time. The average person now had money to spend on popular culture. Since the late nineteenth century, sports, theater, movies, books, and music began to compete for the attention of masses of people.

Politicians could soon be seen throwing out the first ball at opening days at baseball games. Play became acceptable as a release for tensions derived from work, different from the old Protestant Work Ethic, which in a sense preached work to relieve work-related tensions. Soon Americans organized and structured their play, as they did their work, to avoid the spontaneity associated with emotion and sin.

In 1929, the bubble broke. America found herself confronted with the challenges of the Great Depression. Americans questioned the belief in the unending productivity of a saintly society. As the Saints lost fortunes and jumped from windows, politicians began to read the pulse of a newly emerging value system—a fanatical concern to prevent poverty and disease. The New Deal's welfare state emerged.

With Franklin Delano Roosevelt's election to the presidency in 1932, the federal government took an ever increasing role in promoting the general welfare. The Roosevelt administration followed the economic theories of **John Maynard Keynes**—*a British economist who sought to improve capitalism by a system of orderly and predictable economic activity through a government-managed economy*. Keynesian theory held that recessions or depressions were caused by under-consumption and over-production. Therefore, to get the economy back on its feet, the government should take an active role by pump priming the system with aid to the consumers.

World War II brought on even greater amounts of government spending in aid to industries and to consumers. War industry also demanded labor, and with the large number of people serving in the armed forces, employment reached almost 100 percent and the Great Depression finally ended.

At the end of the War, America was again on the road to abundance, this time with government deposit insurance, disaster loans, price supports, unemployment insurance, social security, *ad infinitum*. Both producers and consumers looked to Washington for guidance and direct financial help.

The circle pin era.

Success was still respected when based upon merit, but a little help from government certainly was acceptable. I guess people, similar to the days of the absolute monarchies, saw government as the hand of God aiding the Saints' march on to their salvation. The Jeffersonian idea that the government which governs least governs best had given way to a belief in the goodness and benevolence of government.

America's materialistic work ethic, her meritocracy, and her industrial revolution peaked in the 1950's. Alvin Toffler, in his book *Future Shock* (New York: Random House, 1970), identifies this era, when I attended school and which I remember so well, as the apex of the industrial age of uniformity. As a school boy, I confronted two worlds, Fonzie's or Rich Cunningham's, the hood heading for the blue-collar work force or the collegian preparing to wear his grey flannel suit as a white-collar executive. Each group appeared to dress alike and to groom alike. Sure there existed a few pariahs—outsiders—like the beatniks who demanded diversity on their terms, but most of us whites only had the choice between two roles.

I recall my college classrooms, where all the guys sported flat-top haircuts or crewcuts, while wearing button-down collar shirts, chino pants with belts in the back, and saddle shoes or white bucks. A style we called Ivy League and a few years ago reappeared as Preppy. Women in my class always seemed to wear madras blouses, pleated skirts, loafers with pennies in them and circle pins! We joked that the circle pins symbolized their virginity. I have not seen any women wearing circle pins in recent years.

Boys headed for blue-collar occupations wore blue jeans, T-shirts with the cigarettes held tight against their shoulders with rolled-up sleeves, motorcycle jackets, garrison belts (with sharpened buckles in case of a gang fight) and boots with metal toes (the better to stomp someone with). The women of this group, the future childbearers, displayed their falsies through tight sweaters, their allegiance through the oversize jackets with their boyfriends' gangs' name, and their legs through peddle pushers.

The fifties were the culmination of a civilization born of the Protestant Work Ethic and the Industrial Revolution: each person stamped from the same mold in order to adapt to a society based on mass production and conforming to Puritan values. Individuals remained a part of a community, a compact group to be assimilated into the nation.

The media and politicians generally ignored racial, ethnic, cultural, and sexual diversity. An assimilated society created a smooth organic process identical to the predictable machines of the industrial age. To admit to the existence of diversity might draw the nation apart, throwing a wrench into the machines of mass production.

The 1960's introduced a revolution. Toffler writes of the new age as the coming of super-industrialism, an era of diversity. For example, at the height of industrialism, let us say, a machine could cut out of layers of cloth one hundred suits in ten minutes—all the same grey flannel style. In the super-industrial age, a laser can cut out one hundred suits in a minute and each suit will be completely different.

In the age of diversity, the choice between alternatives is infinite. Students in the 21st century can select among hundreds of lifestyles and patterns of dress. When I went into an ice-cream store in my youth, I could have vanilla, chocolate or strawberry flavors. Howard Johnson's offered a little more variety with their 28 flavors, always the same. Today you can get any flavor ice-cream you want from Yankee Doodle Dandy to Zucchini.

Super-industrialism provides an unending expansion of individual choices between alternatives. And, if freedom is the ability to choose between alternatives, freedom expands. This is especially true politically not only for the elite saints, but as each particular develops its own intrinsic worth in a diverse society, each individual becomes a saint and few, if any, sinners exist.

An age of diversity.

During the fifties, when I attended school, every male attempted to be Jack Armstrong, all-American boy, and every woman wanted to be Doris Day, all-American housewife. We still believed in the Horatio Alger myths. Anyone, we held, could obtain material success as long as he or she maintained his or her virtue and morality. We might have added: being white, blonde, blue-eyed, Protestant and male added to one's merit. The era of uniformity bred skin lighteners, hair straighteners, nose-jobs, and name changes, as minorities tried to conform and obtain God's governmental sanction. It also brought about identity crises combined with weekend drunkenness, big Cadillacs in the ghettos, and hundreds of other escape valves as the "sinners" of America failed to assimilate.

The sixties brought welcomed change. People who lived in America's fringe society demanded participation in her material rewards while maintaining their cultural identity. Minority groups marched, demonstrated, and burned in their drive to bring God's government to the side of all the saints. A counter-culture emerged which, instead of holding it all in, decided to let it all hang out. A belief that the Puritan value system, the Protestant Work Ethic, had created an uptight, hypocritical, racist, sexist, imperialist system brought millions into the streets joined by a few courageous politicians. "Tell it like it is" became the battle cry of the youth who refused to compromise their political, social, and educational counter-culture values.

The Puritan sense of an individual within a community evaporated into the demands for a nation of diverse communities. Politicians found it difficult to lead as they failed to know to which group to appeal. Their sainthood was brought into question as the radicals shouted them down. The radicals, the counter-culture, the emerging nationalities destroyed the political heroes by emphasizing only their racism, sexism, and colonialist attitudes.

Anti-heroes emerged who followed Dionysius (Greek god of wine, song, dance, feeling, spontaneity, emotion) rather than Apollo (Greek god of intellect, rationality, controlled thought, structured action). Abbie Hoffman, Jerry Rubin and a few other anti-establishment individuals formed the *Yippies—Youth International Party whose political dogma during the 1960's combined nihilism with being hippies*. They laughed at the traditions and values of America's past. When they took to the streets, they did so as a joke, but the remnants of the uptight Puritans could only take them seriously and came down on them with bricks and clubs.

Saul Alinsky, in his chapter on "Tactics" in his 1971 book *Rules for Radicals*, argued that humor could destroy the credibility of a political opponent, especially when that individual is an uptight hypocrite. He also said that this type of politician, when confronted with ridicule, loses his/ her cool and shows his/her true colors, advancing the ultimate purpose of the radical activist. The Yippies

The counter-culture.

Requiem for Martin Luther King, Jr.

and their allies in **The New Left**—*a radical-liberal movement, particularly of college students and some professors in the 1960's and early 1970's that challenged the established political, social, cultural, and economic norms*—unknowingly used the techniques of Saul Alinsky to attract the attention of the news media, gaining recruits, and sowing the seeds of distrust about traditional American values and government. As middle America and hardhats yelled, "America, love her or leave her," the hang-up from the Puritans who sent their dissidents out into the wilderness, the radicals answered back "America, change her or lose her."

Actually, a great optimism existed among the young and the minorities in the sixties. They felt they could and would bring about a society of true equal opportunity, where everyone could compete to become saints.

Martin Luther King, Jr., the name sake of the 16th century revolutionary cleric who had indirectly led to the American value system, led marches and demonstrations throughout the South. His non-violent tactics contrasted drastically with the firehoses, attack dogs, and clubs of the Southern establishment. Politicians from other parts of the country took up the cause and for the first time since Civil War days, major civil rights legislation passed Congress in 1964 and 1965 and was signed into law by President Lyndon Johnson, himself from the South. Blacks and their allies believed this to be a start and only a start.

Demands for equal opportunity began to change to egalitarian concerns as some blacks rejected the doctrines of Martin Luther King, Jr. and turned to violence. It was one thing for white America to yell racism in the South, but when blacks identified the oppression of the Northerners, and demanded change, often violently, a white backlash came into being.

Tragically, in May, 1968, Martin Luther King, Jr., winner of the Nobel Peace Prize, was assassinated in the prime of his life—39 years of age. He had accomplished so much, not only for blacks but for all Americans, that most people thought he must be ancient. Frustration in black communities exploded into rage, but worse, the hopes of millions for a society of true equal opportunity

The human potential movement era.

diminished and the calls for equality of condition as the only way out from the racism of America prevailed.

For white liberal Americans, a similar tragedy hit the month after Martin Luther King, Jr.'s death when Robert Kennedy also died by an assassin's bullet. Kennedy had just won the California Democratic Party presidential primary and seemed destined for the White House. His murder reminded many people of the assassination of his brother John, five years before, and dashed their renewed dream of a society which would eliminate poverty, illiteracy, disease, and war.

For many liberals, the murders of the Kennedy brothers and Martin Luther King, Jr. appeared to validate the radicals' argument that America would never permit a change in her historical saintly rule. Almost to underscore the feeling of helplessness and frustration, the Democratic Party nominated for the presidency Vice-President Hubert Humphrey, who had been identified with the war policy and failures of the Johnson Administration. The voters elected the Republican, Richard Nixon, the epitome of the old Puritan cultural values and hypocrisy, to be President.

A few people maintained their hope that America's political system could still be changed through political involvement or protest. The publication of *The Pentagon Papers* identified the lies and duplicity of the United States Government. Nixon's decision to end the Vietnam War right before the 1972 election seemed to terminate any remaining optimism for outward reform or change in the political system.

A few groups in the early seventies, like the feminists and gays, continued to push for political equality. Most liberals and counter-culture radicals turned instead to the ***human potential movement***—*a myriad of groups and organizations whose purpose was to change people internally, helping them love themselves, and in this fashion helping them love others, thereby creating a more humane political world.*

In the late sixties, as the counter-culture turned on and tuned out, the human potential movement began to attract recruits. By the early seventies, people like Werner Erhard, with his EST (Erhard Seminar Training), stacked away millions of dollars in foreign banks, playing with middle America's continuing anal retentiveness. People attending EST had to hold it all in for 48 hours as they let everything else out, learning that only they were at fault for their lives. The cost for this fulfilling weekend came to about $250. In similar groups, people

The Me Generation and the Sexual Revolution—An era before AIDS.

pounded pillows while screaming at imaginary relatives to release their unconscious and find true love—themselves. Others meditated, chanting mantras, bringing the pariah activities of the fifties to middle America.

Be it through EST, Transactional Analysis, Transcendental Meditation, or a hundred other groups, liberal Americans tried a new way to cope with the super-industrial age, the age of diversity, and the resulting anxieties which raised blood pressure, promoted ulcers, caused heart attacks, and maybe even sustained an individual's cancer. More conservative Americans turned to traditional religion as a panacea for the ills of society.

In a search for stability, in a transitional period of value change, many young people became so-called Jesus Freaks, and more recently have called themselves Born Again Christians. While the remnants of the anti-war demonstrators marched, and a few hippies continued to reject the cleanliness is next to godliness culture, the Jesus Freaks, many dressing in rags and unkempt as they imagined Jesus and his followers, preached love, while giving people the index finger. In a sense, they were a part of the human potential movement, as they rejected organized religion, gathering in congregations to get high on Jesus in order to find love internally to share externally.

The super-industrial age had provided numerous options in products and lifestyles. Americans of all ages and positions began a search for direction and truth. In the sixties, after Michael Harrington, in his *Poverty in America*, had identified fifty million people living at poverty level and twenty million going to bed hungry, President Lyndon Johnson had declared his "War on Poverty." America, in an age of abundance, had moved to share some of its wealth with the poor through extensive government programs.

By the seventies, middle America also decided to share its wealth with itself. To create a more productive citizenry, in a period when too many Americans seemed directed towards being television robots, feeding off the media, America began to provide low-cost or free human potential programs through her public institutions. Adult education programs expanded and in California, for example, junior colleges officially became community colleges, providing leisure courses, art and music programs, and job retraining for local community members, rather than simply preparing students for university programs.

Soon the realities of the costs of providing butter and guns, promoting the general welfare, and providing for the national defense, hit home with two devaluations of the dollar and high inflation. Arab oil blackmail in 1973, brought home to Americans the vulnerability of an economy which used fifty-five percent of the world's resources for six percent of the world's population. As Americans lined up at the gas stations and ecological activists warned about the limitations of our resources and the consequences of pollution to life on our planet, people began to question their priorities.

Sadly, the human potential movement's goal to create a world of altruistic individuals had become misdirected. The advice of writers like Father John Powell in his *The Secret of Staying in Love* (Niles, Illinois: Argus Communications, 1974) to love oneself first in order to love others became distorted into narcissism. The search for self-love turned to egotism rather than egoism. Where both the egoist and egotist are self-centered, the egotist is indifferent to the well-being of others, while the egoist can share his/her being. The "You're O.K., I'm O.K." generation in their search for a higher consciousness (see Charles Reich, *The Greening of America*, New York: Random House, 1970), became what Tom Wolfe, in an August 30, 1976, article in *New West* (pp. 27–48), called the **Me Generation**— *the decade of the seventies—felt by many to be an age of narcissism whose chant was "Me, Me, Me."*

A transient society saw the divorce rate soar, marriage become an overnight affair; and children become a burden as people sought material goods. "I want to do my own thing!" became the slogan for new generations. The traditional desire to work it out and to provide a creative compromise disintegrated to "you live your life and I will live mine." Communication between people, especially the young, almost ceased behind loud music, dancing without partners, and "slam bam, thank you mam" attitudes.

Middle America demanded everything, now. Similar to the early movements of many Third World and counter-culture people in their chauvinistic stage, believing they had a guaranteed right to the resources of America, many white, middle-class Americans now insisted upon equality of condition, rather than equal opportunity.

In many ways, President Richard Nixon symbolized all of the negative characteristics of the Me Generation. His only concern as President seemed to be his own aggrandizement of power. He ignored many of his own party's candidates in the 1972 election to assure his own victory. The abuses of power of his administration culminated in the Watergate scandals which finally forced his resignation. Millicent Fenwick, former New Jersey Congresswoman, in a political speech summed up Nixon's Watergate in a famous quotation: "Every society on earth has corruption. It is the nature of human society. But my country was lost because we had corruption without indignation!"

Nixon embodied the equality of condition mentality. Unable to recognize and certainly unable to admit his own weaknesses, he even called up a Superbowl coach and suggested certain football plays. He continued to exclaim: "I am not a crook!" This leads me right into the **Machiavellian Work Ethic**— *the idea that the least amount of work done to achieve the greatest profit is the smartest approach to life; and anything done in the name of making a profit is justifiable.*

With sainthood bestowed on everyone due to the condition of being alive, many Americans felt they deserved the good life—translation, material rewards. It mattered not whether they worked to earn them. On the contrary, some argued that the rich never worked anyway and earned their place in society by ripping people off. Mean-

AIDS awareness quilt at Ohlone.

while, television shows reinforced this attitude by presenting entrepreneurs as desensitized individuals who often engaged in immoral and illegal activities. A member of the Danish parliament, interestingly, introduced legislation to condemn the producers of the television show *Dallas* for trying to destroy the American peoples' respect for businessmen. He implied that the extreme left-wing had taken control of the Hollywood television studios and were using their productions as a way to bring revolution to the United States. I doubt whether the television producers were doing anything more than the rest of the media—presenting Americans with what they wanted to see, hear, or read.

Super-industrialism, the age of diversity, the Me Generation, and the developing equalitocracy brought on the Machiavellian Work Ethic. The uncontrolled inflation fueled the flames. Many people decided to get back their fair share of the pie by ripping off their companies. Employee theft became a major problem, as some workers padded their incomes through an underground economy in stolen goods. I do not mean to imply that employee theft never existed in bygone days—it did! The difference came in its acceptance and spread. An employee known to be taking items from a company years back would have been turned in or ostracized by his colleagues for his immorality. Now, the thieving employee seemed to become a hero and a person to imitate.

Because of the inflation and the constant pressure to buy new products some people rationalized that if they worked too hard they would not obtain overtime pay. So they cut back on their productivity, enabling them to work weekends and holidays at time and one half or double time. Other workers simply pressured their unions to demand more money for less work.

The salesman ethic of the post–World War I era continued into the seventies and expanded into the speculator ethic as millions of people looked for ways to make quick bucks without expending too much energy. Worst of all, from my own perspective, was the degradation of work and merited success. Psychologists and others bantered about words like workaholic to imply that people who spent their lives striving for success at their jobs were sick. I realize that they used such language to aid those individuals who placed undue stress on their systems, leading to physical or mental illness, but the layman's interpretation simply said: "Work ain't worth it!"

Many efficient workers reported that their coworkers insisted they slow down as their hard work made them look bad. If they continued their pace, their co-workers warned, they would face the consequences.

Interestingly, the more people avoided work, the greater became the demand for laboring style clothing. For the first time in history, even the upper classes began to sport working class clothing in the form of blue jeans, albeit with designer names on their backsides. John Calvin seemed to be replaced by Calvin Klein. Instead of buying season tickets to the opera, businesses now bought their managers passes to football games. This switch in clothing styles and attitude was probably brought on by an automated society retraining laborers for service oriented industries.

The saints of the meritocracy, many of whom like Thomas Edison, John David Rockefeller, Andrew Carnegie, lived full lives despite their passion for work. Working hard, working long hours, struggling to achieve success, is not, a priori, destructive to health or society. Only when individuals strive to achieve success on someone else's level rather than on their own terms does work become a burden. The Machiavellian Work Ethic, however, simply needed to degrade labor to advance the goals of minimal work to obtain maximum wealth.

By the end of the seventies, spreading from California, came the pyramid movement. Numerous individuals shelled out a thousand dollars in the hopes of getting to the top of a list and obtaining sixteen thousand dollars. Only a few could win. The vast majority had to be losers. Few players seemed to care about the losers, only their own selfish gain. Even at my college, the police arrested a number of my colleagues as they ran the scam out of a $400,000 home owned by a group of educator-investors. One professor, a member of the local school board, got arrested for staffing a walkie-talkie to warn those inside of any impending police raids. He failed and, with six others, paid a substantial fine. Not one element of society, not even the sacred halls of academia, first established in this country by the Puritans, appeared unaffected by the Machiavellian Work Ethic of unearned income.

The sophisticated ads for consumer items and the easy availability of credit completed the destruction of the spiritual and materialistic work ethics. "Never a creditor nor borrower be," nor any of the other adages identified with Puritanism made sense to the immediate gratifiers of the Me Generation. "Save for a rainy day," made even less sense when investment in banks lost money due to low interest rates. High taxes on interest earned, and the demands for keeping up with the Joneses in an inflationary economy led to increased spending.

The Amuse Me Generation.

Beginning with the New Deal's desire to get us out of the Depression by pump priming the economy, expanded by the Johnson Administration's War on Poverty during the sixties, reaching its apex with the Human Potential Movement's desire to create productive citizens, and fractured by the inflation, all levels of society brought demands for government programs to better their own existence. Welfare became a panacea to meet the increasing demands of the poor, the middle class, and even the very rich.

Politicians responded by providing government aid in the form of direct handouts to such diverse interest groups as beekeepers (over a million dollars a year), ski-resort operators (when it failed to snow—supposedly a natural disaster), food stamps for college students, and on *ad infinitum*. The number of tax exemptions provided all segments of society (obviously the poor benefited the least) increased two-fold as political leaders answered the cries of their constituents.

I do not mean to imply that all these programs were unnecessary, although I believe many were—especially much of the welfare to the rich. I am simply attempting to identify the changes that occurred in the value systems of Americans during the seventies and the resulting political implications.

Factionalism—conflict within a country between individuals or groups producing dissension rather than the resolution of problems—soon worried political party leaders. They realized that individuals had stopped turning to the traditional party machinery to resolve conflict. People now turned to single interest groups to promote their views. In the decade of the seventies, the number of such groups nearly doubled, reaching in excess of three thousand.

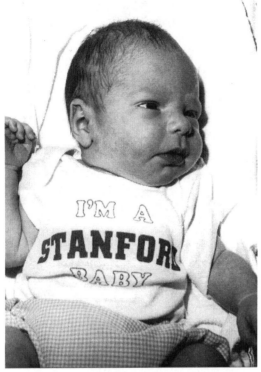

A newborn YUPPIE—a search for status.

Tied to the emergence of the new single issue or veto groups (as they are at times called) were the *political action committees (PACs)—an interest group's fundraising branch that distributes money to candidates and more recently has spent its cash in an attempt to secure the victory of its cause.*

Religious groups like the former Moral Majority and the Christian Coalition enlisted the support of fundamental and evangelical Christians to spread millions of dollars into a political battle to preserve what some have called America's anal retentive society. Although Congress tried to limit PAC Presidential contributions to $1000, the Supreme Court on March 18, 1985, in a 7–2 decision, declared that limiting a group's right to seek to influence voters on behalf of one candidate violated the First Amendment's protection of free speech.

In previous decades, factions existed, but most Americans, whether supportive of interest groups or not, worked within the two-party system to bring about creative compromise. Aided by laws which limited candidate and party spending, the PACs and other groups often raised large sums of money appealing to people's selfishness or fears, while refusing eclectic causes.

Single-interest group pitted itself against single-interest group, refusing to compromise on any portion of their programs. America's news media lamented the lack of political leadership to bring an end to this fragmentation of the political process.

Time ran its cover story on the cry for leadership on August 6, 1979. Five years previously, *Time* had contained a similar article questioning the ability of political leaders to confront global problems, blaming it on leadership's diminished vision. In August, 1979, *Time* turned its attention to the question of leadership and national issues.

Examining the American Dream, Lance Morrow, author of the cover story, reminded readers that Alexis de Tocqueville in 1835 had warned against the possibility of our values degenerating from spiritual to material—a land of plenty could become a land of wretched excess where equality of condition would prevail. Morrow saw the problem resting, using my terms, with the demands of a selfish generation living in a super-industrial era of excess, an age of diversity and equality of condition, creating the **entitlement ethic**—*the view that people are entitled to everything everyone else has.*

With government unable to fulfill all of its promises, it must disappoint everyone. Americans soon refused leaders the element they need most for success—continued support. In other words, Americans became next to impossible to lead. With the fragmentation of society into single-interest constituencies, armed with their computer mailing lists, zeal, and moral righteousness, leaders lost the talent to bring about compromise.

Politicians, even Presidents, exemplified by Jimmy Carter, first tried to appease everyone—an obvious impossibility. Carter, attempting to maintain the programs of the New Deal, the Fair Deal, the New Frontier, and the Great Society, failed to be all things to all people. He found himself engulfed in a tax revolt caused by the high inflation and inspired by America's Me-Generation attitudes.

A student speaks to promote recycling cans and bottles.

Tax revolts were not uncommon, historically. Successful ones were, however. California's Proposition 13, penned by Howard Jarvis and Paul Gann, succeeded in drastically reducing property taxes. Land taxes in California had climbed drastically because of inflated values of homes and the state reaped the profit, proudly displaying a five billion dollar surplus. Enraged homeowners flocked to the initiative. Although badly needed, the problem with Proposition 13 lay in its failure to define the limits of the spending cuts and left this to the legislature and politicians.

People calling for the elimination of frills and waste soon found their own necessities of life listed as frills. On my campus, to provide one example, a member of the elected Board of Trustees demanded that the college stop tuning harps and pianos. If students wanted these courses, she implied, let them take private lessons. Rationalizing the benefit to campus students and the community, the same person joined other Board members on expensive junkets to conferences in Washington D.C., Hawaii, and other sections of the nation.

This highly publicized taxpayers' revolt and the Reagan Administration's drive to reduce federal spending did not mean that middle Americans rejected the new pluralism of the age of diversity. Norman and Emily Rosenberg in their book *In Our Times* (New Jersey: Prentice-Hall, 1982) argued that an examination of the tax revolt showed that the voters still endorsed government programs directed to the truly needy.

Senior citizens in the U.S. are no longer confined to old-age homes.

Californians in recent years have rejected other initiatives by Paul Gann and Howard Jarvis, the co-authors of Proposition 13, which would have cut even deeper into government resources. Apparently, the voters felt enough was enough. They wanted not less government, but better government.

Look Out For #1 told the story of the 70's. Politicians failed to take up the challenge of leadership as the call for entitlement proved too great and so they took their own entitlements.

At the end of the decade, political scientist Samuel Huntington wrote a report for the Tri-Lateral Commission. Huntington linked the failure in leadership to the egalitocracy, whose unreasonable and unattainable demands emasculated the political and economic system—an explanation of President Carter's inability to bring the country together, except for a short time during the Iranian crisis. Jimmy Carter, by the end of his tenure in office, had received the lowest job rating of any President since polling began. Interestingly, after Jimmy Carter left the presidency he became one of our most popular ex-presidents for his altruistic work and statesmanship.

In 1980, the smallest percentage of eligible voters in decades turned to Ronald Reagan for leadership to pull the country out of the quagmire of entitlement. While Jimmy Carter wanted to keep alive the New Deal, it appeared that Ronald Reagan intended to return America to her pre–Franklin Delano Roosevelt days. Some political observers argued he wanted to return to the simpler times of the 1920's materialistic American Dream. Others insisted that Reagan hoped to go back as far as the spiritualistic American Dream of the Puritans' City on the Hill.

Ronald Reagan at least inspired enough white Americans to win the election with statements like, "I'd like to return to the time when we didn't know there was a black problem." At least one group of saints felt it was time to identify sinners once again.

Hands Across America, 1986—eliminate poverty through self-help movements.

President Reagan's New Federalism faced the realities of fifty years of federal expansion. Perhaps the Reagan Administration managed to slow the growth of big government, but the progress towards eliminating it has been almost nil. Many of the wealthiest Americans have had their taxes reduced, yet families with incomes below $50,000 a year were paying higher proportions of their income to government when Reagan left office in 1989 than when he was elected.

Ronald Reagan's approach to leadership differed from Jimmy Carter's. While Carter tried to bring all things to all people, Reagan courted the support of ultra-conservatives. Reagan compromised on a few issues, but he seemed determined only to back ultra-conservative economic theory and to give verbal support to ultra-conservative moral issues—prayer in schools, anti-abortion, elimination of sex education, teaching creationism in the schools, aid to private schools in the manner of tax exemptions and so forth.

His personal charisma and television image gave him a landslide victory in the 1984 presidential election. Ronald Reagan won support in his bid for reelection from almost every segment of American society. New saints and old sinners seemed to desire a regression to an uncomplicated past.

President Reagan's shortcomings as a leader have become apparent. Instead of trying to bring diverse forces together, developing creative compromises, and expanding the dimensions of vision, he chose to support one element of American political life almost exclusively, implying that the wealthiest Americans were the one and only Saints.

Personally, I doubt if America, considering the deep changes in our society caused by super-industrialism, the age of diversity, and the egalitocracy, could ever return to a simpler past. A number of people called the early eighties *The*

Amuse Me Generation—*the early 1980's era when people's goals were to be participants in activities and work that were fun and relaxing.* Maybe Ronald Reagan's career as an actor and his sense of humor were reflective of what people desired in a political leader. Amuse Me Generation people enjoyed their leisure time in a more productive manner and demanded more leisure time, introducing a *leisure ethic*—*where people are more interested in free unoccupied time to rest or indulge in recreational activities rather than work.*

The selfishness of the Me Decade continued in the types of individualistic activities people engage in: the Rubic's Cube, video games, video tape machines and cameras, computers, reading *101 Uses For Dead Cats.* Yet, instead of being egotistical as the Me Generation, causing a dropping out, popping out, copping out, the Amuse Me Generation became egoistic, **Yuppies**—*Young Upwardly Mobile Professionals; a term used in the mid-1980's to describe those who sought selfish luxuries for their own fulfillment.*

The New York Times (December 13, 1987) argued that the Yuppie generation ended with the stock market crash of October 19, 1987. Yet *The New York Times* admitted that eras do not end in a day. The greed of the gilded, impudent age symbolized by Black Monday, the day the stock market failed, should have crystallized people's discomfort with their unbridled pursuit of self-interest, according to the historian Arthur M. Schlesinger. The 1990's saw an adjustment between altruism and selfishness. Selfishness did not end, but the life of the Yuppie no longer seemed so simple. They were confronted with the influx of energetic, highly skilled immigrants from Asia and Eastern Europe.

The activities of the eighties did, however, inspire creativity and active involvement. Where much of the media of the seventies tended to be hot media feeding on an individual and not demanding participation, the media of the eighties seemed to demand the active participation of cool media, to borrow Marshall McLuhan's analogies developed in *Understanding Media: The Extensions of Man* (1964). People joined together to test their skill at video games, individuals developed programs for their home computers to share with others, and families recorded their events with their video cameras.

The dawning of the electronic '80s also produced a nostalgic era. In 1984, the popular game Trivial Pursuit sold upwards of 20 million games. A board game craze and the return of traditional toys renewed pastimes shared by both parents and children. The mid-80's change reflected the new conservatism in America, symbolized by the re-election of Ronald Reagan. The technology of the high-tech society produced the need to "reach out and touch someone." Ronald Reagan, appearing more touchable than Walter Mondale and emphasizing a simpler past, in which people could take refuge from the uncertainty of a digital world, won a landslide victory in the 1984 presidential election.

In the 1988 presidential election, neither candidate seemed to "reach out and touch someone," but George H. W. Bush seemed more personable than the cold, unmoving Michael Dukakis. Governor Dukakis appeared controlled and calculated—in a debate with George Bush, he lacked emotion while responding to a question about the possibility of his wife being raped and murdered.

In 1992, Democratic Party candidate Bill Clinton defeated George H. W. Bush for the presidency. A few months earlier, Republican President George Bush seemed untouchable in his bid for re-election. Many Democrats whom the media considered top contenders choose not to challenge the popular Gulf War President. The virtually unknown Bill Clinton had the winning magic—the ability to reach out and touch people—an ability George Bush lacked. Of course, I cannot discount another cause for Clinton's success, the declining economy and Clinton's campaign strategy: "It is the economy, stupid!"

Bill Clinton's plans for a more humanized America immediately fell foul to the Republican media blitz on his plan to integrate the military with gays. The neo-Puritan Americans prevailed in their saint-sinner mentality by continually imaging the independent and successful Hillary Clinton as the female anti-Christ. By the 1996 re-election campaign, the outspoken, hard-working humanist Hillary Clinton became a traditional First Lady. She began doing woman's work—becoming an advocate for children. Her book, *It Takes a Village*, became a best seller and the theme of her very popular Democratic Convention speech during the summer of 1996.

In 1996, despite damaging accusations of infidelity and questionable economic deals in Arkansas (Whitewater), President Clinton won re-election. Robert Dole, the Republican candidate and 73 years of age, seemed too dull and old by comparison to the young, warm and politically astute incumbent.

"It is the economy, stupid!" America's economy was the strongest it had been in decades. Inflation and unemployment were near all-time lows. Republicans angered over their inability to attach scandal and non-Puritan values to the popular president, took some comfort in increasing their majorities in Congress.

Watergate gave birth to a politics of vengeance. Many Republicans felt that Democrats hounded Richard Nixon out of the presidency through hypocrisy—

America must face the plight of the homeless.

An American View.

other presidents they argued broke the same laws with impunity. Columnist Russell Baker wrote: "After that, politics was played more fiercely. It was rude, mean, sometimes viciously uncivil. Conservatives yearned for revenge for Nixon." In 2000, the Republican Party's sequel presidential candidate, George W. Bush, squeaked out a narrow victory against the anti-charismatic Democratic Al Gore. America seemed divided on its future or its past. I am not alone in believing that Janet Jackson baring her breast at Superbowl XXXVIII along with the hysterical fear of same-sex marriage contributed to a large increase in Republicans in Congress and George W. Bush's re-election to the presidency in 2004. The Puritans now hoped to be able to restore the United States to yesteryear and finally get even.

From my perspective, political conflicts and scandals are good for America as well as our soul. Thomas Jefferson once wrote something to the effect that "every twenty years the tree of liberty must be watered with the blood of both patriots and tyrants." This call for continuous revolution does not necessitate real blood. A democracy needs conflicts and even scandals to remind those who represent us that they do just that. Power does tend to corrupt, and one way to prevent absolute power from creating absolute corruption is for the people to become indignant and make our politicians "bleed." Then, at least for another generation, the arrogance of power and the abuse of power is reduced.

Thirty years ago, by the end of the seventies, the universal saints in America wanted recognition and status. The age of diversity had produced enough choices for everyone to show off with. People wore the names of manufacturers on their chests or backsides, apparently to prove their predestination for salvation. In 1981, John Brooks in *Showing Off in America; From Conspicuous Consumption to Parody Display* identified this phenomenon. He argued: "They flaunt commercial and industrial objects to prove that they don't have to be serious about such matters."

Maybe, in this egalitocratic manner, we had the beginning of the Amuse Me Generation. I grant that the Amuse Me Generation has found its heroes among some of the names attached to the products they use or wear, mostly from the sports, television or movie industries. Up until the end of the nineteenth century, these areas of endeavor were considered play, but as I indicated earlier, they developed respect during the 1920's.

Popular culture had become the rage as cities were willing to pay millions for football teams, but very little for elite culture, such as ballet. Even in my own city of 200,000 plus people, the city council put aside hundreds of thousands of dollars for soccer fields and softball stadiums. The city council for as long as I can remember has discussed plans to build a cultural arts center. During that period we have seen plenty of movie complexes arise. A sign of the times? Seemingly, we can develop a synthesis—popular culture and elite culture.

The demands of the egalitocracy saints, that everyone be like them, may be replaced by a true age of diversity where pluralism becomes a reality. Certainly, the large emigration to the United States from Asia, Africa and Latin America in the 1990's has added to American diversity. Hard working materially driven immigrants have restored the work ethic. Traditional Americans were forced to reject a leisure ethic and even a Machiavellian Work Ethic as

Another American View.

they were forced to compete in a free market place with the new Americans from throughout the world. Even Republican President George W. Bush (2001–2009) supported increasing visas for techies from other countries. Traditionally, the Republican party has opposed immigration and extended visas. According to CNET News (January 24, 2004) complaints arose from American workers in the high tech industries that they feared for their jobs due to being forced out of work as the proposals did not include a provision that employers must pay a prevailing wage. Near the end of George Bush the Younger's administration, the failing economy that some referred to as a recession saw many of these high skilled immigrants and visa holders began to return to their homelands. There they found more jobs that paid better wages. Yet, they had set the seeds for a new immigrant work ethic that permeated the American society. The leisure ethic was gone and the American Dream was once again based upon achievement through hard work—a Protestant Work Ethic combined with an Immigrant Work Ethic blended with our individualism and Frontier Spirit.

The mores and folkways of the new immigrant groups may also have affected America's social values. Statistics in the nineties indicated that more marriages occurred. While some continued a lifestyle of non-sanctioned marriage, the demand for traditional values seemed to take hold. Divorce rates dropped. People apparently tried to work things out rather than do their thing. The option for divorce still existed when communication failed or individuals grew apart. People in the 1990's, unlike the three previous decades, seemed to want to make a commitment. Some speculate that the AIDS epidemic had a lot to do with ending America's roaming and sexual revolution. The trend continued and by the end of the first decade of the 21st century the divorce rate was the lowest it had been since 1970.

More families are having children, especially more established families with career women in their thirties. Yet some families still choose a new car over a child or decide that life is not worth introducing children to this world.

Other forms of social renewal may be forced on people: The cost of housing has gone beyond the means of most young people. More families will be forced to stay together as the young couples move in with in-laws because they are unable to afford their own homes. A return to extended families might occur. Neighborhoods could remain more intact as people lose their mobility. The difficulty in finding living quarters will cause some couples to work out their differences rather than terminate their relationship in divorce.

The nuclear family will never again mean a father, mother, and children, as more than half of the kids born today will live in single-parent nuclear families. Creative solutions are already being developed, as judges award custody of the home to the children and the parents take turns visiting.

While ultra-conservatives cry out for the family values of the past failing to adapt to the changes of the present, people are still looking to government for

And the future?

guidance and direction. Americans do not want the elimination of government. We just want better government—a government that truly empowers the people.

Voters in California and other states have passed *term limitation initiatives*— *where elected officials are limited to a set number of years in office.* People feel that their elected representatives have lost touch with their needs.

They believe the lack of concern for constituent needs derives from the legislator's desire to appease the vested interest groups. Voters feel that the politician's only care is to get lots of campaign contributions from the PACs to gain reelection. In March, 1992, the U.S. Supreme Court refused to hear an appeal on a lower court's decision that upheld California's Proposition 140 on term limitation.

Americans are enraged at the special privileges and arrogance of members of the federal and state legislatures. Traditionally, voters return incumbents to office in very large numbers. Republicans gained control of both houses of Congress in 1994 for the first time since 1956.

For awhile it appeared that Americans had developed a love affair with the conservative Republican ideology. However, by 2008 the love affair ended due to an arrogance of power. Democratic party pundits argued that the Bush the Younger administration had abused power even far greater than the Nixon White House. The honeymoon was over and the American people voted to "throw the bums out" as they are prone to do every few years to remind politicos—republicans or democrats—that they are responsible to we the people—the ultimate American Dream. In 2008, the Democrats won over-whelming victories in local, state and federal elections. The question arises as to whether they will heed the advice of the comic books: "With great power, there must also come great responsibility."

Term limitation might return people to the ballot box to elect citizen politicians. The number of people voting is in decline. Opponents of term limitation argue that inexperienced legislators will not know how to get things done. The bureaucrats, they argue, will control government. While not voting, more people are engaging in grass-roots politics. John Naisbitt, in his nationwide bestseller *Megatrends* (New York: Warner Books, 1984) discussed this movement from representative democracy to participatory democracy.

Many political scientists fear that the movement towards participatory democracy will just exacerbate factionalism. On many college campuses and in the work place we have seen in recent years a *politically correct movement (PC)—leftist groups and individuals who demand that only their narrow agenda be heard; they feel that any view that differs from theirs denies oppressed people their self-esteem and prevents their access to power.*

In an article Robert Hughes called "The Fraying of America" in *Time* magazine (February 3, 1992, pp. 46–49), he attacked the particularism and separatism of the PC movement. He expressed his belief in diversity and multiculturalism. He feared, as I do, the possible Balkanization of American culture:

> But the desire for self-esteem does not justify every life and exaggeration and therapeutic slanting of evidence that can be claimed to alleviate it. The separatism it fosters turns what ought to be a recognition of cultural diversity, or real multiculturalism, tolerant on both sides, into a pernicious symbolic program. Separatism is the opposite of diversity.

He condemned, in words that I wish I could have written, the refusal of many individuals and groups to take responsibility for their own actions:

> The all-pervasive claim to victimhood tops off America's long-cherished culture of therapeutics. Thus we create a juvenile culture of complaint in which Big Daddy is always to blame and the expansion of rights goes on without the other half of citizenship: attachment to duties and obligations.

A few months earlier, *Time* magazine (August 12, 1991) ran a cover story on "Busybodies: New Puritans" and "Crybabies: Eternal Victims." The busybodies—neo-Puritans—humorlessly try to impose their values and standards on everyone else. John Elson observed: "The busybodies—conformity seekers, legal nitpickers and politically correct thought police—seem to have lost sight of a bedrock American virtue: tolerance, allowing others, in the name of freedom, to do things one disagrees with or does not like, provided they do no outright harm to others." (p. 20)

The crybabies see themselves as eternal victims. Because they are human—equality of condition—they believe society owes them. If they do not get their way, they cry very loud and issue uncompromising demands.

For over a decade, *Time* magazine has expressed its concern about the growing factionalism in this society and our entitlement ethic. *Time* magazine has issued a continuing call for elected officials to set about doing their job again—active leadership and creative compromise.

On August 6, 1979, *Time* cried out for leadership. And, on October 23, 1989, *Time* magazine's cover read: "Is Government Dead?" Under a drawing of George Washington weeping, *Time* added, "Unwilling to lead, politicians are letting America slip into a paralysis." Is it any wonder that people are demanding term limitations?

In Essay II, I proposed that democracy demands both liberty and equality, liberty being the freedom to choose between alternatives, and equality meaning the equality of opportunity. Americans, as Lance Morrow identified in "Feeling Proud Again" (*Time*, January 7, 1985) have always lived with the tension between the values of freedom and equality. Since Franklin Roosevelt's New Deal, Americans have inclined toward equality—in a sense, the ideal of a just society. "In Reagan's America," Morrow said, "the value of freedom has reasserted itself, sometimes at the expense of the gentler instincts."

President Bush, the elder, called for a "kinder and gentler America" and then spent a good deal of his time overseas. President Clinton appeared to symbolize a kinder and gentler America but disappointed most Americans as he waffled on social and political issues. President Bush, the younger, seemed to ignore the whole concept of a kinder and gentler America. Many Americans, tired of sound bite symbolism, want a government that will help us regain some self-confidence and self-worth.

I am, however, optimistic about this first decade of the 21st century—granted with a touch of trepidation. I am not sure how our political system, which moved from a laboring society to a service society in the last thirty years, will respond to the transformation into an information-processing community.

New immigrants compete with skilled, more established citizens to show their sainthood of wealth. Americans are once again gaining respect for a good education and hard work in this competition for high-technology jobs.

Our economy, based on high-tech research and information processing, is still experiencing the pains of unemployment. We can only train a few of the unemployed to work in pure research, or information processing or high technology. America's saints once again view the unemployed as sinners predestined to failure and damnation.

Some unemployed profiteer by selling drugs to those who try to escape reality and stress that the new work ethic of the saints produced—others simply cop out. Government's symbolic talk about the good days will no longer suffice.

I Have A Dream!

My controlled optimism stems from the synthesis I see emerging. Both the private and public sectors are facing the bureaucratic nightmare of overburdened and overgrown institutions. Volunteerism, self-help, and localism, I feel, are reducing selfishness and creating a new sense of community.

Many individuals are again cooperating for the general good of all society. A new consensus will have to recognize the common sainthood of all—a multicultural pluralism.

Self-help movements and the born again drive for excellence sometimes confuses our recent materialistic values with our spiritual beginnings. As high a value as America's new saints place on the ideal of individual liberty, they must never forget the ideal of a just society. Yes, liberty demands freedom from government interference, but justice requires a benevolent government not one simply concerned with Puritan control.

Politicians must find ways to maintain our commitment to the ideals of liberty and equality even when they clash. A meritocracy, that emphasized individual liberty at the expense of equal opportunity, failed the democratic spirit in much the same manner that an egalitocracy, which dictated absolute conformity, destroyed the American Dream. While the state and federal government is eliminating Affirmative Action programs, we can never give up our affirmation to equality.

The Republican Party cannot return us to a pre–New Deal, pre–Great Society existence. The Democratic Party cannot continue the stagnation of the New Deal and the Great Society.

The good old days are past. The good old future is upon us. I look forward to politicians appearing in both parties aiding the creation of a new American Dream that combines the best of the egalitocracy with the best of the meritocracy.

Remember, I only said I was a controlled optimist. I refuse to predict the future as I have too often been in error. I can only point to the good signs among the bad and underline the syntheses that are occurring and that America needs.

I have used this final essay to provide you with a history of the American value system—the American dream of success—and its impact on the political system over the centuries. My emphasis has been on the changes in the Protestant Work Ethic—from a spiritual dream to a material one. I have identified how this change produced a meritocracy where the elite few demanded excellence and held that their excellence would benefit all.

I then examined the transformation in American values since the 1950's to see what the new egalitocracy did to the myths of the self-made man (white, Anglo-Saxon, Protestant)—the Horatio Alger hero, the Frontiersman, the Rugged Individual. I recognized the new ethic of ecumenical sainthood in an age of super-industrialism and diversity, and the resulting universal unrealistic demands on the limited resources of the political institutions.

I tied the lack of political leadership to the ensuing factionalism, the refusal to compromise. Finally, I examined the immediate present and future to introduce a ray of hope with my usual Kirshnerisms.

GLOSSARY

HORATIO ALGER
(1834–1899), Wrote over 100 books and became the most popular author of the last thirty years of the nineteenth century; his heroes maintained their morality and work ethic and were rewarded with success, usually material; the values presented in his books exerted one of the most powerful influences on American culture as they reinforced the Puritan ethic.

AMUSE ME GENERATION
The early 1980's era when people's goals were being participants in activities and work that were fun and relaxing.

JOHN CALVIN
A French theologian who after 1541 took control of Geneva, Switzerland, and introduced a theocracy based upon his concept of only the elect being saved.

DEMOCRATIC CENTRALISM
A concept usually associated with Marxist groups and attributed to Lenin where the various local party assemblies vote on issues and then introduced them to a general meeting of the Central Committee; after a final decision is arrived at, the local party members must adhere to it no matter what their original vote.

EGALITOCRACY
A nation where people receive awards and honors, not for their achievements or excellence, but because they are simply people; equality of condition rather than equality of opportunity.

ENTITLEMENT ETHIC
The view that people are entitled to everything everyone else has.

FACTIONALISM
Conflict within a country between individuals or groups producing dissension rather than the resolution of problems.

HUBRIS
A Greek word meaning excessive pride.

HUMAN POTENTIAL MOVEMENT
A myriad of groups and organizations whose purpose was to change people internally, helping them love themselves, and in this fashion helping them love others, thereby creating a more humane political world.

IMMIGRANT WORK ETHIC
Immigrants to the United States have traditionally worked hard to succeed and to partake of the American Dream.

JOHN MAYNARD KEYNES
British economist who sought to improve capitalism by a system of orderly and predictable economic activity through a government managed economy.

LEISURE ETHIC
Where people are more interested in free unoccupied time to rest or indulge in recreational activities rather than work.

MACHIAVELLIAN WORK ETHIC
The idea that the least amount of work done to achieve the greatest profit is the smartest approach to life; and, anything done in the name of making a profit is justifiable.

ME GENERATION
    The decade of the seventies felt by many to be an age of narcissism whose chant was Me, Me, Me.

MERITOCRACY
    A nation where people are rewarded and honored for their achievements and excellence.

MUCKRAKERS
    A term coined by President Theodore Roosevelt in 1906 to characterize those writers he felt were arousing discontent by uncovering corruption in business and politics during the early 1900's.

NEW LEFT
    A radical-liberal movement, particularly of college students and some professors in the 1960's and early 1970's, that challenged the established political, social, cultural and economic norms.

POLITICAL ACTION COMMITTEES (PACs)
    An interest group's fund-raising branch that distributes money to candidates and, more recently, spends its cash in an attempt to secure the victory of its cause.

POLITICALLY CORRECT MOVEMENT (PC)
    Leftist groups and individuals who demand that only their narrow agenda be heard; they feel that any view that differs from theirs denies oppressed people their self-esteem as well as preventing their access to power.

PREDESTINATION
    God foreordained all souls either for salvation or damnation.

PROGRESSIVE MOVEMENT
    A reform movement from around 1900 to the U.S. entry into World War I aiming to correct abuses which had accompanied the growth of big business.

PROTESTANT REFORMATION
    When Christianity in Western Europe split into numerous groups and the Catholic Church was forced to coexist with other churches, especially the Lutheran, Calvinist, and Anglican.

TERM LIMITATION
    Where elected officials are limited to a set number of years in office.

YIPPIES
    Youth International Party whose political dogma during the 1960's combined nihilism with being hippies.

YUPPIES
    Young Upward Mobile Professionals; a term used in the mid-1980's to describe those who sought selfish luxuries for their own fulfillment.

INDEX